CRITICAL
INSIGHTS

The Joy Luck Club

CRITICAL INSIGHTS

The Joy Luck Club

by Amy Tan

Editor

Robert C. Evans

Auburn University Montgomery

Salem Press
Pasadena, California   Hackensack, New Jersey

Cover photo: © iStockphoto.com/Timur Anikin

Published by Salem Press

© 2010 by EBSCO Publishing
Editor's text © 2010 by Robert C. Evans
"The *Paris Review* Perspective" © 2010 by Karl Taro Greenfeld for *The Paris Review*

∞ The paper used in these volumes conforms to the American National Standard for Permanence of Paper for Printed Library Materials, Z39.48-1992 (R1997).

Library of Congress Cataloging-in-Publication Data
The Joy Luck Club, by Amy Tan / editor, Robert C. Evans.
    p. cm. — (Critical insights)
Includes bibliographical references and index.
ISBN 978-1-58765-626-2 (alk. paper)
1. Tan, Amy. Joy Luck Club. I. Evans, Robert C.
PS3570.A48J6346 2010
813′.54—dc22

                                                        2009026304

PRINTED IN CANADA

Contents_____

About This Volume

Robert C. Evans

This collection of essays on Amy Tan's *The Joy Luck Club* is only the latest of many indications that the book has now achieved the status of a modern (or perhaps "postmodern") classic—a text that is widely read, widely taught, highly valued, and much discussed. Instantly and unusually successful when it was first published twenty years ago, Tan's volume (which she prefers to think of as a collection of stories rather than as a novel per se) has stayed continuously in print ever since and remains perhaps her most widely esteemed work. The purpose of this volume is to help illuminate Tan's book from a variety of some-times contrasting, sometimes complementary perspectives.

The volume opens with a brief essay in which I emphasize the artis-tic excellence of Tan's text—an approach that has not received as much stress in recent criticism as it might have. Joanne McCarthy next offers a helpful overview of Tan's life. Then, Karl Taro Greenfeld, a writer for *The Paris Review*, recalls his personal responses to the book when it was first published and then later, after a lapse of many years.

In the "Critical Contexts" section (which comprises essays entirely new to this volume), Camille-Yvette Welsch begins by surveying the critical reception of Tan's works, particularly *The Joy Luck Club*. I then provide a sense of the cultural and historical contexts of the book, espe-cially developments in the four decades following World War II (when Tan and many of her readers were growing up) as well as events and trends in the late 1980s (when her work was first being written and read). Doris L. Eder then discusses the book from numerous points of view, including structure, narration, style, genesis, (auto)biographical background, fabulous and fantastic elements, themes and variations, and Tan's uses of repetitions, parallels, dualities, and doublings. Fi-nally, to conclude this section, Neil Heims compares and contrasts Tan's book with Michael Cunningham's *The Hours*.

The "Critical Readings" section (which reprints previously published work, arranged in chronological order) opens with a fascinating and insightful interview (conducted by Barbara Somogyi and David Stanton) with Tan herself. Next, Ben Xu uses *The Joy Luck Club* to argue that "the ethnic self, just like the existential self, is neither free nor self-sufficient, and therefore never an authentic or genuine self." Stephen Souris suggests that Tan's book "invites analysis from critical perspectives that theorize and valorize fragmented, discontinuous texts and the possibilities of connection across segments." Esther Mikyung Ghymn contends that "we cannot really believe the stories that the mothers tell about themselves in *The Joy Luck Club*." Ghymn faults many of the characters for being stereotypical, unrealistic, and insufficiently individualized.

In an essay comparing *The Joy Luck Club* to Tan's next book (*The Kitchen God's Wife*), M. Marie Booth Foster asserts that "the quest for voice becomes an archetypal journey for all of the women" in both texts. Patricia L. Hamilton offers a great deal of helpful information about many of the traditional Chinese beliefs mentioned in *The Joy Luck Club*, and Patricia P. Chu argues that a "utopian view of American immigration is the foundation of Tan's text." In this volume's penultimate essay, Catherine Romagnolo uses deconstructive methods to examine the structure of the book, in the process arguing that the work is more politically sophisticated than some critics have alleged. The volume closes with my recent interview of Tan, conducted on the eve of the twentieth anniversary of the publication of *The Joy Luck Club*.

The Joy Luck Club, like any significant creative work, inevitably defeats any single or partial attempt to comprehend it, but such defeats have (ideally) the salutary effect of sending us back to the original text in search of new insights, deeper understanding, and fuller appreciation. If the present volume inspires thoughtful rereadings of Tan's book, it will have accomplished one of its most important goals.

THE BOOK
AND
AUTHOR

On *The Joy Luck Club*

From the time of its initial publication in 1989 until the present day, Amy Tan's *The Joy Luck Club* has been an enormously successful book. It won instant critical acclaim in the popular press, rapidly became an enduring best seller, was even more avidly sought after in paperback than in hardcover, was quickly turned into a well-regarded "major motion picture," and soon became a standard item on college reading lists and a frequent focus of serious academic discussion. Today, twenty years after the book first appeared, it remains the subject of sustained attention and admiration and is widely regarded as a modern "classic." Not everyone, of course, concurs with this view. Indeed, *The Joy Luck Club* has sometimes been censured by critics who find it too saccharine, too neatly resolved, and too much given to stereotypes in its depiction not only of China but also of Chinese people and Chinese Americans. In fact, various Asian American commentators have frequently been among Tan's harshest critics. They have accused her of crafting a book designed to appeal to non-Asian readers (especially educated white women), and various Asian American men have objected to the ways the work depicts (or fails to depict) Asian males. Some critics have even found the book politically suspect, considering it insufficiently progressive. Nevertheless, Tan's text seems to have weathered such criticism well, and there are few signs that interest in *The Joy Luck Club* is likely to decrease anytime soon. If anything, the opposite seems far more likely to occur: Tan's book seems likely to remain one of the enduring works of late-twentieth-century American literature.

Why is the survival of *The Joy Luck Club* so likely? Why has this work proven so enduringly appealing? The simplest reason—but one (surprisingly) that is rarely addressed in any detail in most recent commentary—is that the book is very effectively written. When reviewing the kind of analysis the book has generated, one is immediately struck by how infrequently *The Joy Luck Club* is seriously ana-

On *The Joy Luck Club*   3

lyzed as a work of art. Commentators tend to discuss the text from a wide variety of sociological, philosophical, and theoretical perspectives, studying it in terms of all the recent critical trends (such as race, class, gender, ethnicity, and "subaltern studies," to mention just a few). There is a strong tendency in writing about Tan's book—as in recent writing about many literary texts in general—to treat the work in terms of themes and ideas rather than to examine it closely for the skill and craft with which it is composed. Thus this novel (or body of interrelated stories, as Tan prefers to see it) tends to be read almost as if it were an essay collection, interesting and significant mainly for the topics it explores rather than for the talent and subtlety with which it is crafted as a piece of creative fiction.

This heavy emphasis on the book's themes—on its paraphrasable "content" rather than on its skillful design and memorable phrasing—is a bit of a shame, because this kind of emphasis does scant justice to Tan's real accomplishments as a thoughtful and discerning writer. Anyone, after all, could have written down the "ideas" explored in Tan's book, but only a highly accomplished author—one gifted with a certain degree of innate talent, but one who had also carefully studied and honed her craft—could have produced *The Joy Luck Club*. Of course, it is easy to dismiss any concern with the aesthetic quality of Tan's book as naïve or as highly subjective, but surely Tan wrote (as most serious authors do) out of an intense concern with the individual artistic choices she was making at every level and at every moment. Each word and sentence, each paragraph and chapter, each sound and rhythm was the product of lucky inspiration, careful design, or (more probably) some combination of both. In fact, the most impressive quality of *The Joy Luck Club* is its quality itself—its skillful accomplishment and enduring success as a work of art. In reading interviews with Tan (such as those included in this volume), as well as in reading the brief acknowledgments section that precedes the text of *The Joy Luck Club*, one is impressed by her humility and commitment as a writer—her eagerness to learn from others, her cheerful willingness to subject her work to thoughtful feedback from other writers, and her generosity in paying tribute to the authors and teachers whose advice she has sought. Tan is, in many respects, one of the clearest, most honest, and most insightful of commentators on her own work; her remarks on *The Joy Luck Club* are refreshingly unpretentious and free of jargon, and one senses, in reading them, a serious artist genuinely in love with her craft.

It is easy enough to list quickly some of the features that make Tan such an effective writer. One notices, for instance, on the very first page of the first substantial story, the quick succession and juxtaposition of alternative explanations of the death of Suyuan Woo, the woman who founded and then refounded the Joy Luck Club. The narrator is Jing-mei (June) Woo, Suyuan's daughter:

> My father thinks she was killed by her own thoughts.
>
> "She had a new idea inside her head," said my father. "But before it could come out of her mouth, the thought grew too big and burst. It must have been a very bad idea."
>
> The doctor said she died of a cerebral aneurysm. And her friends at the Joy Luck Club said she died just like a rabbit: quickly and with unfinished business left behind. (19)

Swiftly and deftly, Jing-mei alternates between the masculine (and somewhat censorious) superstition of her father (carefully explained, with all its illogical but prosaic logic); the clinical, brief, and matter-of-fact explanation of Western medicine; and the poetic and sympathetic superstitions of Suyuan's female friends. The phrasing is simple, clear, and straightforward; there is a touch of humor even in dealing with so grim a topic; and the father's tone of voice is convincingly conveyed. Perspectives alternate (as indeed they do throughout this book); no single voice is privileged over another. Each voice, each explanation, is accorded its own measure of respect. Suyuan is presented, successively, as an ambitious thinker, a mere physical organism, and a small, energetic, and unfortunate victim of fate. And all this is accomplished with a few simple but carefully chosen words and with a subtle and intelligent sense of effective contrasts. This one brief passage, then, not only epitomizes many of the methods of the book as a whole but also encapsulates many of the most effective aspects of its style.

Or take, for instance, a passage from a few pages later in which Suyuan herself is speaking, as she remembers the depredations of wartime China during the height of the Japanese invasion:

> We were a city of leftovers mixed together. If it hadn't been for the Japanese, there would have been plenty of reason for fighting to break out among these different people. Can you see it? Shanghai people with north-water peasants, bankers with barbers, rickshaw pullers with Burmese refugees. Everybody looked down on someone else. It didn't matter that everybody shared the same sidewalk to spit on and suffered the same fast-moving diarrhea. We all had the same stink, but everybody complained that someone else smelled the worst. Me? Oh, I hated the American air force officers who said hubba-hubba sounds to make my face turn red. But the worst were the northern peasants who emptied their noses into their hands and pushed people around and gave everybody their dirty diseases. (22)

Writing as good as this doesn't just happen by accident, unless the author is extraordinarily inspired. Whether subconsciously or by deliberate design, Tan manages to make each word—even each syllable—count. Thus the description of the refugees as "leftovers mixed together" not only contributes to the book's heavy emphasis on sensations associated with food but also vividly suggests the refugees' sense of themselves as mere scraps or residue. Meanwhile, when the mother directly addresses her daughter—"Can you see it?"—she addresses us, as readers, too, and the very fact that she addresses us directly helps contribute to the vividness of her words. That extremely short question follows a fairly long declarative statement, and then the question itself is followed by another long sentence that is broken into a series of highly balanced clauses. "Shanghai people" are juxtaposed with "north-water peasants," and the latter phrase, with its hint of authentic dialect, is far more memorable than "peasants from the north" or "northern peasants" would have been. Next, "bankers" are alliteratively juxtaposed with "barbers," but the similar-sounding words help stress the contrasts in the types of jobs and in respective social status. Finally, "rickshaw pullers" are set side by side with "Burmese refugees"—the first phrase suggesting people who are recognizably Chinese, the latter phrase (with its assonance and rhyme) bringing in the strangely unfamiliar.

In a work sometimes accused of being sentimental, Tan does not refrain from including frank physical details, as in the references to "spit," "diarrhea," "stink," and crude nose blowing, nor does she refrain from depicting the least attractive aspects of human psychology. The quoted passage even involves some subtle irony at the speaker's expense, since the mother complains about others' complaints and judges others for being so judgmental. Most impressive, however, is the way in which Tan captures convincingly the distinct sounds of a credible human voice, as when the mother abruptly asks, "Me?" or when she echoes, decades later, the dated "hubba-hubba" dialect of randy American officers—men who thereby treated rudely the very civilians and allies they had been sent to help. In not much more than one hundred words, Tan manages to summon up, quite vividly, a whole society and an entire significant moment in history, even as she also gives us insight into a particular person's mind and creates an utterly convincing tone of voice.

The sheer quality of Tan's writing seems all the more remarkable when one remembers that *The Joy Luck Club* was not only her very first book but also contained some of the very first creative writing she had ever done. The astonishing thing about the book is less the topical issues it explores than the skill, tact, and subtlety with which those issues (along with characters, scenes, episodes, and styles of speech) are put into words. When the topical aspects of *The Joy Luck Club* no longer seem nearly as fresh as they do today, and when the political and social themes it examines no longer have the power to surprise, the book will still endure because of the sureness and power of Tan's talent as a writer. That talent includes not only her ability to deal convincingly with both the tragic and the comic aspects of human existence but also her ability to craft effective and memorable sentences—sentences that accumulate, one after another, paragraph after paragraph, and page after page. It is the quality of Tan's writing that makes most readers want to continue turning her pages, and it is Tan's talent with words that will help *The Joy Luck Club* continue to endure.

Work Cited

Tan, Amy. *The Joy Luck Club*. 1989. New York: Penguin, 2006.

Biography of Amy Tan

Joanne McCarthy

Amy Tan (given the Chinese name of An-mei, or "Blessing from America") is the second of three children born to Chinese immigrants John and Daisy Tan. Her father, educated as an electrical engineer in Beijing, became a Baptist minister. Daisy, child of a privileged family, was forced to leave behind three daughters from a previous marriage when she fled Communist troops.

Tan's older brother died in 1967 and her father died six months later, both of brain tumors. This began a troubled time for her. At fifteen, she moved to Europe with her mother and younger brother, was arrested on drug charges in Switzerland at sixteen, and nearly eloped to Austria with a German army deserter.

Daisy Tan wanted her daughter to be a neurosurgeon and a concert pianist, but Tan felt she could not live up to her mother's expectations. Although her test scores were highest in math and science, she left premedical studies to become an English major. In 1974, she earned a master's degree in linguistics from San Jose State University and married tax attorney Lou DeMattei. She began doctoral studies at the University of California at Berkeley, but after a close friend and roommate was murdered, she dropped out to become a consultant to programs for disabled children. Later she served as reporter, editor, and publisher for *Emergency Room Reports*.

Tan became a freelance business writer in 1983. She wrote sales manuals and proposals for such firms as American Telephone and Telegraph (AT&T), International Business Machines (IBM), and Apple, and by 1985 she was working up to ninety hours a week. Her business writing paid well, and she could choose her projects, but, she has said, "It was death to me spiritually. It was writing that had no meaning to me."

She sought therapy but became discouraged when her psychiatrist fell asleep during her sessions. Instead, she decided to cut her work week to fifty hours, study jazz piano, and write fiction in her spare time. She had just read novelist Louise Erdrich's *Love Medicine* (1984), interwoven stories of an American Indian family, and was inspired to write her own stories. At the Squaw Valley Community of Writers fiction workshop, she met Molly Giles, winner of the Flannery O'Connor Award for fiction. Tan showed Giles what would become Waverly Jong's story, "Rules of the Game," in *The Joy Luck Club* (1989), and Giles became her mentor.

Tan finished three stories in three years. When *The Joy Luck Club* was sold to Putnam in 1987 on the basis of a proposal and three stories ("Rules of the Game," "Waiting Between the Trees," and "Scar"), Tan closed her business and wrote thirteen more stories in four months. She thought her acceptance was "a token minority thing. I thought they had to fill a quota since there weren't many Chinese-Americans writing."

Like the daughters in her books, Tan was ambivalent about her Chinese background. She contemplated plastic surgery to make herself look more Western, and she did not fully accept her dual culture until 1987, when she and her mother went to China to meet her half sisters. She has remarked, "As soon as my feet touched China, I became Chinese."

Writing *The Joy Luck Club* also helped Tan to discover how Chinese she really was. In many respects, it is her family's story. Her mother had formed a Joy Luck Club in China and again in San Francisco. Daisy Tan "was the little girl watching her mother cut a piece of flesh from her arm to make soup, and she was the little girl watching her mother die when she took opium because she had become a third concubine."

Tan's first book was a surprise best seller in both hardcover and paperback. It received the Commonwealth Club Gold Award for fiction, the Bay Area Book Reviewers Award for fiction, and the American Library Association Best Book for Young Adults Award and was a finalist for the National Book Award. In 1993, *The Joy Luck Club* was made into a popular film, cowritten and coproduced by Tan. It was adapted for the stage in 1999.

For nearly a year, Tan tried to start *The Kitchen God's Wife* (1991). Again, her subjects were a Chinese mother and a Chinese American daughter, but this time she focused on the mother's life in China. The novel, based on Daisy Tan's tumultuous past, received *Booklist*'s editor's choice honors and was nominated for the Bay Area Book Reviewers Award. *The Hundred Secret Senses* (1995) followed; it tells the story of Olivia Yee Bishop, a Chinese American photographer, and her irrepressible Chinese half sister Kwan, who believes that she lived another life in the nineteenth century. Tan's next novel, *The Bonesetter's Daughter* (2001), draws in part on the histories of her mother and grandmother in China.

Tan's first nonfiction work, *The Opposite of Fate: A Book of Musings* (2003), is a collection of casual writings that supplement her fiction and her life. The title essay describes her struggle with Lyme disease, which began in 1999 and for several years had a serious impact on her ability to write.

From *Magill's Survey of American Literature.* Rev. ed. Pasadena, CA: Salem Press, 2007. Copyright © 2007 by Salem Press, Inc.

Bibliography

Bloom, Harold, ed. *Amy Tan.* Philadelphia: Chelsea House, 2000. Bloom provides an introduction to this installment in the Modern Critical Views series. Pulls together the comments of contemporary critics.

Cheung, King-kok. *An Interethnic Companion to Asian American Literature.* New York: Cambridge University Press, 1997. An essay collection with a critical overview of Asian American literary studies. Most interesting to readers of Tan's novels are essays by Sau-ling Cynthia Wong, Shirley Geok-lin Lim, Jinqi Ling, and Donald Geollnicht.

Cooperman, Jeannette Batz. *The Broom Closet: Secret Meanings of Domesticity in Postfeminist Novels by Louise Erdrich, Mary Gordon, Toni Morrison, Marge Piercy, Jane Smiley, and Amy Tan.* New York: Peter Lang, 1999. A study of the role of traditionally feminine concerns, such as marriage and family, in the works of these postfeminist writers.

Ho, Wendy. *In Her Mother's House: The Politics of Asian American Mother-Daughter Writing.* Walnut Creek, Calif.: AltaMira Press, 1999. Includes two chapters dedicated specifically to Tan, "Losing Your Innocence but Not Your Hope: Amy Tan's Joy Luck Mothers and Coca-Cola Daughters" and "The Heart Never Travels: The Incorporation of Fathers in the Mother-Daughter Stories of Maxine Hong Kingston, Amy Tan, and Fae Myenne Ng."

Huh, Joonok. *Interconnected Mothers and Daughters in Amy Tan's "The Joy Luck Club."* Tucson, Ariz.: Southwest Institute for Research on Women, 1992. Examines the relationships between mothers and their adult children in Tan's novel. Includes a bibliography.

Huntley, E. D. *Amy Tan: A Critical Companion.* Westport, Conn.: Greenwood Press, 1998. Discusses Tan's biography and analyzes her novels in the context of Asian American literature. Analyzes major themes such as the crone figure, food, clothing, language, biculturalism, and mothers and daughters. Includes useful bibliography.

Lim, Elaine. *Asian American Literature: An Introduction to the Writings and Their Social Context.* Philadelphia: Temple University Press, 1982. The first critical guide to Asian American literature, Lim's book is an essential introduction to the historical and literary contexts of Tan's work.

Ling, Amy. *Between Worlds: Women Writers of Chinese Ancestry.* New York: Pergamon Press, 1990. A chronological and thematic introduction to prose narratives in English by American women of Chinese or partial Chinese ancestry. Includes an extensive annotated bibliography of prose by Chinese American women.

Paintbrush: A Journal of Poetry and Translation 22 (Autumn, 1995). Special issue focuses on Tan and on *The Joy Luck Club* in particular. Includes articles on mothers and daughters, memory and forgetting.

Pearlman, Mickey, and Katherine Usher Henderson. "Amy Tan." *Inter/View: Talks with America's Writing Women.* Lexington: UP of Kentucky, 1990. Provides biographical information on Tan, revealing the sources of some of the stories in *The Joy Luck Club.*

Snodgrass, Mary Ellen. *Amy Tan: A Literary Companion.* Jefferson, N.C.: McFarland, 2004. Presents a readable, engaging introduction to both Tan's life and works. Replete with tools for further research, including study questions, an extensive bibliography, and a glossary of Chinese terms found in Tan's works.

Tan, Amy. "Amy Tan: An Interview." Interview by Barbara Somogyi and David Stanton. *Poets & Writers Magazine* 19, no. 5 (September/October, 1991): 24-32. Excellent interview. Tan speaks about her childhood and her early career as a business writer, her decision to write fiction, her success with *The Joy Luck Club*, and some of the work's autobiographical elements.

the PARIS
REVIEW

The *Paris Review* Perspective_____

Karl Taro Greenfeld for *The Paris Review*

I originally read *The Joy Luck Club* out of a sense of obligation. The novel's tremendous commercial success and cultural and conversational ubiquity—if Oprah Winfrey had had a book club in 1989 she surely would have selected it—marked it as one of those popular books to be resented. I was at my snobbiest when it came to these matters, just out of college, trying to figure out my own literary tastes and preferences. I was sure that novels about mothers and daughters that loomed for seasons atop the best-sellers list were not my kinds of books. Yet it was the first breakout commercial novel by an Asian American author, and as an aspiring Asian American writer myself, I suspected I would have to investigate this matter, if only to confirm my prejudices.

Finally, ill prepared for a long international flight, I gave in and bought a British mass-market paperback edition at a kiosk at Tokyo Narita airport. (That yellowed paperback, with its red cover and "Amy Tan" spelled out in a ridiculous Chinese-restaurant-style font, is sitting beside my computer right now.) The book started: the clever italicized allegories opening each section, the deft alternation of the narrative between daughter and mother, the precise, almost poetic, yet never labored language. But surely, very soon, like so many best-selling novels, it would start to suck.

Instead, by the end of the novel, I was actually crying. Every plot turn hit me with thumping emotional force, even when I saw it coming. I was struck by the way the mothers project their old-country concerns onto their new-country daughters, always asserting a Chinese context around their American lives. It reminded me of the struggles of my own mother—though she is Japanese rather than Chinese—to come to terms with her feckless American son (me). I realized that *The Joy Luck Club* is one of the best novels ever written about the American immigrant song.

Amy Tan had achieved that rarest of all literary accomplishments, a vast and masterful novel that is also a breakout commercial success. If it had merely been a great book, would I have ever felt compelled to investigate it? Probably not. Yet it was the commercial success almost as much as the literary qualities of *The Joy Luck Club* that served as an inspiration and opened the door, however slightly, to subsequent waves of Asian American authors. The book's great success and the good sales of Amy Tan's subsequent novels have shown that the Asian American experience, as specific and seemingly distinct as that might be, is as valid a tableau for American fiction as any other. *The Joy Luck Club* was the first great Asian American novel. It did for the Asian American community what Philip Roth and Saul Bellow did for the Jews or Gay Talese and Mario Puzo did for Italian Americans. It propagated some stereotypes, it destroyed others, it was sentimental and occasionally overwrought, but more than anything else, it said: Our families and our stories are worthy. Pay attention.

I didn't think much about the book for a long time, until a chance meeting with Amy Tan a few years ago in Paris encouraged me to pick up the novel and read it again. Now that I am a father myself, with an immigrant wife—she is German, rather than Japanese or Chinese—and two daughters, I read the book through that prism, looking to see how the dreams of the mothers are transferred onto the daughters, how the daughters must fight to create their own personalities and character. My wife, with her old-country ways, her recipes in a notebook of her mother's handwriting, makes dishes representing the collective wisdom of generations of mothers and daughters. And then, when the cake is baked or the goulash prepared, our daughters—of course!—won't take a bite. The good intentions of mothers always seem to crash against the willfulness of daughters.

I cried again when I reread *The Joy Luck Club*. Not for the happy ending that manages to be perfectly sad at the same time, but for the longing of the mothers. This time I was moved by the steady yearning of the parents for the well-being of their children, even if those children never for a moment consider the sacrifice of their parents. It is a perfect evocation of that bond—a remarkable feat when you consider that Amy Tan doesn't have children. The mothers give, even when their daughters won't take. The mothers give so that they know they did everything they could, so that they are sure their spirits will be passed on. "She will fight me," says Ying-ying St. Clair of her architect daughter, "because that is the nature of two tigers. But I will win and give her my spirit, because this is the way a mother loves her daughter."

I finally realized on this reading that *The Joy Luck Club* is so much more than a book about immigrants or a book about Asian Americans. It is simply a great story about perhaps that greatest of subjects: family.

Work Cited

Tan, Amy. *The Joy Luck Club*. 1989. New York: Ballantine, 1990.

CRITICAL
CONTEXTS

Amy Tan:
A Look at the Critical Reception_____

Camille-Yvette Welsch

Amy Tan is one of a lucky minority of writers whose first book made a major impact in the world of publishing. Her first novel, *The Joy Luck Club*, hit the *New York Times* best-seller list and stayed there for nine months, longer than any other book that year. It was short-listed for the National Book Award for fiction and nominated for the National Book Critics Award. The book also won the Bay Area Book Reviewers Award for fiction in addition to the Commonwealth Club Gold Award. While Tan's initial contract sold the hardcover book for $50,000, the paperback rights earned her nearly $1.2 million. Since then, the book has been made into a major motion picture, translated into more than twenty languages (including Chinese), and adapted into a play (Huntley 11-12, 41).

Tan's popularity might not have been so meteoric if Maxine Hong Kingston's autobiographical work of fiction *The Woman Warrior* had not primed the pump in the 1970s. Until the 1960s and 1970s, Asian American literature had a spotty history, consisting largely of memoirs and autobiographies. Kingston continued the tradition but chose a more fragmented, multivoiced style in which to tell her story. Rather than employing the linear narrative to which the reading public was accustomed, Kingston used a form called "talk-story," which celebrated the oral histories contributed by generations of women kept out of the formal histories created by men both in the United States and in China, among other places. Kingston's book was well received, earning the National Book Critics Circle Award for nonfiction in 1976. Tan's novel seemed to be a kind of literary kin, with its multivoiced, multi-generational series of stories. In *Time* magazine, John Skow wrote, "Growing up ethnic is surely the liveliest theme to appear in the American novel since the closing of the frontier. . . . The Chinese-American culture is only beginning to throw off such literary sparks, and Amy

Tan's bright, sharp-flavored first novel belongs on a short shelf dominated by Maxine Hong Kingston's remarkable works of a decade or so ago, *The Woman Warrior* and *China Men*."

By the end of the 1980s, Chinese American authors had made a name for themselves in the literary world. Kingston continued her success in 1980, winning the American Book Award for *China Men*. Poet Cathy Song won the Yale Younger Poets Prize with her volume titled *Picture Bride*. Poet Li-Young Li read on National Public Radio and received both a Guggenheim and a grant from the National Endowment for the Arts, and Garrett Hongo won the Academy of American Poets Lamont Poetry Prize (Huntley 29). David Henry Hwang's Broadway sensation *M. Butterfly* won several Tony Awards in 1988. With Tan's publication of *The Joy Luck Club* in 1989, Asian American authors had definitively entered both the public consciousness and the literary canon.

Both the public and the critics embraced Tan and *The Joy Luck Club*. *New York Times* critic Orville Schell wrote that Amy Tan "has a wonderful eye for what is telling, a fine ear for dialogue, a deep empathy for her subject matter and a guilelessly straightforward way of writing, [so that her themes] sing with a rare fidelity and beauty. She has written a jewel of a book." Other critics were largely positive, although some found Tan's seemingly happy ending to be problematic, too "easy." Some complained that Tan's fiction did little to address larger political issues and that Tan should have written a book that cast China in a more flattering light.

For Tan herself, the book was less about creating a literary masterpiece than it was about understanding her mother and her mother's memory. No discussion of the origins of *The Joy Luck Club* can begin without an examination of Daisy Tan's life. Born in Shanghai, Daisy grew up the daughter of a wealthy family. Her father, a scholar, had died when she was very young. After his death, Daisy's mother, Jingmei, refused the proposal of a man, who then raped her and made her his concubine, thereby forcing her into exile from her family and her daughter. Daisy was allowed to visit her mother periodically, but that ended with her mother's suicide. When Jing-mei bore the rapist a son, one of his principal wives stole the child and raised him as her own. Jing-mei, overcome with the pain of her position, lost family, and stolen son, killed herself by eating an overdose of opium. Daisy was nine and orphaned. Still, her relatives did their duty by her and settled her in an arranged marriage. She bore her abusive husband four children: a son, who died very young, and three daughters. She left them behind when she fled the marriage and made her way to the United States. Shortly after her arrival in 1949, Daisy met Tan's father, John, also a Chinese immigrant, and married him. Much of this story made its way into *The Joy Luck Club*.

The couple had three children, Peter, Amy, and John, who grew up embracing all things American while trying to deal with the culture and language their parents had brought with them from China. For Amy, being bicultural was painful. She felt ashamed of her Chinese heritage, of her mother's imperfect speech, and of herself for being unable to live up to the high expectations of her parents. When Tan was fifteen, her father and her older brother Peter both died of brain tumors. Tan's mother took her children away from the "diseased" house and traveled with them around the eastern seaboard before leaving for Europe and finally settling in Switzerland. Tan graduated in 1969 and the family returned to the United States, where Amy attended college, first at Linfield College, then at San Jose City College, and finally finishing at San Jose State University, where she earned a B.A. in English and linguistics and then a master's degree in linguistics, thereby ruining her mother's dream that her daughter become a doctor. Tan married Louis DeMattei, an Italian American tax lawyer. She enrolled in a doctoral program but decided to leave it, preferring instead to enter the job market. She floated from job to job before finally settling as a freelance writer.

Eventually, Tan, a self-diagnosed workaholic, decided to cut back on her freelance work to make room for her creative endeavors. She wrote a short story, "Endgame," that gained her entrance into the Squaw Valley Community of Writers. There she met Amy Hempel and

Molly Giles, who encouraged Tan in her work. A little while later, Tan joined Giles's San Francisco-based writing workshop. "Endgame" was published in *FM Magazine* and later reprinted in *Seventeen* magazine. She also wrote a second story, "Waiting Between the Trees," which she submitted to *The New Yorker*. The community of writers was essential to Tan; Giles gave "Endgame" to agent Sandra Dijkstra, who liked the story and encouraged Tan to keep writing. A short while later, after discovering that "Endgame" had been published in Italy without her consent, Tan sought representation from Dijkstra. The agent requested another story. Tan sent "Waiting Between the Trees" with a letter outlining her idea for a novel or series of short stories telling the tales of a group of women of different backgrounds and generations. On the basis of the story and the letter, Dijkstra agreed to become Tan's agent (Huntley 9).

Meanwhile, Daisy Tan was not feeling well. In 1986, she was hospitalized for a heart attack. Though the heart attack turned out to be angina, Tan was so unsettled at the thought of losing her mother without really knowing her that she endeavored to create a closer relationship with her mother. She also agreed to accompany her mother to China and meet her three half sisters. Just before Tan left for China, Dijkstra asked the writer for one more story and an outline for a complete book. Tan created the proposal and then left for China with her mother and her husband. When she returned from China, she had a book deal with G. P. Putnam and Sons and a novel to finish. Tan had originally conceived of the book as a series of stories, but the publishing company thought a novel would be easier to market. Tan quit her freelance job and spent four months completing the text.

At the center of both Tan's life and her first book is the mother-daughter relationship. Tan's own struggle as an American of Chinese descent living between the culture of her Chinese parents and the culture of her native country, the United States, informs the text as well. Much of the critical response to *The Joy Luck Club* reflects these primary concerns. For an excellent critical overview of Tan's first three novels, the history of Asian American literature, and Tan's biography, E. D. Huntley's *Amy Tan: A Critical Companion* is a particularly useful source.

Feminist readings of *The Joy Luck Club* begin with the idea that women find themselves and their relation to each other by interacting with texts by other women. In the case of *The Joy Luck Club*, the mothers' stories represent shifts in their own lives from silent, powerless women to empowered survivors. This forward motion helps to shape the book as the mothers move from China to the United States. That movement also suggests that the Asian women are "prefeminist." The West becomes the beacon of democratic hope, of equality and modernity. The mothers' hopes for their daughters are enacted as they move to the United States, where they believe their daughters will have the opportunity to be recognized as public, relevant people independent of their domestic skills and their husbands. Leslie Bow does acknowledge that the stark dichotomy that figures the West as exclusively enlightened and the East as exclusively patriarchal and oppressive does an injustice to both. The same dichotomy also negates the potential for more fully problematizing gender issues in both countries. Ultimately, Bow suggests, this dichotomy may have helped to make the book more palatable to Western readers. David Leiwei Li concurs. He argues that Tan's insistence on chronicling only the nuclear family is a means by which the author can ignore other, larger political issues and create China as a gender-oppressing monolith. He also suggests that Tan's claims of a matrilineal, genetic inheritance keep the understanding private and familial rather than allowing that Chinese politics and history might have offered a similar kind of understanding.

Yuan Yuan also examines Tan's narrative configuration of China. For the mothers in *The Joy Luck Club,* China is both geographical and historical; for their daughters, it is a culture from which they are removed. The mothers use China and their memories to create myths and legends with which they intend to guide their daughters to an understanding of their lineage, their culture, their inheritance. The daughters must rely on their mothers to offer and explain the stories; the mothers must trust that their daughters will listen. Chandra Tyler Mountain takes the idea a step further, claiming that without the context of China and its symbols, the mothers are unknowable, so that their stories, and subsequently their identities, are lost. It is a political act to remember China and to make it a part of the lives of their daughters. The daughters must reconcile their identities not as Chinese or American but as Chinese American, a hybrid with its own history and culture. These two necessities create much of the tension that drives the novel. In E. Shelley Reid's reading, the book sets up the mothers and daughters as yin and yang, implying a search for balance, particularly for the daughters, who strive to find their identities in the midst of the American society in which they have public lives and the Chinese society in which the nuclear family operates. The daughters must find balance to find enlightenment; they must come to terms with their mothers' lives and culture before they can live fully in their own. Eventually, the daughters come to understand that they can find strength in the stories of their mothers without having to relive those stories.

Wenying Xu continues the examination of myths, claiming that the women in the stories reverse the tradition of using myths to suppress women; instead, revisionary myths are used to empower and enlighten women ("Womanist"). Critic Frank Chin takes exception to these changed myths, alleging that Tan, along with Maxine Hong Kingston and David Henry Hwang, wrote the myths to appear cruel and misogynistic, thereby reinforcing negative stereotypes about China and Chinese men.

Tan's use of multiple narrators and multiple time periods has encouraged a number of readings based on the theories of the Russian philosopher Mikhail Bakhtin, who assumes that a dialogical work is in conversation not only with itself and its own multiple perspectives but also with other works and other authors. The conversation resists single-source authority; instead it encourages change, exchange, and elucidation. Each work has the power to change and expand as other works come into contact with it. This theory became increasingly popular in the 1970s as a lens through which to view intertextuality. This conceptual approach is also well suited to certain elements often found in women's writing that stresses community and multivoiced narratives, as does that of both Kingston and Tan.

Bonnie Braendlin was one of the first critics to apply the Bakhtinian approach to *The Joy Luck Club*. In her reading, the multiplicity of voices suggests a desire for self-definition that transcends the boundaries of generations and ethnicities. Qun Wang uses a study of dialogics to explain how Tan analyzes the effects of traditional Chinese culture on second-generation Chinese Americans. Wang examines the daughters' struggles for balance in the novel and links them back to the Chinese belief in balance for harmony of body and soul. She also looks at the varied effects of American culture on both the mothers and the daughters and their relationships with one another. Marc Singer approaches the study of dialogics in the text by emphasizing the past and the present. He suggests that the juxtaposition of past and present, history and myth, and the methods of presentation offer their own dialogic. Indeed, it is only through hearing all of the stories, myths, and histories, then reassembling them in the mind of the reader, that the book truly speaks, and the narrative structure helps to support that supranarrative.

Stephen Souris uses the theories of both Bakhtin and Wolfgang Iser to interrogate the text. Adding Iser's reader-response theory adds the reader's voice to the dialogic mix. The experience of understanding and grouping choices of the reader dramatically affects the experience of reading the book. Iser's theory insists on an active, intertextual engagement. Souris's reading celebrates the gaps in the narratives, as they require the reader to make the connections between the narratives and within the relationships. Souris also asserts that Iser's theories help to explain how readers experience and read the text. The reader will try to balance negative elements of the text with a more positive counterpoint. In this way, a reader might mourn the loss of Ying-ying St. Clair's aborted son in the story and balance it with the potential the story has to teach the daughters and what it taught the mother. Souris also argues that the structure of the story encourages the reader to have a more sympathetic response to the mothers and their plight as a result of when and how the reader interacts with the text. The reader knows what kind of interaction might happen between the mothers and daughters if only they would talk to each other. Readers experience that loss of potential keenly, and this draws them more deeply into the stories. Souris further adds that readers are in what Iser calls a "feedback loop" in which they must constantly revise their notions of the text in relation to the new information being offered in new chapters.

Another trend in Tan scholarship is to examine her works' portrayals of the East versus the West. Some critics have charged Tan with perpetuating stereotypical Chinese characters, exoticizing China and its people, and demonizing the East. Tamara Silvia Wagner argues that Tan actually interrogates assumptions made by the Occidentalist and the Orientalist by looking critically at the behavior of both Americans and Chinese in the book, although the interrogation is not always sufficiently critical. Boyfriend Rich becomes the tourist at the dinner table, asking about Chinese customs and behaving in ways that seem rude to the Chinese household. At the same time, the mothers criticize and question the Western approaches to parenting and decision making. Wagner discusses the realm of domesticity as a sphere in which both sides, the Chinese and the American, interact and try to understand the assumptions of the other ("Realigning"). In Wagner's essay "'A Barrage of Ethnic Comparisons': Occidental Stereotypes in Amy Tan's Novels," she also looks at Tan's use of more Americanized stereotypes, including Chinese and Jewish, which Tan uses to comedic effect to question the American ideal of the "melting pot." Wagner expresses concern that the stereotypes are not interrogated enough to prevent them from reinforcing themselves through the vehicle of the text. Using the semiotic analysis of the ethnic as theorized by William Boelhower and Werner Sollors, Mistri Zenobia argues that investigating the cultural symbols imported from Chinese culture will help to broaden potential study of the novel, particularly examination of the structure of the book as a metaphor for its larger themes.

Li Zeng uses both Tan and Maxine Hong Kingston to talk about the negotiation of ethnicity. Postmodernism has led to a great interest both in fragmented stories and in stories from outside the mainstream white male perspective. Zeng sees the daughters and mothers in *The Joy Luck Club* as negotiating, respectively, between being Chinese and being American and between being mothers and being survivors. These identities keep the two sets of women from truly knowing each other. What does eventually bridge the gap between them is shared gender experience. In this way, women are knowable across cultures, and the suffering of the mothers is recontextualized to be inclusive of the daughters' lives and fears rather than exclusionary. Ben Xu also assesses the ethnic self in Tan's novel. For the mothers, as for many immigrants, the self is constructed from what they have overcome. They are self-reliant, strong, mindful, and sly. Their daughters, like much of American society, assume that these characteristics are ethnic characteristics when, Xu argues, they are more individuated than that. The mothers do not represent China; they represent survivors. The mothers, in turn, make experiences of the events of their lives; they use those experiences to create identity. In addition, they make sense of what happened to them in terms of the moment, of what is most useful to educate their daughters. In this way, the past and present are constantly acting upon each other. In lieu of the traditional relationship a Chinese daughter might share with her mother, the mothers and daughters now connect as covictims and cosurvivors.

The Joy Luck Club is rich with Chinese cultural symbols, beliefs, and mythology. Examining those beliefs helps to create new readings of the text. Patricia L. Hamilton investigates the use of feng shui, Chinese astrology, and the five elements in the book. These aspects of Chinese culture help to make sense of the actions of the mothers, but they also create distance between the daughters and the mothers as the members of the younger generation do not have the context to make sense of their mothers' actions. This leads to disconnection between them. Still, the belief systems helped the mothers to survive their histories in China and their lives in the United States. Ellen Handler Spitz uses a Western myth—that of Demeter and Persephone—and a psychoanalytic approach to explore the relationship between mothers and daughters in the text. Walter Shear sees the text as reflective of a critical moment in immigrant history, where the traditional Chinese family unit is fractured and must be reconfigured in light of the diaspora. Tan chooses to emphasize healing possibilities in using Chinese culture, history, and stories to overcome the schism.

Clearly the stories of mothers and daughters are central to the understanding of the text and its criticism. Some critics approach those relationships as representative of movements in Chinese American literature and as a larger part of the women's movement. Wendy Ho positions the book in terms of the women's movement. During the 1960s and 1970s, many women of color were dissatisfied with the women's movement as it seemed centrally focused on the concerns and lives of middle-class white women and unsympathetic to the unique concerns of women of color, including Asian American women. The forebears of many Asian Americans were brought to the United States as labor commodities. In 1943, the Magnuson Act finally added women to the quota of Chinese allowed into the United States (Huntley 21). The Chinese who entered had concerns that were markedly different from those of white middle-class women. They contended with racist stereotypes, disrespect shown to themselves and their husbands, and the task of educating their children in Chinese culture and tradition. When the mainstream feminist movement of the 1970s and 1980s called for a reclamation of women's stories, Asian American writers responded, as in the cases of Tan, Kingston, and Fae Myenne Ng. The movement intended to reclaim stories and histories from the patriarchal, imperialist, capitalist traditions. In Tan's novel, the mothers suffer dislocation as their histories and beliefs are independent of their daughters' experience. Unfortunately, differences in social strata, cultural histories, and other matters make it difficult for the younger women to connect with their mothers. However, on a larger scale, Ho sees the book as helping to make mother-daughter connections in the lives of the readers. She explores the public reception of the book and the way in which its mother-daughter stories brought mothers and daughters together across social, economic, and ethnic strata. Some critics have scoffed at the popular response the novel generated and the outreach it has created with readers, claiming it to be "sentimental." Ho argues that this response invalidates the history of women and women's culture. Ho also addresses Tan's assertion that her book is not to be taken as a monolithic explanation of all things Chinese or as a primer for the would-be tourist. Xiaomei Chen adds to this vision of *The Joy Luck Club* as a unifying text by exploring the mother-daughter bond as it connects women and women's literature across generations, cultures, and histories.

Megali Cornier Michael argues that another part of the women's perspective in *The Joy Luck Club* is the privileging of the community over the individual. She uses the novel's San Francisco Joy Luck Club as a primary example of this idea. The club gives the women agency; rather than having consistent losers and winners, the women pull together to offer each other power and support with which they can thrive in their adopted country. They even pass on the sense of community to the younger generation through their support of June and her trip to China. Marina Heung adds to the view of the mother-daughter relationship by positing the mother as the fulcrum between the past and the present. The daughter can understand the two only by engaging the texts/lives of the mother. In this way, the text is transformed from the typical daughter-centered text to a mother-centered text. By the end of the book, the only individual privileged to see all of the stories and their intersections is the reader. In this way, the text moves to become sister-centered as the reader re-creates the connections of the text.

The text's conversion to film has also brought comparative studies. Karen Fang sees *The Joy Luck Club* as part of an ongoing cultural conversation about Asian representation in film. To what extent must the filmmaker present Asian characters in a positive light? Are stereotypes being reproduced ad infinitum, and to what end? How are the women of *The Joy Luck Club* portrayed? Do they move outside of the stereo-types of Asian American women? Do they go beyond the China doll and the dragon lady? Robert Mielke's inquiry focuses on whether the film is as strong in its medium as the novel is as a novel. Ultimately, Mielke asserts, overexplanation and sentimentality rob the film of the complexity and texture the novel possesses, making it a much less suc-cessful example of its genre. Claire A. Conceison opens up a new venue for criticism by examining the process of producing the live the-atrical version of *The Joy Luck Club* across cultures. This process may very well elicit more critique in the future.

Since *The Joy Luck Club*, Tan has published the novels *The Kitchen God's Wife*, *The Hundred Secret Senses*, *The Bonesetter's Daughter*, and *Saving Fish from Drowning* as well as the nonfiction volume *The Opposite of Fate*. She has also written children's books. The critical re-ception of her work has been largely positive, although some critics continue to question Tan's endings and her fragmented style. Still, she has seen great success in the classroom, with the presence of her works on collegiate syllabi a testament to her growing importance in Chinese American literature. Increased interest in postmodernism and frag-mented storytelling styles will likely continue to breed commentary on Tan's work, as will interest in women's history and the history of women of color. Also, the proliferation of books by and about women of color will surely invite comparison of Tan's novels to texts about other immigrant groups and other groups split between American and immigrant identities. Tan's fiction will likely continue to be a staple in women's studies, Asian studies, and literature classrooms for the fore-seeable future.

Works Cited or Consulted

Bow, Leslie. "The Triumph of the Prefeminist Chinese Woman? Incorporating Ra-cial Difference Through Feminist Narrative." *Betrayal and Other Acts of Sub-version: Feminism, Sexual Politics, Asian American Women's Literature.* Princeton, NJ: Princeton UP, 2001.

Braendlin, Bonnie. "Mother/Daughter Dialog(ic)s in, Around, and About Amy Tan's *The Joy Luck Club*." *Private Voices, Public Lives: Women Speak on the Literary Life*. Ed. Nancy Owen Nelson. Denton: U of North Texas P, 1995. 111-24.

Chen, Xiaomei. "Reading Mother's Tale: Reconstructing Women's Space in Amy Tan and Zhang Jie." *Chinese Literature: Essays, Articles, Reviews (CLEAR)* 16 (Dec. 1994): 111-32.

Chin, Frank. "Come All Ye Asian American Writers of the Real and the Fake." *The Big Aiiieeeee: An Anthology of Chinese American and Japanese American Literature*. Ed. Jeffery Paul Chan et al. New York: Meridian, 1991.

Conceison, Claire A. "Translating Collaboration: *The Joy Luck Club* and Intercultural Theatre." *Drama Review* 39.3 (Autumn 1995): 151-66.

Cooperman, Jeannette Batz. *The Broom Closet: Secret Meanings of Domesticity in Postfeminist Novels by Louise Erdrich, Mary Gordon, Toni Morrison, Marge Piercy, Jane Smiley, and Amy Tan*. New York: Peter Lang, 1999.

Dunick, Lisa M. S. "The Silencing Efforts of Canonicity: Authorship and the Written Word in Amy Tan's Novels." *MELUS* 31.2 (Summer 2006): 3-20.

Fang, Karen. "Globalization, Masculinity, and the Changing Stakes of Hollywood Cinema for Asian American Studies." *Asian American Literary Studies*. Ed. Guiyou Huang. Edinburgh: Edinburgh UP, 2005. 79-108.

Gately, Patricia. "Ten Thousand Different Ways: Inventing Mothers, Inventing Hope." *Paintbrush: A Journal of Multicultural Literature* 22 (Autumn 1995): 51-54.

Hamilton, Patricia L. "*Feng Shui*, Astrology, and the Five Elements: Traditional Chinese Belief in Amy Tan's *The Joy Luck Club*." *MELUS* 24.2 (Summer 1999): 125-45.

Heung, Marina. "Daughter-Text/Mother-Text: Matrilineage in Amy Tan's *The Joy Luck Club*." *Feminist Studies* 19.3 (Fall 1993): 597-613.

Ho, Wendy. "Feminist Recovery and Reception: Chinese American Mother-Daughter Stories." *In Her Mother's House: The Politics of Asian American Mother-Daughter Writing*. Walnut Creek, CA: AltaMira Press, 1999. 31-62.

Huntley, E. D. *Amy Tan: A Critical Companion*. Westport, CT: Greenwood Press, 1998.

Li, David Leiwei. "Genes, Generation, and Geospiritual (Be)longings." *Imagining the Nation: Asian American Literature and Cultural Consent*. Stanford: Stanford UP, 1998. 111-25.

Michael, Megali Cornier. "Choosing Hope and Remaking Kinship: Amy Tan's *The Joy Luck Club*." *New Visions of Community in Contemporary American Fiction: Tan, Kingsolver, Castille, Morrison*. Iowa City: U of Iowa P, 2006. 39-71.

Mielke, Robert. "'American Translation': *The Joy Luck Club* as Film." *Paintbrush: A Journal of Multicultural Literature* 22 (Autumn 1995): 68-75.

Mountain, Chandra Tyler. "'The Struggle of Memory Against Forgetting': Cultural Survival in Amy Tan's *The Joy Luck Club*." *Paintbrush: A Journal of Multicultural Literature* 22 (Autumn 1995): 39-50

Reid, E. Shelley. "'Our Two Faces': Balancing Mothers and Daughters in *The Joy*

Luck Club and *The Kitchen God's Wife.*" *Paintbrush: A Journal of Multicultural Literature* 22 (Autumn 1995): 30-38.

Schell, Orville. "'Your Mother Is in Your Bones.'" *New York Times* 19 Mar. 1989, late ed.: A3.

Shear, Walter. "Generational Differences and the Diaspora in *The Joy Luck Club.*" *Critique* 34.3 (Spring 1993): 193-99.

Shen, Gloria. "Born of a Stranger: Mother-Daughter Relationships and Storytelling in Amy Tan's *The Joy Luck Club.*" *International Women's Writing: New Landscapes of Identity.* Ed. Anne E. Brown and Marjanne E. Goozé. Westport, CT: Greenwood Press, 1995. 233-44.

Singer, Marc. "Moving Forward to Reach the Past: The Dialogics of Time in Amy Tan's *The Joy Luck Club.*" *Journal of Narrative Theory* 31.3 (Fall 2001): 324-52.

Skow, John. "Tiger Ladies." *Time* 27 Mar. 1989. http://www.time.com/time/magazine/article/0,9171,957340,00.html

Souris, Stephen. "'Only Two Kinds of Daughters': Inter-Monologue Dialogicity in *The Joy Luck Club.*" *MELUS* 19.2 (Summer 1994): 99-123.

Spitz, Ellen Handler. "Mothers and Daughters: Ancient and Modern Myths." *Journal of Aesthetics and Art Criticism* 48.4 (Autumn 1990): 411-20.

Stanton, David. "Breakfast with Amy Tan." *Paintbrush: A Journal of Multicultural Literature* 22 (Autumn 1995): 5-19.

Wagner, Tamara Silvia. "'A Barrage of Ethnic Comparisons': Occidental Stereotypes in Amy Tan's Novels." *Critique* 45.4 (Summer 2004): 435-45.

_____. "Realigning and Reassigning Cultural Values: Occidentalist Stereotyping and Representations of the Multiethnic Family in Asian American Women Writers." *Asian American Literary Studies.* Ed. Guiyou Huang. Edinburgh: Edinburgh UP, 2005. 152-75.

Wang, Qun. "The Dialogic Richness of *The Joy Luck Club.*" *Paintbrush: A Journal of Multicultural Literature* 22 (Autumn 1995): 76-84.

Xu, Ben. "Memory and the Ethnic Self: Reading Amy Tan's *The Joy Luck Club.*" *MELUS* 19.1 (Spring 1994): 3-18.

Xu, Wenying. "Amy Tan." *Asian American Novelists: A Bio-bibliographical Critical Sourcebook.* Ed. Emmanuel S. Nelson. Westport, CT: Greenwood Press, 2000. 365-73.

_____. "A Womanist Production of Truths: The Use of Myths in Amy Tan." *Paintbrush: A Journal of Multicultural Literature* 22 (Autumn 1995): 56-67.

Yuan, Yuan. "The Semiotics of 'China Narrative' in the Con/Texts of Kingston and Tan." *Ideas of Home: Literature of Asian Migration.* Ed. Geoffrey Kain. East Lansing: Michigan State UP, 1997.

Zeng, Li. "Diasporic Self, Cultural Other: Negotiating Ethnicity Through Transformation in the Fiction of Tan and Kingston." *Language and Literature* 28 (2003): 1-15.

Zenobia, Mistri. "Discovering the Ethnic Name and Genealogical Tie in Amy Tan's *The Joy Luck Club.*" *Studies in Short Fiction* 35.3 (Summer 1998): 251-57.

The Joy Luck Club:
Cultural and Historical Contexts_____

Robert C. Evans

When Amy Tan's *The Joy Luck Club* was first published in hardcover in the early months of 1989, the book seemed in many ways a perfect reflection of its era. By the time the work was chosen in the fall of that year as one of five finalists for the National Book Award, ensuing events—especially in China itself—had made the text seem in some ways even more timely than when it had first appeared. Whether by accident or by design, Tan had produced a work that mirrored many of the central developments of life in the 1980s, not only within the Chinese American community in particular and within the Asian American community in general, but also within the United States and in the world as a whole. Of course, the timeliness of the book cannot by itself explain its enormous initial success, let alone its continuing perennial appeal. Ultimately the impact of the work depended then (and still depends, and will depend increasingly) on Tan's talent as an artist—as a literary craftsperson skilled in the use of words, gifted with an aptitude for structure and design, and endowed with convincing insight into human psychology and behavior. These are the qualities that will help keep *The Joy Luck Club* continually alive and will help make future readers still want to read it. Nevertheless, the book will also always retain some interest because of the ways in which it captures and conveys the specific cultural and historical contexts of its time.

The Baby Boomers

Tan herself (who was born in 1952) has attributed part of her novel's success to the fact that she wrote as a "baby boomer" and presumably appealed to other members of that very large and highly influential generation (Somogyi and Stanton 29). "The baby boom" is a term used to describe the enormous jump in the birthrate that followed the end of

World War II (in 1945). The boom continued during the first decade or so of renewed prosperity that followed the cessation of the war. U.S. soldiers returning home were often eager to marry, settle down, and start families, and the many children born in these years enjoyed conditions of peace, prosperity, and increasing well-being largely unknown to their parents. Those parents had suffered through the Great Depression, which preceded the most catastrophic war in human history. In contrast, the generation raised in the 1950s and early 1960s experienced a much easier and more privileged lifestyle than their parents had, and this was generally true across all demographic groups. New kinds of opportunities of all sorts were opening for nearly all segments of society, and these positive changes are obviously reflected in the generally affluent lifestyles of the younger generation of characters in *The Joy Luck Club*, who face challenges far less daunting than the ones faced by their parents. Tan's book manages to convey many of the typical traits of the baby boomers while also paying a moving if belated tribute to the elders who had prepared the way for the boomers' relative success. Tan offers subtle satire of the so-called yuppies (young urban—or upwardly mobile—professionals), a group much in the news in the 1980s, while also gently and lovingly mocking some traits of the older generation as well.

Significantly, the very differences between the experiences of the prewar and postwar generations had led, in many cases, to the so-called generation gap—a broad sense of widespread tension between the two groups. These tensions became especially prominent in the 1960s. Parents often came to feel that their children failed to appreciate the advantages they had enjoyed and failed to honor properly the parents who had made those advantages possible. Young people in the 1960s and 1970s, in turn, often came to feel that their parents were "out of touch" with new, more "progressive" ways of thinking, feeling, and behaving, especially with the desire among many young people to experiment with new lifestyles, to challenge traditions, and to "do their own thing." In the United States, in particular, differences over the Vietnam

War, over the breakdown of "law and order," and over a broad trend toward "liberalism" in many aspects of life helped exacerbate this kind of generational friction. The "gap" between the generations was memorably (and popularly) summarized in 1965 when one twenty-four-year-old leader of a student rebellion commented that "we don't trust anyone over 30" (qtd. in Platt 343). That statement soon became a slogan for many young people during the later 1960s.

By the late 1980s, of course, the young radicals of the 1960s were themselves rapidly approaching or were well into middle age. In any case, they were well over thirty. Anyone born in 1946 was forty-three years old when *The Joy Luck Club* first appeared. Many such people now had rebellious children of their own and could appreciate the experiences of their parents in new and unexpected ways. They now knew what it was like to struggle to earn a living, pay taxes, and raise children who did not always appreciate their guidance. In addition, many of the parents of these suddenly middle-aged baby boomers were now in their twilight years. Many were increasingly frail and sickly, and some—like Suyuan Woo, the recently deceased mother of Jingmei (June) Woo in *The Joy Luck Club*—had already died. Tan's novel thus spoke, potentially, to two whole generations of readers who sought to bridge the "generation gap" while there was still time to do so.

In particular, the book helped baby boomers appreciate the struggles and wisdom of their elders—elders who would eventually come to be called "the greatest generation" because of all the sacrifices and suffering they had endured (see Brokaw). Tan's text allowed members of her age group to look back on their own childhoods with a combination of nostalgia for times past, appreciation of their parents' virtues, and understanding of their parents' foibles. *The Joy Luck Club* is very much a book about what it means to grow older oneself and about what it also means to see one's parents age, weaken, and die. In both respects, then, the book reflects the specific concerns of a particular (and very large) group of readers of the late 1980s, but it also reflects an enduring human experience. In that sense, the book is unlikely ever to seem irrelevant. One need not be Chinese American or female to appreciate this dimension of *The Joy Luck Club*; one need only be an ever-aging person of any sort with ever-aging parents of one's own.

The Women's Movement

Clearly *The Joy Luck Club* also reflects the rise of feminism and the growing social, political, and economic influence of women from the 1960s to the 1980s. Although further progress obviously remained to be made, by 1989 the women's movement could look back on more than two decades of gains in profeminist legislation, in solid advances toward economic equality, and in substantial changes in popular thinking about women's social roles. Few people in the late 1980s would have disputed the idea that women should receive equal pay for equal work, nor would many people have challenged the idea that women should have equal opportunities to excel in whatever professions they choose. Men (especially husbands and fathers) had far less automatic or dictatorial influence over women's lives in the United States in the late 1980s than was true in earlier decades, and *The Joy Luck Club* depicts its younger women as either already free from male domination or in the process of winning or asserting such liberty. One daughter (Jing-mei Woo) is unmarried and has a reasonably successful career as a business writer; another daughter (Waverly Jong) has already been divorced and is an accomplished tax attorney; yet another daughter (Rose Hsu) has gained enough self-confidence by the end of the book to assert herself in her dealings with her philandering husband, who is seeking a divorce; while the fourth daughter (Lena St. Clair) also learns, thanks to her mother's influence, to begin to assert herself in her disappointing relationship with her rich but penny-pinching husband, Harold Livotny. If anything, the main tensions the book depicts, at least in its chapters focusing on the United States, are not tensions between men and women (whether fathers and daughters or husbands and wives) but tensions between mothers and daughters. Much of the book is concerned with showing the ways those tensions are overcome or resolved, so that by the end of the text all the main female characters seem to have achieved deeper and fuller appreciations of one another.

The book is, in many respects, a celebration of the power and resourcefulness of women, especially their ability not only to survive but also, eventually, to thrive under difficult circumstances. *The Joy Luck Club* is a tribute to the older women it depicts even as it acknowledges the economic and social gains achieved by their daughters. At the same time, however, the book is not pugnaciously or stridently feminist; it does not depict all men as inevitably or universally oppressive. The tone of the text is not combative, and so it can appeal to male readers as well as to females. Nearly all the major characters in the work, both men and women, have flaws as well as strengths, vices as well as virtues, and are therefore recognizably true to life. Tan manages to help all readers—both male and female—appreciate the strengths (while acknowledging the foibles) of their parents (especially their mothers). At the same time, she depicts the value and potential of the younger sisterhood of women, who nevertheless have shortcomings of their own.

Multiculturalism

By the late 1980s, the United States—thanks in part to a significant change in immigration laws in the 1960s—was becoming an increasingly multicultural society. The Civil Rights movement that had come to prominence in the same decade had helped produce real growth in the economic, social, and political power of African Americans, and a growing influx of Hispanic immigrants (especially from Cuba and Mexico) had also helped change the face of the country, not to mention the patterns of its speech and the flavor of its popular culture. Between 1980 and 1988, moreover, there had been a 70 percent increase in the Asian population of the United States. A Census Bureau report from early 1990 indicates that the "Asian population grew nearly seven times as fast as the general population as well as three times as fast as the black population." Asian Americans, according to the same report, "numbered about 6.5 million on July 1, 1988, up from 3.8 million eight years earlier" (Barringer). Asians, moreover, were less likely to suffer discrimination in housing than were blacks (Hays), and prejudice against Asians in employment opportunities had declined significantly since the 1960s ("Study Finds"). Both factors helped contribute to growing Asian American success.

Nevertheless, Asians did suffer various kinds of discrimination, often due in part (ironically) to their increasing prominence, both at home and abroad. The rise of Japan as an economic superpower had led many Americans to feel threatened by competition not only from that country but also from other progressive Asian nations, such as Korea and Taiwan. Moreover, by the late 1980s mainland China, which had been crippled for decades by its adherence to strict Maoist communism, had begun to abandon various old dogmas and had thus begun to come alive economically. Numerous analysts began predicting that China, too, might soon become an economic powerhouse and a significant global competitor for the United States.

Finally, even (or especially) within America itself, Asians had increasingly become a group to be reckoned with. Thus an article from August 1986 reported that although "Asian-Americans make up only 2.1 percent of the population of the United States, they are surging into the nation's best colleges like a tidal wave." Social scientists sought various ways to account for this astounding academic success (Butterfield). In any case, and however the achievement of Asian American students was explained, it helped lead to a backlash of sorts, and claims of anti-Asian bias and quotas in admissions to higher education began to arise (Lindsey, "Colleges"; see also Johnson). For this reason and others, Asian Americans felt a growing need to assert themselves politically (see Gurwit; Iritani; Lindsey, "Asian-Americans"). By the late 1980s, Asians were becoming an increasingly visible—and forceful—presence in American society.

To complicate matters even further, the academic success of Asian

Americans led many commentators to label them as a "model minority"—a label that not only caused problems within the Asian American community itself (especially among young people who did not live up to the stereotype of "the docile whiz kid" [Lee; see also Bernstein]) but also exacerbated tensions between Asian Americans and members of other minority groups. Unease between Asian Americans and African Americans, in particular, could be especially acute ("Black-Asian Tension"). Intermarriage was far more likely to occur between whites and Asians than between Asians and blacks—a fact clearly reflected in Tan's book. Moreover, many non-Asian Americans tended to lump all Asians together rather than appreciating the significant differences that exist (for instance) among various national and linguistic groups. Important differences also exist between recent immigrants and longtime U.S. citizens and between Asians of higher and lower economic classes. The number and complexity of all these differences often made it difficult for Asian Americans to unite and act as a coherent political and cultural force (Gross). Thus Asian Americans, when viewed as a homogeneous group, seemed increasingly powerful, but the Asian American community itself was in reality far less coherent and united than it seemed to many outsiders.

The Joy Luck Club reflects, in many ways, the various multicultural contexts just described. The book helps remind non-Asian readers, for example, of the significant conflict that existed throughout much of the twentieth century between China and Japan. The original Chinese Joy Luck Club was born, after all, during the time of Japan's invasion of China, and the lives of many of the book's main characters were directly and adversely affected by that war with the Japanese. If any non-Asian reader needed reminding that all Asians are not the same, Tan's book definitely helped serve that purpose. At the same time, by describing the lifestyles of the younger generation of characters in *The Joy Luck Club*, Tan also showed how thoroughly many Asian Americans had already become assimilated into broader American society and how completely (for good or ill) they had embraced many of the values of the larger culture. If many non-Asian Americans were worried, at this time, by the rise of a Japanese superpower, Tan's book helped show how totally "American" a large segment of the Asian American community had already become. Intermarriage between Asians and whites is common in Tan's text (although black characters seem almost entirely absent), and racial discrimination by whites against Asians is stressed far less forcefully than it might have been. In addition, Tan's work helped illuminate the kinds of tensions that could exist within the Chinese American community itself and especially within Chinese American families. In some ways the book confirms many of the stereotypes associated with the "model minority" (although a son of at least one of the Chinese families has been arrested as a thief [Tan 35]), but in describing Jing-mei, in particular, Tan shows that not all Asian Americans desire (or are able) to live up to the stereotype of the "docile whiz kid." Tan depicts the emotional and psychological costs often paid by children who are expected to become high achievers; at the same time, however, she also helps explain why high achievement by their children was so important to so many first-generation Chinese immigrants.

The total effect of *The Joy Luck Club* is to humanize nearly every one of its major characters. The book takes non-Asians inside a community they tend to know only from the outside; it shows how much Asians and non-Asians have in common, especially in terms of family dynamics. Paradoxically, although the work focuses on a community that would have seemed somewhat mysterious to many non-Asian readers in 1989, the ultimate effect of the text is to emphasize the kinds of family bonds and tensions, as well as the kinds of interpersonal friendships and conflicts, that characterize most human relationships. *The Joy Luck Club* was published at a time when many Americans were increasingly interested in learning about Asians both inside and outside the United States, and the book helped reveal the ways in which China and Chinese Americans could seem both intriguingly different and reassuringly familiar.

The Rise of China

Through one of those strange (but not infrequent) accidents of history, *The Joy Luck Club* happened to be published in one of the most important of all years in the history of China's relations with the outside world. By the spring of 1989 China was embroiled in widespread and unexpected social turmoil—turmoil that made it seem possible, for a brief time, that a wholesale political and cultural revolution might occur. Suddenly Americans became even more interested in China than they had already been throughout the 1980s.

Following the Communist revolution of 1949, China had remained poor and economically stagnant. After the death of dictator Mao Zedong in 1976, however, reform-minded Communists under the leadership of Deng Xiaoping began to liberalize the economy, making it more competitive and more efficient. These new leaders adopted many aspects of the capitalism that had worked so well in many other countries. By the early to mid-1980s, China's economy had begun to improve rapidly, but by 1988 rampant inflation was a serious concern. "To solve this problem the Chinese Communist Party (CCP) instructed the government to call a temporary halt to economic reform in September 1988" (Starr 179). By the spring of 1989, however, events had begun to spiral out of control. "Concern over inflation and corruption brought the populace into the streets of every major city in China once demonstrations began in mid-April" (Starr 179). The more the government tried to reimpose order, the larger the demonstrations became. "By May 17 more than 1 million people were demonstrating each day, including not only students but also workers, professional people, and government officials" (Starr 181). Students even erected a crude but inspiring thirty-foot-tall Statue of Liberty in Tiananmen Square, the center of government power in Beijing. Many people—especially in the United States and in Western Europe—strongly sympathized with the demonstrators and hoped that their protests might lead to significant further liberalization in China. Instead, however, in "the early morning hours of June 4" government "troops opened fire, and by dawn, had brought this episode in China's democracy movement to a bloody halt" (Starr 181).

The Joy Luck Club undoubtedly benefited from the American obsession with China throughout much of 1989. The book reflects the optimism that existed prior to mid-1989 about the prospects for greater friendship between China and the United States and for renewed ties between the population of mainland China and the population of Chinese immigrants in the United States. Tan's book showed that many Chinese Americans (especially among the younger generation) had already become strongly assimilated into the mainstream of American society, and an unspoken implication of the book is that China itself—after its long isolation—might eventually become part of the larger family of modern, democratic nations. When Jing-mei travels to China with her father at the end of the book and embraces her long-lost Chinese sisters (Tan 287-88), the episode not only enacts a private family reunion but also symbolizes the new contacts that had begun to grow up between China and the West. Tan's novel was written during a period when the prospect of greater ties between China and the United States seemed not only realistic but also inevitable. The book was read, however, especially in the latter half of 1989 and into 1990, by numerous people precisely when those ties seemed sorely strained and close to breaking. Tan's book depicts (especially in its chapters focused on the mother characters) the tragedies caused by political turmoil in China in the first half of the twentieth century. Ironically, by the second half of 1989 this emphasis on the tragedy of unrest in China must also have seemed strangely and unpredictably relevant to many of the novel's readers.

The Reagan Revolution

For lack of a better term, the phrase "the Reagan Revolution" can be used to summarize a variety of developments (both foreign and domestic) that occurred in the 1980s and that helped provide important historical and cultural contexts for *The Joy Luck Club*. Republican Ronald Reagan, who was elected president of the United States in November 1980 in a landslide victory over Democrat Jimmy Carter, occupied the White House until January 20, 1989, when he was succeeded by his own vice president, George H. W. Bush. Throughout the 1970s, confidence in the United States had seemed to be in decline, both inside and outside the United States. The Vietnam War had been a fiasco, Richard Nixon had resigned the presidency in disgrace, the economy was crippled by stagnation and inflation, and communism seemed to be making aggressive inroads throughout the world. Perhaps most humiliating and infuriating to many Americans, on November 4, 1979, a group of radical Iranian students had seized control of the U.S. embassy in Tehran and held fifty-two Americans hostage for 444 days with the approval of the revolutionary Iranian government. The continuing crisis, along with the poor economy, were two main causes (among many) of Carter's electoral loss to Reagan. During his inaugural address on January 20, 1981, Reagan was able to announce that the Iranians had finally agreed to free the hostages, who in fact were on a plane on their way home even as he spoke. Many Americans attributed this outcome, as well as many other positive events over the next eight years, to Reagan's declared intention to revive and reassert American power and self-confidence.

By the time Reagan left office in January 1989 (right around the time of the initial publication of *The Joy Luck Club*), he seemed to have had—at least in his eyes and the eyes of his supporters—a remarkably successful presidency. The economy was growing rapidly, U.S. military might had been restored, Americans were far more optimistic than they had been in years, and Reagan's conservative ethic—which emphasized the importance of strong family ties, hard work, and "traditional values"—had won many new adherents. For better or for worse, the country seemed a different kind of place than it had been in the radical 1960s or in the depressed, depressing 1970s. Reagan had accomplished many of his domestic and foreign policy goals, and the whole tide of human history seemed to be moving in directions he had favored. Most significant, communism seemed to be in rapid decline, and the prospects for democratic freedom and the growth of capitalism had rarely seemed brighter. As one contemporary observer wrote, in attempting to sum up this memorable year, "The signposts of history have changed, . . . and seldom more radically than in 1989. They are now pointing toward democracy and away from dictatorships of all kinds, but especially the Communist version" (Senser 25). Even the defeat of the prodemocracy movement in China seemed, to many, merely a postponement of inevitable and positive change, and in fact it was possible for one influential intellectual (and an Asian American at that) to suggest, in the summer of 1989, that "what we may be witnessing is not just the end of the Cold War [against communism], or the passing of a particular period of post-war history, but the end of history as such: that is, the end point of mankind's ideological evolution and the universalization of Western liberal democracy as the final form of human government" (Fukuyama 107). Subsequent events (especially those of September 11, 2001) would, of course, prove this prediction highly premature, but in 1989 the United States, and many of the foreign and domestic principles associated with Ronald Reagan, seemed to be in the ascendant.

Amy Tan's *The Joy Luck Club* can be seen as reflecting many of these developments in various ways. Her book's implicit celebration of family ties and family values would have pleased many Reaganites; the respect the book shows for the work ethic, along with the belief in the American Dream embraced by so many members of the novel's older generation, would also have appealed to many conservative readers. Meanwhile, the younger characters in Tan's book rarely lodge any fundamental protests against the political or economic conditions of their time. They may feel uncomfortable in some ways in their relations with their own parents (especially their mothers), but for the most part they seem comfortable and uncomplaining members of the American middle class. Moreover, the parents use the Joy Luck Club partly as an opportunity to play the stock market (Tan 29)—a Reaganite pastime if there ever was one. Tan, of course, often seems to be subtly satirizing the materialism of many of her characters, especially the younger ones, particularly the "yuppified" Waverly Jong and Harold Livotny. Her younger characters, however, also seem recognizably liberal, especially in their attitudes toward abortion, premarital sex, and interracial marriage. Perhaps what is most intriguing about Tan's book, however, when it is viewed from an explicitly political perspective, is how radically apolitical it seems. Reagan—a highly controversial president—is never mentioned. Mao Zedong is never mentioned, let alone defended or condemned. To the extent that the book has a political "ideology" at all, it seems to take for granted that Western, "liberal" economic and political values will ultimately prevail but that the wisdom inherited from the traditional past (whether of the West or of the East) will never lose its relevance. Little in Tan's book would have offended Ronald Reagan, and many of its themes and values might have pleased him—a claim that is offered neither as criticism nor as praise but simply as a dispassionate observation.

Other Contexts

The Joy Luck Club reflects the history and culture of its time in many more ways, of course, than the ones just mentioned. It seems worth noting, for instance, that the most popular television program in the United States in both 1988 and 1989 was *The Cosby Show*, which featured the minor tensions and strong emotional bonds existing among the members of a prosperous African American family. The widespread popularity of this show indicated that Americans in general would welcome a warm and humorous look at the lives of a minority family practicing "traditional values" and committed to the American Dream. (In 1988, the second-most popular program was *A Different World*, a spin-off of *The Cosby Show*, while in 1989 the second-most popular program was *Roseanne*, which likewise featured strong family ties, not to mention an exceedingly strong and eccentric mother figure.) The winner of the Academy Award for Best Motion Picture in 1989 was *Rain Man*, a film in which Tom Cruise, playing a materialistic and self-absorbed yuppie, gradually becomes less selfish as he develops genuine affection for his previously unknown, and exasperatingly autistic, adult brother. Once again, then, the theme of family bonds played an important role in a major work of American popular culture. The following year, the Academy Award for Best Picture was won by *Driving Miss Daisy*, a film set mainly in the 1950s and 1960s that focuses on the developing friendship between a black chauffeur and the cantankerous elderly white woman for whom he works. Miss Daisy is the sort of strong-willed (but ultimately lovable) older mother who would have seemed instantly recognizable to readers of *The Joy Luck Club*, while the film's emphasis on the growth of cross-racial understanding—on the dawning realization of how much all Americans have in common, whatever their ethnic differences—might also have appealed to many of Tan's initial readers. These are just a few additional ways in which Tan's book, first published in 1989, catches and encapsulates the spirit of its particular historical and cultural moment—a moment it nevertheless ultimately transcends.

Works Cited

Barringer, Felicity. "Asian Population in U.S. Grew by 70% in the 80's." *New York Times* 2 Mar. 1990.

Bernstein, Richard. "Asian Students Harmed by Precursors' Success." *New York Times* 10 July 1988.

"Black-Asian Tension Studied." *New York Times* 13 Oct. 1985.

Brokaw, Tom. *The Greatest Generation*. New York: Dell, 2001.

Butterfield, Fox. "Why Asians Are Going to the Head of the Class." *New York Times* 3 Aug. 1986.

Fukuyama, Francis. "The End of History?" *The Geopolitics Reader*. 2d ed. Ed. Geróid Ó Tuathail, Simon Dalby, and Paul Routledge. New York: Routledge, 2006. 107-14.

Gross, Jane. "Diversity Hinders Asians' Power in U.S." *New York Times* 25 June 1989.

Gurwit, Rob. "Asian Americans Seek Clout: Violence, Judicial Results Stir Demands for Change." *Seattle Times* 30 Dec. 1990.

Hays, Constance L. "Study Says Prejudice in Suburbs Is Aimed Mostly at Blacks." *New York Times* 23 Nov. 1988.

Iritani, Evelyn. "Asian-Americans Find It's Time to Flex Their Political Muscle." *Seattle Post-Intelligencer* 6 July 1988.

Johnson, Julie. "Wider Door at Top Colleges Sought by Asian-Americans." *New York Times* 9 Sept. 1989.

Lee, Felicia R. "'Model Minority' Label Taxes Asian Youths." *New York Times* 20 Mar. 1990.

Lindsey, Robert. "Asian-Americans Press to Gain Political Power." *New York Times* 10 Nov. 1986.

_____. "Colleges Accused of Bias to Stem Asians' Gains." *New York Times* 19 Jan. 1987.

Platt, Suzy, ed. *Respectfully Quoted: A Dictionary of Quotations.* New York: Barnes & Noble, 1993.

Senser, Robert A. "Communism in Flux: The Democratic Revolution." *The Americana Annual 1990.* Danbury, CT: Grolier, 1990. 24-35.

Somogyi, Barbara, and David Stanton. "Amy Tan: An Interview." *Poets & Writers Magazine* 19.5 (1991): 24-32.

Starr, John Bryan. "China, People's Republic of." *The Americana Annual 1990.* Danbury, CT: Grolier, 1990. 179-83.

"Study Finds Less Bias Against Asian Workers." *New York Times* 18 July 1988.

Tan, Amy. *The Joy Luck Club.* 1989. New York: Penguin, 2006.

The Structure of *The Joy Luck Club*:
Themes and Variations_____

Doris L. Eder

> In these frail vessels is borne onward the treasure of human affections.
>
> —George Eliot, *Middlemarch*

> All of us are like stairs, one step after another, going up and down, but all going the same way.
>
> —An-mei Hsu in *The Joy Luck Club*

With the publication of *The Joy Luck Club* in 1989, Amy Tan brought Asian American fiction into the literary mainstream. Both a commercial and a critical success, the book was serialized in four different magazines and won many literary awards, including the National Book Critics Circle Award, the Los Angeles Times Book Prize, the Bay Area Book Reviewers Award, and the Commonwealth Club Gold Award. In 1993 it was made into a film with a screenplay cowritten by Tan, and it has been adapted into a stage play in both China and the United States. The book had sold more than four and a half million copies by 1996 and has been translated into two dozen different languages (Huntley 10).

Structure

For me the most fascinating aspect of *The Joy Luck Club* is its structure. The book consists of a sequence of sixteen linked stories that, together, form a novel, though by no means a conventional one. The stories are arranged in four sections. The narrators are paired Chinese American mothers and daughters, members of the Joy Luck Club established by one of these mothers, Suyuan Woo. Suyuan's story is told by her daughter, June (Jing-mei) because Suyuan has died just before the novel opens. The other stories are recounted by An-mei Hsu, Lindo

Jong, and Ying-ying St. Clair. The maternal narratives wrap around and envelop their daughters' stories—those of Jing-mei, Waverly Jong, Rose Hsu Jordan, and Lena St. Clair. June/Jing-mei's narratives, which predominate, serve as a "frame" around the series that brings the sequence full circle.

In their wide-ranging geographic scope and extended time span, the stories that make up *The Joy Luck Club* encompass two generations of mothers' and daughters' lives and also include anecdotes about grandparents. The novel moves from cities in eastern and southern China (Shanghai, Guilin, and Wuxi, for example) during the 1920s and 1930s, and the onset of the Sino-Japanese War, to San Francisco in the latter decades of the twentieth century. The novel shuttles back and forth between past and present, one of its challenges being to unite the two.

Tan's first novel resembles a complex mosaic or rich tapestry and is brilliantly organized and articulated. *The Joy Luck Club* blends different genres and modes of narrative. These include autobiography and biography, fable or parable, fantasy, realism, comedy, and tragicomedy. The frame story grounds the novel in the present; its fabric is realistic. The mothers' stories leading off from this contain more fabulous or fantastic elements than the daughters' stories, so Tan's placement of them first means that the work shades gradually from fantasy into realism and back again, though all is contained within the tough integument of the frame story. *The Joy Luck Club* may be called postmodern. Its mode is not magical realism because, though it contains many fantastic and exotic features, these are realistically grounded. An argument can be made for the work being postmodern, for, as Bella Adams observes, the "how" of the story shapes its "what": how the novel is narrated determines its content, which is further modified by readers' differing perceptions (Adams 36).

The Joy Luck Club differs from conventional novels in that it lacks a principal character or a traditional plot. Jing-mei Woo comes closest to being the protagonist and is certainly the principal narrator; as stand-in for the author, she is given more narrative space than anyone else in the book. In addition to presenting seven different narrators, *The Joy Luck Club* is also remarkable for its wry humor, most of which inheres in Tan's use of Chinese *gong gu tsai*, or "talk-story." Talk-story might be described as the narrative staple of the work. Talk-story encapsulates Chinese oral wisdom that is often passed down in the form of apothegms or proverbs. It is the patois the four Chinese aunts speak as they exchange gossip in a kind of pidgin English that is sometimes right on target. For example, An-mei Hsu reproves her daughter for confiding her troubles to a "psyche-atric," not to her mother, while Ying-ying St. Clair describes her daughter's and son-in-law's profession to her sister-in-law as "arty-tecky." E. D. Huntley sees talk-story as enabling women, who have been condemned for most of their lives to silence by a patriarchal society, to unburden themselves in a manner that maintains a comfortable distance between speaker and audience. It has been therapeutic for Chinese women and has empowered them (Huntley 32).

Narration

The Joy Luck Club presents a large cast of characters. If it is increasingly true that most of us nowadays live multiple lives, not a single existence, the Chinese women in this work have each led at least two radically discontinuous lives—one in pre-Communist China, the other in the modern industrial United States. So we are presented with different lives lived by different personalities.

An overarching theme of *The Joy Luck Club* is the conflict between two generations and between two different nations and their utterly dissimilar cultures. The conflict between mothers and daughters is one of Tan's habitual themes. A second theme is the difficulty these women of different generations experience in communicating with each other. The mothers find their heritage and their life's experiences—which, for their own and their daughters' sakes, they want desperately to impart to their children—incommunicable. This is so because the families and societies in which these mothers grew up were so different in form, constituents, and customs from the ones in which their children live as to render them, in their daughters' eyes, too fantastic to be believed. Credibility is an issue. Tan needs these different first-person accounts rather than a single, third-person narrative or one presented from an omniscient viewpoint. Multivocal and multiperspectival novels are an Asian American tradition. Some critics find that the Chinese voices in *The Joy Luck Club* sound too much alike; Charlotte Painter has expressed the wish that, given the consistency of her themes from first to last, Tan had used the third person. However, Tan's predilection for the immediacy of the first person, evident in all her fiction, dictated her choice.

To understand the author's dilemma in conferring credibility, ask yourself how brash, pert little Waverly Jong (named after her street is San Francisco) is to comprehend the kind of life her mother led in Ningpo and Tientsin as the daughter of a widow who had been raped and compelled to become a concubine to a rich merchant. Waverly's mother shares with all these mothers a longing for her offspring's success and fulfillment. Intensely proud of Waverly, she is sad, indeed shamed, that her pride in her daughter is not reciprocated. She had hoped Waverly would make the best of the heady combination of "American circumstances and Chinese character. How could I know these two things do not mix?" she asks herself. She is convinced that only her daughter's hair and eyes remain Chinese, that otherwise she is "American-made" (254-55). Similarly, how can the more empathetic June (Jing-mei Woo) understand her mother's abandonment of two baby daughters on her flight from Kweilin to Chungking during wartime? What experience has she of war, invasion, disease, or famine?

Readers may share similar quandaries in confronting the extraordinary experiences of these women. The discontinuities and incommunicability of their experience—migrants as they are between two different universes—must be pieced together from a welter of different scenes, events, and relationships. The book is a kind of puzzle, which makes reading it both challenging and involving. As Nancy Willard remarks in her review of *The Joy Luck Club*, "If the book has a plot, it is [the] characters' slow progress from confusion to understanding" (97). Another critic, Jeffrey F. L. Partridge, detects as the master plot of all Tan's work a foray into a mysterious, exotic, and tragic past to discover family secrets and bring back this knowledge so that, integrated into the present, it will bring about a better future.[1]

Style

As complicated in structure as *The Joy Luck Club* is, a contrasting and remarkable aspect of the book is the simplicity of its style. Amy Tan has said that when she began writing as a child she emulated her father's simple, honest sermons.[2] (John Tan was a Baptist minister and engineer who died of a brain tumor when Amy Tan was in her teens.) Another reason for her style's limpidity or lucidity is that Tan wrote this book for her mother and in memory of her grandmother. Through it she hoped to explain herself to her mother and her mother to herself. The dedication reads simply: "You asked me once what I would remember. This, and much more" (vi). Tan's mother, Daisy, did not understand English well. Like Suyuan and Jing-mei, their fictional counterparts, Daisy Tan addressed Amy in Chinese; Amy responded in English. The theme of incommunicability is further underlined by June/Jing-mei when she says: "My mother and I never really understood one another. We translated each other's meanings and I seemed to hear less than what was said, while my mother heard more" (37). As Julie Lew has observed, Tan deliberately devised a language for this book that would not draw attention to itself but simply tell a story. Still, this is the art that conceals art: Tan is a compulsive reviser who rewrites passages as many as twenty times if she thinks it called for (Lew 23). Her straightforward, seemingly simple prose style is in no way facile, and the book's structure is no less cunning.

Genesis

The Joy Luck Club originated in a short story titled "Endgame," which corresponds to the section in the book in which Waverly Jong becomes a junior chess champion ("Rules of the Game"). When Tan began writing the novel, she believed she was writing a collection of short stories, and it was as such—under the provisional title "Wind and Water"—that the work was sold by her agent, Sandra Dijkstra, to the publisher.[3]

(Auto)biographical Background and Elements

Exploring biographical and autobiographical elements in Tan's work, we recognize that her first foray into fiction has its roots in familial experience. *The Joy Luck Club* and Tan's second novel, *The Kitchen God's Wife*, recount the stories of her mother (Daisy) and grandmother (Jing-mei). In *The Joy Luck Club*, Daisy Tan's experience of losing her Chinese daughters is given to Suyuan Woo, June/Jing-mei's mother, while the story of Tan's grandmother, that of a young widow raped and disowned by her own family, then becoming the concubine of a rich merchant and eventually committing suicide—ironically to ensure her son's and daughter's future—is given to the mother of An-mei. (In *The Kitchen God's Wife*, this becomes the story of Winnie Louie, mother of Pearl.) The ambivalent relationship between Suyuan and Jing-mei reflects the author's own relationship with her mother, who also had overweening ambitions for her daughter; in the novel, Jing-mei seems to make a point of thwarting her mother's aspirations (Huntley 6). It would be impossible to identify all the fictional motifs, scenes, and episodes culled from life for this book. The Joy Luck Club itself (echoed by Amy Tan's "A Fool and His Money" club) was begun in wartime as a social and investment gathering to cheer up its members. It finally provides the means for June to travel to China to be reunited with her family. The book was completed about the time Amy Tan visited China with her mother to be reunited with her long-lost sisters.

The years immediately preceding publication of *The Joy Luck Club* were tumultuous for Tan. After several years employed in helping the developmentally disabled, she had become a medical writer, then set up her own company as a business writer. A workaholic, Tan was clocking ninety-hour workweeks when she suffered a sort of breakdown and sought out a psychotherapist. However, her analyst kept dozing off as she told him her problems, so she decided to devise her own therapeutic regimen. This took the form of intensive reading, trying her hand at writing fiction for the first time, and listening to and playing jazz piano. Tan joined a writers' club and fell under the spell and influence of Louise Erdrich's *Love Medicine* (1984).[4] Like *The Joy Luck Club*, *Love Medicine* has an oral quality and comprises a series of family narratives, but these are related by Native Americans. *The Joy Luck Club* is also frequently compared to a work by another Chinese American writer, Maxine Hong Kingston. Published thirteen years before *The Joy Luck Club*, Kingston's *The Woman Warrior* is a conspectus of different genres that blends fact and fiction, memoir and novel, and contains mythic and folkloric elements, as Tan's work does.

In the mid-1980s Daisy Tan was stricken with angina, and Amy Tan resolved to take her mother to China to see the daughters from whom she had been parted for more than a quarter of a century. Tan was also determined to listen to her mother as she never had before. Comparing fact and fiction, we note that, whereas Daisy was mortally ill, in *The Joy Luck Club* Suyuan dies; Suyuan's anxiety about handing on her Chinese heritage to her daughter parallels a real-life concern of the Tans. When Amy Tan arrived in China, immediately and for the first time, she felt Chinese. This is reflected in June/Jing-mei's response to setting foot in her ancestral homeland at the end of *The Joy Luck Club*. The novel begins with Jing-mei taking her mother's place at the eastern end of the mah-jongg table—"the East is where things begin"—and ends with her journey to her ancestral homeland and reunion with and recognition of her bonds to her motherland and her lost sisters.

Fabulous and Fantastic Elements

Fantasy plays an important role in the book, and many of its scenes have a dreamlike, fairy-tale air. Tan carefully prefaces each section with a fable or parable that epitomizes the mood or drift of what follows. Consider the epigraphs or fables that preface each of the novel's four main sections: "Feathers from a Thousand *Li* Away," "The Twenty-six Malignant Gates," "American Translation," and "Queen Mother of the Western Skies." The first epigraph or vignette evokes a duck purchased in a Shanghai market that stretched its neck, striving to become a goose, and eventually metamorphosed into a kind of swan too beautiful to eat. (Swans in Chinese symbolism usually represent heterosexual love, but Tan's supersensual swan symbolizes Suyuan's love for her daughter.) After the swan's owners emigrate and pass through customs, all that remains of this bird is a single feather that its owner wishes to bequeath to her daughter when she can explain her gift in perfect American English. That day never comes, but the essential Chinese meaning of such a seemingly ephemeral gift from afar is that it carries with it all the giver's affection.[5]

The cautionary epigraph prefacing the second section of the book is admonitory and foreboding. "The Twenty-six Malignant Gates" are the gates of hell.[6] A constantly repeated motif in *The Joy Luck Club* is the mirror, and the third section of the book, concerned with the daughters' unhappy marriages, begins with a mirror episode. Feng shui forbids placing a mirror at the foot of a marriage bed, for, as the mother warns: "All your marriage happiness will bounce back and turn the opposite way" (147). Instead, this mother installs a mirror above her daughter's bed so that reflections from one mirror will bounce back into the other, multiplying her daughter's "peach-blossom happiness," or amatory good fortune. When Waverly Jong takes her mother to her hairdresser, Mr. Rory, to be coiffed for her wedding, Lindo regards both their faces in the mirror. She recalls how her mother looked into the mirror with her when she was ten years old, telling her fortune through her daughter's features. Now Lindo recognizes how double-faced she has become, how to show her American face she must conceal her Chinese face (254-56). Throughout the stories in the "American Translation" section, mothers and daughters regard themselves and each other in mirrors, the usual effect being the transformation of other into self, or vice versa. A similar effect is achieved at the novel's end when Jing-mei first catches sight of her Chinese half sisters. At first they look both familiar and foreign to her, but then her father takes a Polaroid snapshot of the three and, as they watch the photo develop, Jing-mei remarks, "I know we all see it: Together we look like our mother. Her same eyes, her same mouth, open in surprise to see, at last, her long-cherished wish" (288). It is as though Suyuan has been summoned from the dead to this family reunion.

In the vignette leading into the stories gathered under "Queen Mother of the Western Skies," a mother plays with her granddaughter. The theme of this little fable is how to gain wisdom without losing innocence. The title refers to a beneficent goddess, Syi Wang Mu, who conferred the peach of immortality on the Emperor Wu.[7] This section of the book opens with An-mei's story "Magpies," in which she recalls her mother warning her not to weep, for the turtle in their pond will swallow her tears and transform them into pearly eggs from which will hatch magpies that will fly away, chattering and laughing. The gist of this beast fable is that the tears of those who bewail their fortune nourish the happiness and laughter of others.

In Tan's fiction, as in Chinese thought, ghosts are omnipresent. Traditionally, Chinese females who lost their virginity before being married, women who eloped or committed adultery, even widows who were remarried were all regarded as ghosts, not as human beings. In *The Joy Luck Club* An-mei's and Ying-ying's stories are ghost haunted. Amy Ling has developed a new definition of Chinese ghosts (*gui*) as all that remains when the spirit has been taxed to the utmost, made to suffer "the worst that it can endure" (Ling 135). The sufferings of An-mei's mother and of Ying-ying reduce them to the status of ghosts—literally in the former case, metaphorically in the latter. An-mei's narrative "Magpies" illustrates both the identities and the status of Chinese women, who, for centuries, were dependent first on their fathers, then on their husbands; lacking both, they became nonpersons. It also dramatically exemplifies how the only revenge a woman could take on a brutal or malevolent spouse was to commit suicide and haunt him as a revenant from the next world. Wu Tsing's second wife exerts a stranglehold over him through her "pretend-suicides," and An-mei's mother finally secures her son's and daughter's futures by killing herself and threatening to haunt the rich merchant.

It is interesting to note that Tan's immersion in Chinese thought and symbology can be traced to the untimely deaths of her father and brother when she was fifteen. Both died of brain tumors within a few months, whereupon Daisy Tan "reverted completely to the customs and belief systems of her Chinese upbringing" (Huntley 5). She invoked geomancy and feng shui to find out if their home was contaminated by evil energies and influences, and shortly afterward she took her remaining son and daughter to Europe, where Amy attended finishing school in Switzerland.

The Joy Luck Club contains many allusions to Chinese folklore, symbology, and other beliefs, notably to the Chinese zodiac, the five elements, and feng shui. The Chinese zodiac comprises twelve animals: rat, ox, tiger, rabbit, dragon, snake, horse, ram, monkey, cock, dog, and pig (these were the animals that came to the Buddha when he summoned them). According to belief attached to the Chinese lunar calendar and the zodiacal animals that preside over it, one's birth date determines one's character. Thus in the novel Lindo Jong is portrayed as a horse whose principal characteristics are practicality, shrewdness, diligence, and candor, while Ying-ying is a tiger with a dual nature (alternately fierce and passive). That Waverly and Jing-mei are both rabbits is revealed in their sensitivity—Waverly positively chafes at criticism.

Also influential are the five elements (*wu-hsing*)—wood, fire, earth, metal, and water. These correlate to human organs and temperaments:

an excess of one element may be be tempered by the addition of others. In *The Joy Luck Club*, Lindo seems to have an obsession with metal. An-mei cautions her daughter Rose that there is too much wood in her, with the result that she listens too much to others and is too easily swayed by them. Wood symbolizes life, femininity, creativity, and organic material. Fire represents energy and intelligence. Earth stands for stability and endurance, while metal engenders competitiveness, business acumen, and masculinity. Water is the element "of all that flows . . . symbolizing transport and communication." As for feng shui, it has been defined as "the art of living in harmony with the land, and deriving the greatest benefit, peace and prosperity from being in the right place at the right time." It is a way of channeling the energy of the *ch'i* or life force; the mothers in *The Joy Luck Club* studiously follow the precepts of feng shui.[8]

Themes and Variations

Among the many themes of *The Joy Luck Club* are the search for identity, as well as loss of identity or face; the conflict between mothers and daughters; the conflict between Chinese and American cultures, or between East and West; the effort to connect past with present; and the difficulty of communicating across the barriers of age, generation, class, and gender. These thematic concerns are intertwined. Despite much misfortune, devastating losses, and the traumatic separation of parents from children and wives from husbands, the mothers in this novel, in general, show more sense of their own identities and self-worth than do their American progeny. Given habitual American emphases on individualism and self-reliance, this may appear paradoxical.

Suyuan is separated from her first husband and children. An-mei Hsu is parted for many years from her mother and then, when reunited with her, loses her little brother. She then goes to live in a strange household where she finds another brother of hers has been appropriated by one of her stepfather's concubines as her own son. She is witness to her mother's suicide, which is motivated by the mother's simultaneous desire to end her own life and to try to ensure better fortune for her son and daughter.

Lindo Jong is betrothed, at the age of two, to an infant boy. At twelve years of age she is married to him, only to discover that her husband dislikes and fears women so much that their marriage will never be consummated. Still, she is bound to this "man" and to the imperious mother-in-law who has reduced him to this state. Lindo's most important discovery, made on her wedding night, is that, no matter how miserable her circumstances, she is her own person: "I had genuine thoughts inside that no one could see, that no one could ever take away from me. . . . I would always remember my parents' wishes, but I would never forget myself" (58). Lindo keeps her own counsel, even finding a way of persuading her in-laws that this marriage will prove fatal to the health and happiness of their son and heir, so that they release her from it. So resourceful is she that she contrives to make her way from China to the United States, where she marries again and has seven children.

Only one of the first-generation Chinese women in *The Joy Luck Club* has no sense of identity: Ying-ying St. Clair. Her minimal sense of self is apparent in the narrative "The Moon Lady." This is a haunting story in which the little girl is separated from her family at the Moon Festival and falls into the lake at Wushi, to be fished out and placed on board another boat. As her rescuers seek her parents' floating pavilion, Ying-ying spies a little girl her own age crying loudly as she points at her, "That's not me! I'm here. I didn't fall in the water." Even though Ying-ying has been rescued and is reclaimed by her parents, she says, "I never believed my family found the same girl" (79, 82). Later she enters into a miserable marriage, is abandoned by her husband, and vengefully aborts his son. As a grown woman in San Francisco, now married to the Caucasian Clifford St. Clair, Ying-ying remains virtually a ghost. She passes on her sense of spiritlessness and self-alienation to her daughter, Lena.

The four daughters all, in their different ways, are seeking their own identities and striving to ensure that these will be as different from their mothers' as possible. Interestingly, for those daughters who are married, their marriages seem almost as unhappy and ill-fated as those contracted for their mothers by matchmakers or dictated by fell circumstance. Rose marries Ted, a dermatologist. She was attracted to Ted by his brashness and decisiveness because she is indecisive and vacillating, always able to find as many reasons for not doing something as for doing it. For years Rose has delegated all decisions and responsibility to her husband. (One reason she does so is because she feels undermined by guilt over the death of her baby brother, Bing.) As Rose's marriage falls apart, she is afraid to tell her mother because she knows An-mei will insist she hang on to her husband—even though both parents and in-laws were initially opposed to the match. Rose does not "find" or assert herself until her husband serves her with divorce papers and insists on her signing them and signing over their house as well. Discovering that Ted wishes to marry someone else, Rose suddenly refuses to be expunged and stands firm, telling her former husband that she will be staying on in their house and that he cannot simply uproot her from his life.

After a childhood haunted by maternal terrors, Lena St. Clair marries Harold, an architect. She is self-victimized in this marriage, as Rose is in hers. Lena works in Harold's firm and has helped him become its proprietor. She has continually sacrificed her interests to Harold's. Initially they split all their bills fifty-fifty, but Lena eventually winds up paying the lion's share for everything, and she earns only a seventh of what Harold earns. Her mother, Ying-ying, discovers this marriage is rotten to the core when she comes to stay with them. She determines to try to set her daughter free by confiding the secrets of her own unhappy youth. Both Ying-ying and Lena were born in the Chinese year of the tiger, and thus their nature is dual, one side full of passive suffering, the other fiercely predatory. Ying-ying resolves: "I will gather together my past. . . . I will look at a thing that has already happened. The pain that cut my spirit loose . . . I will use this sharp pain to penetrate my daughter's tough skin and cut her tiger spirit loose. She will fight me because this is the nature of two tigers. But I will win and give her my spirit, because this is the way a mother loves her daughter" (252). Tan perceives that traumatic events in the past—if confronted, understood, and assimilated—are able to "unlock" or rejuvenate the present.

Despite—or because of—their horrific experiences, Suyuan Woo, Lindo Jong, and An-mei Hsu all possess stronger senses of identity and more self-assurance than do their daughters Jing-mei, Waverly, and Rose. (The pair lacking any sense of self or confidence, Ying-ying and Lena St. Clair, are the exceptions.) The reason for this difference between the generations is that these mothers are survivors who have been tested and tempered by their lives' experiences, whereas their daughters have led relatively easy lives, are untried, and have many options. Indeed, the array of choices available to them in American society exerts a paralyzing effect on them. There is another reason, too: as Patricia L. Hamilton points out, the daughters lack a "worldview that endows reality with unified meaning." This is not the case for their mothers, who "inherited from their families a centuries-old spiritual framework, which, combined with rigid social constraints regarding class and gender, made the world into an ordered place for them. . . . In the face of crisis the mothers adhere to ancient Chinese practices by which they try to manipulate fate to their advantage" (Hamilton 348). Thus it is that the more liberated and individualistic daughters do not possess the iron in their souls exhibited by their mothers, whose existences at times came close to slavery.

The normal conflict between generations is exacerbated in *The Joy Luck Club* by the fact that the mothers are immigrants, displaced persons, while their daughters are all trying to assimilate. The mothers and daughters share in common that they are now Chinese Americans inhabiting radically different worlds. It is tempting for these Americanized daughters to regard their mothers as fossilized and as having nothing relevant to teach them. And, as a result of feeling marginalized, their mothers try all the harder to realize themselves vicariously through their daughters. Mother-daughter conflict is most marked in the narratives of Jing-mei and Waverly Jong, who, like their mothers, are rivals as well as friends. Lindo Jong's desire to have her daughter capitalize on the liberality of American circumstances with Chinese savvy has already been cited. Both Lindo and Suyuan are exasperated by their daughters' failure to fulfill their ambitions for them. Suyuan wants Jing-mei to realize her fullest potential, to be "best quality." Lindo preens herself so on Waverly's prowess at chess—she is a junior chess champion—that Waverly throws a tantrum, objecting to being "shown off" by her mother, refusing to compete in any more tournaments, even temporarily running away from home. When Waverly comes back, her mother ignores her, treating her as a "nonperson." Temporarily, bouncy Waverly, seemingly so sure of herself, also loses her identity. In later life she blames her mother for her first failed marriage and is terrified that Lindo will put off her new boyfriend, Rich. All the daughters wish to be loved for themselves, not as projections of their mothers' hopes.

Repetitions, Parallels, Dualities, and Doublings

The novel is full of dualisms, doublings, parallels, and repetitions. The personalities of the members of each mother-daughter pair or dyad are similar yet different, just as affinities and antagonisms exist among the Joy Luck Club mothers, "aunts," and daughters. Suyuan and Jing-mei are intimate yet antagonistic, as are Lindo and Waverly; attraction-repulsion is evident in the relationships between Suyuan and Lindo, and between Waverly and Jing-mei. That the love between these mothers and daughters is shot through with ambivalence and rivalry is what renders Tan's characters so lifelike and convincing.

Doubling is present in many of the story titles—for example, "Half and Half," "Two Kinds," "Double Face," and "A Pair of Tickets." Dualities are everywhere to be found: East/West, yin/yang, Chinese/American, past/present, age/youth, mothers/daughters, life/death. What is remarkable are the skill and seamlessness with which Tan interweaves these characters and their stories, using many different genres and narrative modes. As one reviewer has observed, *The Joy Luck Club* marries "Chinese subtlety and American ingenuity" (Koenig 93).

Notes

1. See chapter 1 in Partridge's *Beyond Literary Chinatown*.
2. Tan mentioned this in a 1990 *Booklist* interview with Donna Seaman.
3. See the entry for Tan in *Current Biography*, Feb. 1992.
4. Ibid.
5. See Wendy Ho's "Swan-Feather Mothers and Coca-Cola Daughters: Teaching Amy Tan's *The Joy Luck Club*" (333) and David Leiwei Li's "Genes, Generation, and Geospiritual (Be)longings."
6. For this and many other fascinating details, see the glossary of Chinese words, phrases, and ideas offered by Molly Isham in "A Reader's Guide to Amy Tan's *The Joy Luck Club*."
7. Ibid.
8. See both Patricia L. Hamilton's "*Feng Shui*, Astrology, and the Five Elements: Traditional Chinese Belief in Amy Tan's *The Joy Luck Club*" and the aforementioned article by Molly Isham.

Works Cited

Adams, Bella. *Amy Tan*. Manchester, England: Manchester UP, 2005.

"Amy Tan." *Current Biography* Feb. 1992: 561.

Hamilton, Patricia L. "*Feng Shui*, Astrology, and the Five Elements: Traditional Chinese Belief in Amy Tan's *The Joy Luck Club*." *Contemporary Literary Criticism* 151 (2002): 343-53. (Repr. from *MELUS* 24.2, Summer 1999.)

Ho, Wendy. "Swan-Feather Mothers and Coca-Cola Daughters: Teaching Amy Tan's *The Joy Luck Club*." *Contemporary Literary Criticism* 155 (2002): 328-36. (Repr. from *Teaching American Ethnic Literatures*. Ed. John R. Maitino and David R. Peck. Albuquerque: U of New Mexico P, 1996.)

Huntley, E. D. *Amy Tan: A Critical Companion*. Westport, CT: Greenwood Press, 1998.

Isham, Molly. "A Reader's Guide to Amy Tan's *The Joy Luck Club*." *Asian Pacific American Heritage: A Companion to Literature and the Arts*. Ed. George J. Leonard. New York: Garland, 1999. 447-72.

Koenig, Rhoda. "Heirloom China." *Contemporary Literary Criticism* 59 (1990): 93-94. (Repr. from *New York Magazine* 20 Mar. 1989.)

Lew, Julie. Review of *The Joy Luck Club*, by Amy Tan. *New York Times* 4 July 1989: 23.

Li, David Leiwei. "Genes, Generation, and Geospiritual (Be)longings." *Imagining the Nation: Asian American Literature and Cultural Consent*. Stanford: Stanford UP, 1998. 111-25.

Ling, Amy. *Between Worlds: Women Writers of Chinese Ancestry*. New York: Pergamon Press, 1990.

Painter, Charlotte. "In Search of a Voice." *Contemporary Literary Criticism* 59 (1990): 98-99. (Repr. from *San Francisco Review of Books*, Summer 1989.)

Partridge, Jeffrey F. L. *Beyond Literary Chinatown*. Seattle: U of Washington P, 2007.

Seaman, Donna. Interview of Amy Tan. *Booklist* 1 Oct. 1990: 256-57.

Tan, Amy. *The Joy Luck Club*. New York: G. P. Putnam's Sons, 1989.

Willard, Nancy. "Tiger Spirits." *Contemporary Literary Criticism* 59 (1990): 97-98. (Repr. from *Women's Review of Books* July 1989.)

The Interplay of Unity and Diversity in *The Joy Luck Club* and *The Hours*_____

Neil Heims

Narrative Unity

Amy Tan published *The Joy Luck Club* in 1989. Michael Cunningham's *The Hours* came out nine years later, in 1998. These two novels seem, at first, to be quite disparate undertakings. *The Joy Luck Club* centers on several generations of people in a community of Chinese immigrants who are living, in the 1980s, in and around San Francisco. It concerns their current lives and interactions, and it explores the currents of memory and history that flow through those lives and have shaped them. *The Hours* is an extended variation on the style, the themes, and the characters of Virginia Woolf's 1925 stream-of-consciousness novel *Mrs. Dalloway*. *The Hours* is composed of several internal variations, too, all on the theme of the tension between inner realities and outer demands, telling similar and sometimes interweaving stories with characters and situations that reflect and refer to one another.

Both *The Joy Luck Club* and *The Hours* are intricately designed narratives comprising discrete, independent sections that can stand on their own, but that, when brought together in the minds of readers, constitute organic, unified, complex, and whole narratives. *The Joy Luck Club* is a collection of sixteen autonomous but overlapping narratives presented by seven narrators. It is a kaleidoscopic story presented from multiple perspectives that complement, enrich, and complete one another. The stories are told by and are accounts of four mothers and four daughters. But one of them, Suyuan Woo, has just died shortly before *The Joy Luck Club* begins. Her story is folded within her daughter Jing-mei's narratives. A mother's voice delivered through her daughter's voice reinforces an essential and defining theme of *The Joy Luck Club*. *The Joy Luck Club* is a novel centrally concerned with the continuity of the spirit from one generation to the next, its influence, and how it is passed on. That is also a central concern of *The Hours* within the world of the book and within the context of actual literary tradition, within the world in which the book appears. The spirits of Virginia Woolf herself and of her novel *Mrs. Dalloway* haunt the characters in *The Hours* and help shape the plot, the theme, and the tone of *The Hours* itself as a work of literature.

The Hours is a novel that tells a story that draws on three historical periods and is constructed of three independent but connected, interweaving narratives presented by one narrator. The narrator of *The Hours*, unlike the narrators of *The Joy Luck Club*, is not a first-person narrator or involved in the events of any of the three stories. The narrator exists only as the narrative, as pure consciousness that can enter into and reveal any of the characters in the book. The narrator is present not as an individual but as a tone of voice or as a style that hardly changes no matter which narrative is being unfolded: the one concerned with the period contemporary with the novel's composition, 1998, set in Greenwich Village, called "Mrs. Dalloway"; the one called "Mrs. Brown," set in Los Angeles in 1949; or "Mrs. Woolf," set in the London suburb of Richmond in 1923, concerning the intersection of Virginia Woolf's life and her beginning the composition of *Mrs. Dalloway*.

If *The Hours* were a piece of music, its tempo markings would vary between *andante* and *largo*. The narrative throughout is slow, abundant, extensive, and pensive. It takes the reader on a walk through the consciousness of its characters. *The Hours* is a fantasia that dwells on the phenomenological identity of the person perceiving something and the thing that is perceived, how the thing perceived becomes the consciousness of the person perceiving, whether that perception is active or passive. Consider Ritchie's tragic bond with Laura, his mother, in "Mrs. Brown," as he follows her, when he is a child, with his soul more than his eyes; or his life's work, as a grown man, Richard, in "Mrs. Dalloway," searching for her in his poetry and prose and recasting her in Clarissa Vaughan.

Or consider how Cunningham's description of Clarissa Vaughan's morning walk through Manhattan's Greenwich Village to SoHo suggests an implicit analogy between the movement of the wind and the working of Clarissa's mind. His prose creates a seamless connection between Clarissa and her environment and presents an image of her mind's peregrinations. Cunningham turns the phenomena of the environment into an emblem for the process of her consciousness: "Wind worries the leaves, showing the brighter, grayer green of their undersides, and Clarissa wishes, suddenly and with surprising urgency, that Richard were here beside her, right now—not Richard as he's become but the Richard of ten years ago" (*The Hours* 19). Or consider the passage (beginning on page 164) when Virginia Woolf feels the possible onset of one of her maddening headaches and sets off on her own to the train station to go to London, although her husband, Leonard, advised by her physician, believes that for the sake of her health and stability, she ought not to. Her walk is presented through her perception of herself, her thoughts, the people she sees, and the environment she traverses as her walk occurs.

Such narration tells two stories, the story of what she does and sees and the story of how she perceives the things she does and sees, not only what she feels but what her apparatus for feeling, her sensitivity, is like. The same technique is employed in the passage when Laura Brown returns to Mrs. Latch's house to pick up Ritchie. Cunningham's description of everything she sees and hears—the "two painted plaster squirrels . . . attached to the gable over the garage," the "peculiar ticking sound" that her "car emits," for example (188)—serves less to describe her environment than to describe her consciousness at that moment, which is nothing but an internalization of her awareness of her environment. The implication for a reader is that this awareness exists in place of the blankness she is in herself, at that moment. She has no inner consciousness of self. The external is predatory and has devoured the inner. That is her malaise, as it is Virginia Woolf's in *The Hours*, and it is what Clarissa Vaughan, like her precursor, Clarissa Dalloway,

---

does not succumb to despite the way the world impinges upon their consciousness. Unlike Laura Brown, whose inner life is usurped by her world, both Clarissas meet the world from within their strong interiority.

Although in *The Hours* there is not an absolute narrative connection made between some characters in one segment and some characters in another, there are significant resemblances. Characters, too, are often vehicles for recurring motifs in *The Hours*. Often these are motifs borrowed from *Mrs. Dalloway* as well, but in these motific recapitulations there is additional variation. Clarissa Vaughan, for example, is set up to mirror Mrs. Dalloway as she sets out to buy flowers herself for the party she will give for Richard that evening. And Cunningham's narrative tone is informed throughout by an echo of Virginia Woolf's prose. Clarissa Vaughan also is made to realize, with her companion, Sally, the relationship that evaded Mrs. Dalloway with the Sally of her youth. Mrs. Dalloway's Sally, in Woolf's novel, remains with her only as the memory of an explosive kiss they shared, once. That kiss, in *The Hours*, becomes a summer kiss Clarissa and Richard shared in their youth and again a kiss that autumn that Clarissa refused. Clarissa Vaughan, however, is also made to mirror Leonard Woolf, in his loving and frustrated ministrations to Virginia, in her ministrations to Richard. And the kiss itself appears and reappears throughout *The Hours*, not only as the kiss between Clarissa and Richard but also as the kiss between Laura and Kitty in the "Mrs. Brown" section and the kiss between Virginia and Vanessa in the "Mrs. Woolf" section.

Laura Brown echoes Virginia, in her uneasiness with domestic confinement and her momentary escape from it. But Laura actually gets to flee in her car to a hotel for a few hours. Virginia, without a motorcar, manages only to get to the train station before Leonard catches her. Richard not only mirrors Virginia Woolf as a lyrical writer, sick unto death, and as an explorer of consciousness and lost moments in his writing, but also as a haunted, ravaged soul who takes his own life as she did. He also reminds a reader of *Mrs. Dalloway* of Septimus Smith, the tormented young man home from the war who sees no way out of his wretchedness, no escape from the ghosts of his past existential shocks, except defenestration. Whereas Septimus Smith, moreover, may be read as tormented by homosexuality, amorphous and unnamed, Richard has been openly bisexual. The stories recounted in the "Mrs. Dalloway" and "Mrs. Brown" sections of *The Hours*, as well as *The Hours* itself, could not exist without *Mrs. Dalloway*, just as the stories of the characters in *The Joy Luck Club* could not exist without the precursor stories of their parents and grandparents.

The characters in the several sections of *The Joy Luck Club* do not mirror each other. They encounter each other and create their identities in the struggles in which they engage to liberate themselves from the forces of each other's influence. In their interactions, within their own sections and across them, the characters in *The Joy Luck Club* exert powerful influences on each other and serve as foils in shaping each other's identities. Children are repeatedly defined as haunted by their parents, especially girls by their mothers, and are caught in struggles to escape mothers' influences or to integrate family, historical, and cultural influences and their own essential individuality. Sometimes they must grapple with the ambiguity of not being able to distinguish between influence and essence. In depicting her characters, Tan demonstrates that there is no clear demarcation between what is influence and what constitutes essence. There is only the struggling identity into which outer influences and individual essence have somehow coalesced.

The force of influence and the struggle against it, in *The Joy Luck Club*, define both casual and fundamental encounters and conflicts. Both the apparently casual and the obviously significant provoke great emotional storms within Tan's characters. This dialectical cluster that presents the struggles between influence and essence that engage the characters in *The Joy Luck Club* occurs in several instances in Jing-mei's narrative "Best Quality" in the third section, "American Translations." The first exchange is an instance of mutual competition and subversion that, as an undercurrent, has defined a friendship of more than thirty years:

"Suyuan!" called Auntie Lindo to my mother. "Why you wear that color?" Auntie Lindo gestured with a crab leg to my mother's red sweater.

"How can you wear this color anymore? Too young!" she scolded.

My mother acted as though this were a compliment. "Emporium Capwell," she said. "Nineteen dollar. Cheaper than knit it myself."

Auntie Lindo nodded her head, as if the color were worth this price. (*The Joy Luck Club* 203)

A second exchange, at the same dinner, is between the daughters of these two old friends—Jing-mei, the narrator of this section, Suyuan's daughter, and Lindo's daughter, Waverly. Beginning with an apparently trivial remark, their exchange quickly becomes a far more significant and painful one than the one between their mothers. It is, like their mothers', an episode in an ongoing, stealthy power struggle. It clearly defines the parameters of each one's identity and the role each plays in formulating and forming the identity of the other. Their exchange begins innocently enough, but the innocence of Waverly's question is soon revealed as the subterfuge of a past master of chess moves and strategies, which the reader knows she is from *her* previous narratives, "Rules of the Game," and "Four Directions." Jing-mei is telling the story now: "'Nice haircut,' Waverly said to me from across the table." That's the opening gambit, trivial in itself, a compliment. Jing-mei greets it with thanks and generously extends the compliment to her hairdresser: "David always does a great job." Waverly's next move is provocative and undercutting. "You mean you still go to that guy on Howard Street? . . . Aren't you afraid?" Jing-mei senses a trap but walks into it. "What do you mean, afraid? He's always very good," she says. But Waverly is not talking about hairstyling now. "I mean," she says, "he *is* gay. He could have AIDS. And he is cutting your hair, which is like cutting a living tissue. . . . You should go see my guy, Mr. Rory. He does fabulous work, although he probably charges more than you're used to" (204). This retort is a masterful work of one-upmanship deriving three put-downs from what was, apparently, an insincere or, at least, a condescending compliment: (1) my hairdresser is better than your hairdresser; (2) you are putting yourself at risk; (3) I have more money than you. Waverly has unleashed a collection of assaults simultaneously from several directions, and all of them wound.

Although nothing is explicitly revealed about her catty tactics in her rivalry with Jing-mei, just as her ignorant bigotry, too, goes unremarked, a reader with recall can make connections. In "Four Directions," the section in the third part of *The Joy Luck Club* that Waverly narrates, she quotes her mother, Lindo, offering this advice about defeating an opponent at chess. "You don't have to be so smart to win chess. . . . You blow from the North, South, East, and West. The other person becomes confused. They don't know which way to run" (170). Earlier, in Waverly's second-section narrative "Rules of the Game," Lindo tells her daughter, "Blow from the South. . . . The wind leaves no trail. . . . Throw sand from the East to distract him" (96). The delicacy and subtlety of method that Tan employs in character development are the results of the narrative unity she achieves through intersecting parts that form a constellated whole without using explicit explanatory narration. Character is revealed in *The Joy Luck Club* incrementally and indirectly, not by the writer's revelations but by the reader's realizations, as it is in the actual world.

With her skill at moving stealthily, at coming from all directions at once, Waverly infuriates Jing-mei, undoes her, and sets her up for a worse defeat. "I was so mad," Jing-mei writes,

> that I wanted to embarrass her, to reveal in front of everybody how petty she was. So I decided to confront her about the free-lance work I'd done for her firm. . . . The firm was now more than thirty days late in paying my invoice.
>
> "Maybe I could afford Mr. Rory's prices if someone's firm paid me on time," I said with a teasing grin. (204)

Her move seems to work. Waverly looks flustered, and Jing-mei proceeds blindly in what she thinks is a victory, led on a course by her adversary that will take her to defeat and humiliation. Waverly checks her by an admission that shows she was flustered for Jing-mei's sake, not out of embarrassment for herself. "Listen, June," she says, prodded by Jing-mei, whom she calls by her Americanized name, "I don't know how to tell you this. That stuff you wrote, well the firm decided it was unacceptable" (205). She adds the coup de grâce by reciting Jing-mei's copy in the mock-heroic voice of a stentorian radio or television announcer.

Jing-mei's humiliation by Waverly's attack on the style of her copy is compounded when her mother intervenes, saying, "True, cannot teach style. June not sophisticated like you. Must be born this way" (206). At this point, the reader of *The Joy Luck Club* has the advantage over Jing-mei and understands Suyuan better than her daughter can, just because the reader has read *The Joy Luck Club* and Jing-mei has not. Suyuan is not complimenting Waverly. In fact she is graciously demeaning her. She has already shown this talent for subterfuge in her earlier exchange with Lindo. Her words are the mark of a very dry sarcasm that can make one utterance sound like its opposite. In her rage and shame, Jing-mei forgets that one characteristic of Chinese etiquette, as revealed repeatedly in *The Joy Luck Club*, is to devalue to others the things one values, as Lindo has done earlier when, bursting with pride at Waverly's prowess at chess, she attributes it to nothing but luck. Another characteristic the reader has learned to associate with the etiquette of behavior laid out in *The Joy Luck Club* is to attack without seeming to, as it were, to inflict a fatal wound with a bladeless knife that also does not seem to have a handle. Suyuan is actually expressing contempt for Waverly's style and sophistication, for her smug and somewhat nasty disposition. These are far less worthy, in Suyuan's eyes, than Jing-mei's simplicity and transparency. When they are alone, in fact, Suyuan, holds the mirror up to her daughter.

Regarding the poor crab Jing-mei had considerately chosen at dinner, Suyuan says, "Only you pick that crab. Nobody else take it. I already know this. Everybody else want best quality. You thinking different." This, Jing-mei realizes, is praise coming from her mother, "proof of something good." Tan's narrative strength lies in the fact that the reader understands this not because of what Jing-mei says but because of the reader's understanding of the way the culture of the novel operates—an understanding that the reader has acquired by reading the novel. This understanding is the result of the developing unity of the several narratives that makes the reader culturally insightful. At this textual moment, the reader understands the linguistic code and the tone of the culture of *The Joy Luck Club* better than does Jing-mei. She says of her mother, "She always said things that didn't make any sense, that sounded both good and bad at the same time." But that is not so. Suyuan's frame of reference is her internal value system, not the external, American value system, which she dismisses as she makes short work of Waverly. "Why you want to follow behind her," she says, "chasing her words? She is like this crab. . . . Always walking sideways, moving crooked" (208).

In the episode at the table regarding hairdressers and advertising copy, Waverly is positioned as a foil for Jing-mei. But she is more than that because of the reader's previous encounters with her and because of her later appearance, with her mother, Lindo, in "Double Face," at the hairdresser's in the last section, "Queen Mother of the Western Skies." The reader's first acquaintance with Waverly in "Rules of the Game" shows her concerned with having "invisible strength," "winning arguments," and gaining "respect from others." She is with her mother in the market, and her mother thwarts her desire to have a bag of salted plums. She learns from Lindo that to get what she wants she must exercise guile, to "bite back your tongue" (89), and seem not to want what she wants. At the beauty parlor, years later, Lindo describes the success of her daughter's integration of her teaching, not entirely pleased by the results: "My daughter's eyes and her smile become very narrow, the way a cat pulls herself small just before it bites" (256). And in the last encounter between Waverly and Lindo at the end of this section, the reader sees just how clearly Waverly knows what she herself is like and what her weapons are. Talking about the "crooked" nose she has inherited from her mother, Waverly says, "Our nose isn't so bad. . . . It makes us look devious." "She looks pleased," Lindo observes. Waverly explains, "We're looking one way, while following another. We're for one side and also the other. We mean what we say, but our intentions are different." Lindo asks, "People can see this in our faces?" "Well, not everything that we're thinking," Waverly explains; "They just know we're two-faced." "This is good?" Lindo asks. It is, Waverly explains in a moment of self-revelation, "if you get what you want" (266).

Tan's approach, narrative juxtaposition rather than direct exposition, is so delicately nuanced that the reader does not leave *The Joy Luck Club* with the sense that June is a hero and Waverly a villain; rather, the reader recognizes that the human character is complex and various, essential and shaped by circumstances.

Structural Unity

In both *The Joy Luck Club* and *The Hours*, clusters of separate narratives are preceded by prologues that direct the reader's focus. *The Hours* begins with a prologue set not in one of the three time periods in which the other sections of the novel occur but in 1941. With a lyrical attention to pastoral details, limned in a muted palette composed of the earth tones of rural England at the end of March, Cunningham shows Virginia Woolf in her last hours as she accomplishes her suicide. The problem of suicide and the presence of death inform the plots of all of the sections of *The Hours*. As she begins writing *Mrs. Dalloway*, Virginia Woolf senses that Mrs. Dalloway will kill herself, but as the work takes shape in her mind, the suicide is displaced from Mrs. Dalloway onto Septimus Smith, and the reader must see in her conjuring the plot of *Mrs. Dalloway* a premonition of Woolf's own end. Laura Brown in her section flirts with suicide but rejects it, removing herself from the environment of her family but not from the world of the living. And in the section titled "Mrs. Dalloway," Laura is a living ghost who haunts her son, Ritchie in "Mrs. Brown" and Richard in "Mrs. Dalloway." He completes the act of annihilation his mother had backed away from, his suicide echoing Septimus Smith's in its method as well as Virginia Woolf's in its motivation.

Each of the four sections of *The Joy Luck Club* is composed of four narratives. Each of those sections—"Feathers from a Thousand *Li* Away," "The Twenty-six Malignant Gates," "American Translation," and "Queen Mother of the Western Skies"—is introduced by a brief parable. Each parable functions something like a key in a musical composition, determining the emotional mood, tone, or tendency of the narrative. The first prologue begins, appropriately, with the invocation of an old woman's memory, represented by a swan. The feathers of the swan are made to represent the stories that the immigrants from China bring with them to pass on to their children. This prologue emblematically represents the entire novel the reader is beginning and elucidates its context and function. The second prologue is a parable of intergenerational conflict, of a mother's anxiety and a daughter's adventurousness, of the closed wisdom of the past and its uncanny and confused influence in the present. The third prologue continues the theme of generational and cultural tensions and extends it infinitely by imagining the future as a reflection of the present. The fourth prologue stretches beyond the accidents of actual events to the renewal of the possibility for joy through the renewal of the spirit in the renewal of life inherent in the birth of children.

In addition to gaining coherence from these prologues, *The Joy Luck Club* is unified by a frame around the entire novel, a frame embedded in the narrative itself. The story itself of *The Joy Luck Club* is framed by Jing-mei Woo's story of her passage from childhood into womanhood. She is shown moving away from alienation from her mother, Suyuan, to reconciliation with her. In the last section, "A Pair of

Tickets," she becomes her mother's surrogate and spiritual reembodiment, after her mother's death, when she visits her long-lost sisters in China, who are her tickets back to her mother and into the future. It is a reconciliation achieved by her becoming her mother's deputy in her mother's lifelong attempt to find the two babies she abandoned in China when she fled the Japanese invasion and occupation of China that began in July 1937. When the three sisters are reunited, the reunion suggests the reconstitution of their mother.

Jing-mei's story of the abandoned babies begins and ends *The Joy Luck Club*. It frames the novel and sets forth and resolves a major theme of the novel, the bond between parents and children. Jing-mei's is the book's dominant narrative. It frames the others. Jing-mei narrates the first and the last sections of the novel, and hers is the final narrative of each of the two inner sections. Each of the other characters narrates two sections, whereas Jing-mei narrates four. Her narrative appears in each section. For the others, the mothers' narratives appear in the first and last sections, while the daughters' narratives appear in the middle sections. Thus Jing-mei is placed among both the mothers and the daughters, embodying the continuity of the spirit across the generations by virtue of carrying her mother's identity as well as her own.

Motific Unity

When speaking of narrative, the question may arise, What exactly is being narrated? The usual response, of course, is that a story is being narrated. While that seems like a reasonable and straightforward answer, another question can follow: What exactly is meant by the word "story"? Usually, "story" suggests a series of events and occurrences that happen to and affect a group of characters, build to a climax or to a point of revelation or conclusion, and then subside. But in both *The Joy Luck Club* and *The Hours*, more than a story is being narrated. These are novels that reflect the consciousness of sets of characters as that consciousness is made manifest through a series of unfolding events and occurrences. The result in both books is an aesthetic unity that brings together the diverse stories and the independent sections of the novels and makes connections between the several actions and the various actors those narratives chronicle.

The stories of these novels are engaging and important because they give incidents meaning by revealing character and culture and the fundamentals of the human experience that are realized and expressed through character and culture. An important narrative apparatus, aside from the actual recounting of events, one that gives depth and resonance to the experience of the characters, is the presence and recurrence of images. Recurring images and objects are motifs that become imbued with referentiality and serve, by concrete representation, to recount and illuminate the inner worlds of the characters that people the stories. They contribute to the reader's sense of the continuity of the characters' experiences by their recurrence. They forge a unity in the diversity of apparently discrete experiences by linking them together. Images of things also convey the tokens of a culture and the sensibilities by which that culture actualizes itself in the experience of its people. In *The Joy Luck Club,* recurring images serve as emblems of social and psychological situations, and they contribute to the narrative unity of the novel.

Consider the blue sapphire ring, for example, that appears in *The Joy Luck Club* in Rose's narrative "Half and Half" in the second book, "The Twenty-six Malignant Gates." Rose's mother, An-mei, throws the ring into the sea as an exchange offering, hoping that the "Coiling Dragon" that lives in the sea—the personification of the power of the sea—will be made to forget about her child, Bing, who has drowned. She hopes to distract it by the beauty of the ring and, thereby, induce it to return Bing to her, accepting one treasure in place of another. It is a magic ritual, informed by cultural mythology, performed by an afflicted mother, and, of course, it does not succeed. To the reader, the ring has no more significance than as a token in this desperate ritual, like the sweetened tea that An-mei poured into the sea beforehand in order to "sweeten the temper of the Coiling Dragon" (129). But this ring itself is the vessel of meaning, the repository of a lesson, and the token of a guiding wisdom that An-mei's mother handed to her years earlier, when An-mei was a child in China.

The ring reappears later in "Magpies" in the last section of *The Joy Luck Club*, but chronologically much earlier than its first appearance in "Half and Half." Wishing her daughter to realize the difference between superficial allure and real value, An-mei's mother, Rose's grandmother, gives An-mei the blue sapphire ring after she shows her that the string of pearls that a rival and more highly regarded concubine had given to the girl—with the aim of directing to herself devotion that ought to be directed to An-mei's mother—is worthless glass. This "heavy ring of watery blue sapphire, with a star in its center so pure that I never ceased to look at the ring with wonder" (231-32), is the ring that An-mei throws into the sea in the desperate attempt at barter to bring her son back from death. The significance of the ring in both episodes is enhanced in each case by its role in the other. The way the importance of the ring is revealed in the novel removes the ring from linear time and makes it a token of timeless, cultural consciousness. As great as the value of the ring is, it has no more power than a glass pearl to penetrate the border that separates life from death. When An-mei sacrifices it to the sea, she is summoning up all the power of her mother's love, which did propel her mother across life's border and into death for An-mei's sake. As a vehicle that unifies time, removes time from the realm of history, and reveals time's psychological dimension, the ring undoes the linear, sequential character that usually defines time. That dimension is replaced by the dimensions of experience and perception. The coincidence and concurrence of apparently disparate time periods are compressed into the meaning of the star sapphire. Time is replaced by tradition. Tradition brings the past into the present as a present force.

Adding to the resonance of An-mei's gesture of throwing the sapphire into the sea, and revealing even more fully the way diverse times and gestures can be conflated, is the incident that An-mei relates at the end of her first narrative, "Scar." She tells the story of how her mother, when *her* mother, who had rejected her, was dying, in order to restore her to life, cut a piece of flesh from her own arm, boiled it in a soup, and fed it to her mother. As An-mei's son, later, was irretrievable from death by An-mei's ritual sacrifice of her spirit's flesh, so her mother's filial sacrifice of that piece of bodily flesh did not save her grandmother's life.

A similar coalescing occurs toward the end of *The Hours* with regard to identity, and that melding of identities also subverts the force of time as an agent of differentiation by distance. In the antepenultimate chapter of *The Hours*, describing how Virginia Woolf finally plots *Mrs. Dalloway*, Cunningham achieves narrative simultaneity. As he writes about Clarissa Dalloway and Septimus Smith, about a single, life-haunting kiss, and about a strong, young poet of a man "ground under by the wheels of the world," about someone "loving her life of ordinary pleasures, and someone else, a deranged poet, a visionary, [who] will be the one to die" (211), the words jump over the boundaries of the separated stories and refer equally to two sets of characters that never meet but live the same experience.

Both *The Joy Luck Club* and *The Hours* bring together patterns of common cultures and show the interplay of those cultures and the individuals through which they flow, anatomizing not only the nature of those cultures but also the humanity of the individuals who are determined by them and struggle with them.

Works Cited

Cunningham, Michael. *The Hours*. New York: Picador, 1998.
Tan, Amy. *The Joy Luck Club*. London: Minerva, 1989.

CRITICAL
READINGS

Amy Tan:
An Interview

Barbara Somogyi and David Stanton

In 1985, Amy Tan was a frustrated but well-paid freelance business writer, devoting 12-hour days to proposals for companies like IBM and AT&T. Attempting to cure her work addiction, she began seeing a psychiatrist. When her doctor fell asleep during their first three sessions, however, Tan decided to look elsewhere for a cure.

She resolved to pursue her long-standing dream of writing a novel. Later that year, she attended the Squaw Valley Community of Writers workshops and met Molly Giles, a fiction writer and winner of the Flannery O'Connor Award. It was at those workshops, and during subsequent meetings of a writers group Giles held in San Francisco, that Tan began to develop the stories that became her first book, *The Joy Luck Club*.

Since its publication in March 1989, *The Joy Luck Club* (Putnam) has been a #1 national best-seller in both hardcover and paperback. Its softcover rights sold for a reported $1.2 million, and it turned Tan from an unknown into a wealthy and respected author. The book tells the story of the Joy Luck Club—four Chinese women who immigrated to San Francisco in the 1940s and who meet once a week to play *mah jong*. When the group's founder, Suyuan Woo, dies, her daughter, June, is invited to take her place.

The book is also the story of June and the other Joy Luck daughters. In many ways, it is Tan's own story. Born in Oakland and raised in the Bay Area, Tan always considered herself an American first and foremost. She even took to wearing a clothespin on her nose at night in an attempt to make it thinner. Her mother, Daisy, was an embarrassment to her: demanding, stubborn, unafraid—distinctly Chinese.

In 1986, however, Daisy suffered a heart attack. Having already lost her father and brother, Peter, to cancer nineteen years earlier, Tan vowed that if her mother lived, they would travel together to China and visit their relatives still living there. It was that trip that inspired much of *The Joy Luck Club*.

Tan's new book, *The Kitchen God's Wife*, was published in June to high acclaim. Book club rights for the novel sold for a reported $425,000—an astonishing amount—and a movie deal for the book is imminent, with Oliver Stone producing and Wayne Wang directing.

Success has had its price for Tan; she is reported to prefer fax communication to the telephone because of the number of "unsolicited" calls she has received. She remains, however, generous and unpretentious in person. She seems somewhat detached from her almost unbelievable success and, at the time of this interview, was hard at work writing *The Kitchen God's Wife* on her laptop computer. The conversation took place in May 1990 in Tan's New York City hotel room.

Somogyi: I wonder if you could tell us a little about the history of The Joy Luck Club—in what order you wrote the different chapters and how the book came to be published.

Well, the book was sold on the basis of a proposal and three chapters—"Rules of the Game," which was then called "Endgame," "Waiting Between the Trees," and "Scarf." My agent had asked me to write a proposal for the book, so I spent a few hours creating a two-sentence summary of each chapter. I hope that doesn't sound cavalier, but I really did not think there was a chance of the book being published. For the last chapter, "A Pair of Tickets," I wrote, "A woman goes to China to meet her sisters with expectations and discovers something else." That's all I knew about that one. What they all had in common is that I knew these characters would discover something about themselves but I didn't know what it was.

When the book was sold, I went back and started with the very first story. I didn't go in the same order that I had outlined them; I just went with the story that seemed to want to be told next, and it seemed to alternate between mother and daughter. I'd write a mother's story, and then I'd hear the daughter saying, "Well, let me tell my side of it." And the very last story I wrote was the one that's last in the book.

Stanton: Were you afraid with the book's format that the reader might get lost? Is that the idea behind having a list of the characters in the front of the book?

You know, I have to say the book was actually written as a collection of short stories, not as a novel, and I still think of them as stories. It never occurred to me that people were going to say, "Wait a minute—this has to follow here," because with a collection of short stories you don't worry as much about how the stories are connected. They're connected by theme or emotion or community.

It wasn't until the book was out in galley form and the first reviews came out that the reviewers called it a novel. And Putnam's said to me, "You know, everybody is calling this a novel." And I said, "But that's not what I wrote." So we compromised; on the jacket flap [of the hardcover], it's called a "first work of fiction." The only place you see the word "novel" on the hardcover is in the *Publishers Weekly* review blurb.

Stanton: I read that your parents expected you would become both a neurosurgeon and a concert pianist, and it made me wonder what your mother thinks of your writing. Does she consider it a legitimate career?

It's funny—after this book was published, my mother started saying, "I always knew you'd be a writer." She said I always had a wild imagination. That wild imagination used to be, "That's why you're so bad! You're always getting into trouble." But now she's decided that all her life she knew I'd be a writer.

I remember years of disappointment for my mother when I didn't go into premed. There was some hope that the "Dr." would be in front of my name if I finished my Ph.D. in linguistics, but I dropped out of that, too. My mother started feeling that maybe I was doing okay for myself when I became successful as a freelance business writer and my husband and I were able to buy her a place to live. That's really what success is about in Chinese families—it's not success for yourself, it's success so you can take care of your family. And I had achieved that finally; I was able to show her: "I can do well enough to take care of you for the rest of your life; you don't have to worry." And that was long before I wrote the book.

Stanton: Exactly what kind of business writing did you do?

I wrote everything from manuals for AT&T salespeople on how to sell "Reach Out America" plans to business proposals for companies doing consulting for Fortune 500 businesses. I had a real strong batting average on these proposals, so that's often why people hired me. One of the last things I wrote was a book for IBM called *Telecommunications and You*, which is twenty-six chapters on telecommunications geared to systems engineers and CEOs of major corporations.

Stanton: Did you really work ninety hours a week at one point?

I worked ninety hours a week for about two months. My mother kept saying, "You're going to kill yourself!" And I couldn't stop. I kept searching for this thing, this click that would make me feel I had finally done enough—either the right project or working hard enough or earning enough money or feeling that I had written the best thing. I never found it, so I kept working harder and harder and taking on all these jobs.

I finally realized that I was looking up the wrong tree and that I had to do something else. That's when I started taking jazz piano and writing fiction. I wanted to create something for myself—not for clients, not for money.

Somogyi: Was the crossover to your own writing hard?

No. You cannot imagine the elation I felt to leave that stuff behind—I kept dreading having to go back. I remember my husband

and me walking at night, and I would say, "Well, I'll have to go back to work on such-and-such a day." Then something would happen, a foreign sale, and I'd say, "Well, that buys me a little more time; maybe I can not go back for six months instead of four." And it kept stretching out and stretching out, and I remember one time thinking, "Maybe I won't have to go back until next year. Wouldn't that be great?"

I had wonderful clients. I could choose the projects I wanted; they paid me well. It was so good that I couldn't give it up, and yet it was death to me spiritually. It was writing that had no meaning to me. I didn't care if IBM made another hundred million dollars. And I kept thinking, I'll look back on my life, and I'll say, "You wasted your life. What did you do? You wrote this stuff for other people, and it didn't mean anything to you."

Stanton: Are most of the stories in The Joy Luck Club *based on things that actually happened, or are they stories that you made up in the vein of things you heard?*

I think that everything in there is true emotionally to what has happened in my life. Amy Hempel and I were talking about this—how we get into our stories—and we think along similar lines. First there's a question, and often it takes a long time for the question to surface out of false starts. The question is always related to my life, so that's autobiographical in a sense. Then there's an image, which is often something from my life or something that my mother talked about in a story to me. And the image leads into a scene. The scene starts to become more fictionalized, but I would say the question and the image to me are the most important things—and the language that surrounds them—and that's all from my life.

The heart of *The Joy Luck Club* is definitely autobiographical, but I could list factual things that are not true—that I did not grow up in Chinatown in San Francisco, that I have never played chess. My mother did not lose her babies in (Guay Lin); she's never been in

Guay Lin except with me in 1987. But she did lose three daughters in China in 1949. She was the little girl watching her mother cut a piece of flesh from her arm to make soup, and she was the little girl watching her mother die when she took opium because she had become a third concubine.

And then the other part, of course, is that my mother is still alive—I'm not like June Woo. And my mother is far funnier and more interesting than any of the mothers in the book. (Laughs.)

Stanton: I wonder if you think that the book's success in this country has something to do with the fact that many people here have a history that they are ignoring and would like to be in touch with more.

I think that's partly true. The strongest reason, I think, is that I'm a baby boomer—in fact, I think that, to the month, I am the baby boomer age—and I think I wrote about something that hit a lot of baby boomer women whose mothers have either just recently died or may die in the near future. They felt that their misunderstandings, things that had not been talked about for years, were expressed in the book. There are so many mothers I know who gave the book to their daughters, and daughters who gave the book to their mothers, and marked passages of things they wanted to say.

Somogyi: Were you concerned about the lack of male voices in the book?

I was. I kept thinking I should have more balance, that I should put some strong male figure in there. Then I said, "No, you have to stay focused on what this book is about. You have to make some choices." That is a flaw in the book, but for me to correct the flaw would have thrown the book in another direction, and I couldn't do it at that point. The men are in there almost as pawns for bringing up the conflicts between the mothers and daughters; that's sort of unfortunate.

I don't think of the men as being as unsympathetic as a lot of people see them. People always say, "The men are weak," but really many of them by other standards are very strong men. The flaw, the weakness, is that we only see the moment in the relationship when they are seen as not that sympathetic. I think there are other dimensions to those men that I could have enlarged upon to make them more sympathetic, but it would have made the book lopsided in another sense.

Somogyi: It's ironic, though, because you think of the stereotypical Oriental woman as submissive and quiet, but the book portrays the older women as the strong ones.

What I've heard a lot from the Chinese-American community is how true the portrayals of the mothers are. Not the specific details, but the mothers' having unusual stories in their past that often are not told, and also that sheer strength over the will of their daughters. From other people's point of view, these mothers would be seen as little old Chinese ladies walking around in Chinatown with funny clothes, funny speech—invisible. And you would think that they're quiet. If you asked my mother what does she think of my book she would tell you, "Oh, very nice." And you would think Daisy Tan is a very shy, quiet woman. But if you would have lunch with her, go shopping with her, you would see her in action; her personality would come out. I mean, it used to embarrass me, how she could fight back. Every Chinese woman that I know is strong like that. Just determined as hell.

Stanton: Do you think of the daughters in the book as weak? So many of them seem powerless with their mothers, and yet if we met them right now, I wonder if we would see it.

If you met them, they would be very strong, successful women. It's the feeling I have with my mother; she is this tiny woman—four-foot-ten, eighty-five pounds—and with her slightest word, I am reduced to emotional trauma. (Laughs.) Mothers have that power.

The lives of the mothers seem so much more dramatic or exotic because of the time and the setting, but I think that in many respects they go through the same kinds of difficulties, only with the daughters there are too many choices. The mothers had no choice; the daughters have too many choices, and all of their difficulties and conflicts are sort of deflected to the outside world. That may be seen as greater weakness, but I almost think the struggle is more complex.

Somogyi: It seems that the superstitions of the parents are exotic and lend themselves to storytelling.

I think it is not so much the superstitions as the images that seem foreign to Americans. We have so many superstitions in American life, too. I was thinking of the lottery—people basing their luck on numbers. And they pick these numbers very religiously. They are staking their lives—a chance for life to change in a very dramatic way—on these numbers. And that is what superstitions are about. It is the possibility that your will or wishes can be imposed on a symbol and that you can change your life forever—hopefully for the better. It's the same thing.

Stanton: Can we talk about the writers' group you belong to and how that helped and influenced you?

The group is led by Molly Giles, a writer I met at Squaw Valley Community of Writers in 1985, when I first started writing. I showed Molly the story "Rules of the Game," which was called "Endgame" then—13 pages covering the life of a woman from age 5 until 35. Molly said, "Well, what you have is not a story." She pointed out that it was the beginnings of about a dozen or more stories, and she started circling bits of stories—this is a story . . . this is a story . . . this is a story. She also said, "You have several voices going on here; it's not consistent." And she showed me—this is a voice . . . this is a voice.

It was wonderful, because those are the kinds of questions I went to Squaw with—what is voice? I also had gone to Squaw because I needed to answer the questions, "Should I continue to write fiction? Is this challenging? Is this interesting to me?" And she brought out so many things I could work on for the rest of my life. I realized that, yes, this is what I want to do.

I asked Molly, if she ever conducted a workshop in San Francisco, to please let me know. I kept asking and asking. And I sent her revisions of that story; she gave me wonderful comments on it. In 1987, she said she would do a private group, and we started meeting once a week, oftentimes in my house. The core group is about five or six people; we read our stories out loud—whatever we've written the week before. We don't tell each other how to write the stories; we respond as readers. The idea is always to improve. I belonged briefly to one group where one of the women said, "Well, I believe we're all good writers, and that we should not criticize each other, we should just support and encourage one another." That's not what I need. I need to get better. The group is a support in the sense that you have to feel committed enough to what you're writing that you would read something aloud and face embarrassment once a week. It keeps your writing on schedule, and it also helps sharpen your own editorial process. Molly has the sharpest eye, the keenest ear for false steps, insincere voice, inconsistencies. She's also a wonderful writer at the same time—a good teacher and a good writer. A rare combination.

Somogyi: How often are you able to meet with the group now?

I haven't been able to meet as often because I've been on the road, but when I'm in town I meet once a week. I still read my stuff out loud and get roasted like everybody else.

Stanton: I wonder if you could tell us a little about your revision process.

I read everything out loud when I revise, because everything to me has to sound in a certain rhythm. So when I revise, which is probably about 12 to 20 times per page, I either read it aloud from the screen or print out a hard copy and read that. I'm not an ecologically sound writer (laughs); I figured out that I went through 7,000 sheets of paper writing *The Joy Luck Club.*

Somogyi: Were there more revisions on the first stories—the ones you were working on for several years?

I didn't revise those as much as the later stories because I didn't think they would ever be published. Some of those stories went through a few drafts on the screen, but maybe only three revisions on hard copy, which for me was very few.

Somogyi: Can you tell us a little about your next book?

It's hard to talk about it, because each page can change the whole rest of the book. The title is *The Kitchen God's Wife*, and it's a single narrative of a woman. The question, going back to how I write, is what in our life is given to us as fate, and what is given to us as sheer luck of moment, and what are choices that we make, so that at the end of our life, what do we take responsibility for, what do we regret, and what gives us peace in our heart? And so this book is those questions in the shape of the story of a woman about whom something is revealed, a secret that she's always wanted to keep hidden, and at that moment she looks at her life—her past in China, her life in America—and asks these questions and reconsiders her life.

Memory and the Ethnic Self:
Reading Amy Tan's *The Joy Luck Club*_____

The Chinese-American milieu in a San Francisco neighborhood furnishes the main contingent of characters in Amy Tan's *The Joy Luck Club*. What the four families in that book, the Woos, Jongs, Hsus, and St. Clairs, have in common is mother-daughter relations. The mothers are all first generation immigrants from mainland China, speaking very little English and remaining cultural aliens in their new world. The daughters are all born and educated in America, some even married to "foreigners." Within the microcultural structure of family, the only means available for mothers to ensure ethnic continuity is to recollect the past and to tell tales of what is remembered. Lamenting the failing marriage of Lena, her daughter, and Lena's unfamiliarity with the "Chinese ways of thinking," Ying-ying St. Clair voices the anxiety and helplessness shared by all the mothers in the book:

> All her life, I have watched her as though from another shore. And now I must tell her everything about my past. It is the only way to penetrate her skin and pull her to where she can be saved. (274)

In her mother's eyes, because Lena, without a memory of the past, allows herself to be borne by the bustle of life, she doesn't know who she is, and cannot hold herself together. It may be true that through her mother's memory, Lena will learn to share a belief in certain rules, roles, behaviors and values which provide, within the family and the overseas Chinese community, a functional ethos and a medium of communication. But will she, even if she unexpectedly finds herself confronted by an hour which has a special connection with her mother's past, have access to her mother's deeply buried anxiety, psychic need, specific mental habits, and life-world perception? Can she really share her mother's unrepeatable life-experience? Can she ever

Memory and the Ethnic Self   **93** learn how to overstep her own existential limits through her mother's story? What if she has to take cognizance of a barrier in her present existence that will eternally be a barrier between her and her mother? These questions can be asked not only about Lena but also about all the other daughters in *The Joy Luck Club*. I will take a close look here at the conflict between the two generations of the book and the existential unrepeatability that separates them. Through examining the complexity of the operations of memory, I will also explore how the recollection and narration of the past are related to a present sense of ethnic identity.

* * *

"Memory" is an intellectually seductive concept, capable of drawing on diverse literatures, from the cognitive concerns of speculative philosophy to experimental psychological probes of the processing-storage-retrieval function of mind.[1] Yet because the intellectual roots are so diffuse, and the connotations quite varied, I should clarify the two basic assumptions that I make when I use this term in my discussion of ethnic identity in *The Joy Luck Club*: first, a premise of the narrative construction of memory, and second, an emphasis on its social-psychological mechanism.

Most of the philosophical thinking on memory lapses almost inadvertently into the idiom of the static picture by conceiving of memory as a particular content of the mind, as an "image," a "presentation," an "impression," and so on.[2] However, it is not just that we have "images," "pictures," and "views" of ourselves in memory, but that we also have "stories" and "narratives" to tell about the past which both shape and convey our sense of self. Our sense of what has happened to us is entailed not in actual happenings but in *meaningful* happenings, and the meanings of our past experience, as I will explore and defend in my reading of *The Joy Luck Club*, are constructs produced in much the same way that narrative is produced. Identity, as well as the implicated self-definition and self-narrative, almost certainly will be activated from memory. Recent social-psychological studies have shown that self-images bring forth a host of intricately related self-knowledge and self-identity, whose information, values, and related beliefs are socially situated as well as psychologically useful.[3] Such understanding of the social-psychological mechanism of memory narrative is also implied in recent studies of narrative. Hayden White suggests that, in the narrative of individual life as well as in the narrative of history, the meaning of a given set of events, which he recognizes as taking the form of recurring tropical enfigurations, is not the same as the story they consist of (White 111). Using, as a guideline, his differentiation of two kinds of narrative meanings without committing to his tropological explanation of them, we may, in memory narrative, distinguish its *life-story* from the *existential perception* it entails. If the life-story is marked by a seeming actuality, the existential perception is what transforms the casual daily events into a functioning mentality or an existential concern that is not self-evident.

This bifurcate view of memory narrative permits us to consider a specific life-story as imagery of existential themes or problems about which the story is told, and the existential perception as a comprehensive context in which meaningful questions can be asked about the factual events of that life-story (what, how, and especially why). A functioning mentality, such as the survival mentality which characterizes all the mother characters in *The Joy Luck Club*, hardly enters into view with factual occurrences. It manifests itself only in the distribution of existential themes of the memory narrative. Memory narrative does not represent a perfect equivalent of the events it purports to describe. It goes beyond the actuality of events to the determination of their coherency as an existential situation, and this general picture of life in turn assigns exemplary values to the events which are awakened in memory by a functioning mentality.[4]

This awakening of memory by a person's present mentality is illustrated by Ying-ying St. Clair's story of her childhood. When Ying-ying was four years old, she got separated from her parents on a Moon Festival trip to a scenic lake, and while watching a performance of Moon Lady, she made a wish which she could not remember for many decades. It is only after her first broken marriage, and a second one to a kind but alien Irishman, and many "years washing away my pain, the same way carvings on stone are worn down by water," when she was "moving every year closer to the end of my life," that she remembers that, on that night, as a child of four, she "wished to be found" (64, 83).

Of the four mother characters in *The Joy Luck Club*, Ying-ying had the happiest childhood. Her family was very wealthy and took good care of her. Her getting lost from her family on a festival trip was no more than a small accident with no harmful consequences. However, this insignificant incident in her early childhood is remembered as an emblem of her unfortunate life. This is the memory of a survivor of bad times, who has lost her capacity to remember a different life even though she did once experience it. The memory itself has become a psychic defense, which helps to justify her social disengagement, her fatalistic perception of the world as a system of total control, and her fascination with extreme situations and with the possibility of applying their lessons to everyday life.

Ying-ying's survival mentality is typical of all the women characters who belong to the Joy Luck Club. All the Club Aunties have experienced two kinds of extreme situations: one kind is famine, war, forced marriage, and broken family in China, and the other is cultural alienation, disintegration of old family structure, and conflict between mother and daughter in America. In order to survive the drastic changes in their lives, these women need to maintain a psychological continuity, a coherent picture of life-world, and a continuity of self. Such a need requires the assuring structure of memory narrative: life-story narrative, with the genre's nominal continuity of aims and intentions, and hopes and fears. Memory is for them a socializing, ego-forming expression of anxieties, hopes, and survival instinct.

Indeed, the Joy Luck Club itself, with a magnificent mah jong table at its center, is an expression and embodiment of that survival mentality and its strategies of psychic defense. Suyuan Woo, mother of the book's first narrator, started the first Joy Luck Club in wartime Kweilin as a refugee running away from the triumphantly advancing Japanese troops. In times of trouble, everyday life became an exercise in survival, both physical and mental. If "hero" means someone who takes decisive action during a time of crisis, then for Suyuan Woo, whose life was in crisis, survival itself became a decisive action—a heroic action, albeit a pathetic and disenchanted one. In order to hang on to living, the club members in Kweilin tried to "feast," to "celebrate [their] good fortune, and play with seriousness and think of nothing else but adding to [their] happiness through winning" (11). As Suyuan herself explains:

It's not that we had no heart or eyes for pain. We were all afraid. We all had our miseries. But to despair was to wish back for something already lost. Or to prolong what was already unbearable. (11-12)

Suyuan starts the second Joy Luck Club in San Francisco in 1949. This time she is a refugee fleeing from the triumphant Communists in China. This second club is both a memory of the first club and a renewed means of survival. For those new club members newly immigrated to America, "who had unspeakable tragedies they had left behind in China and hopes they couldn't begin to express in their fragile English," the happy moments of playing mah jong are the only time they can "hope to be lucky"—"That hope was our only joy" (6, 12).

If the mah jong club reflects and is part of the Club Aunties' survival endeavor, it is not just a common sense survival that describes the difficulty of making ends meet or alludes to the fear of poverty. It expresses the perception that they are all survivors in the sense that they have lived through dark times and have emerged in the new world. It indicates the urgency to hold one's life together in the face of mounting pressures, which are seen in the dire light reflected from their memories of specific events that once victimized them in earlier times. Understanding is made necessary when one encounters the unfamiliar, the unknown, the uncanny. The process of understanding ordinarily begins with the displacement of the thing unknown toward something that is known, apprehended, and familiar. The process of understanding thus begins with an experiential shift. The domain of the unknown is shifted, by renewing the old strategy of survival, toward a domain or field presumably already mastered. All the stories included in the first section of the book are about mother-narrators' experiences of victimization. These old memories help shift the narrators, especially in an unfamiliar environment, to a growing belief that people are all victimized, in one way or another, by events beyond their control.

However, memories are not one-way tracks, as some early philosophers would like to suggest.[5] If the past casts a shadow on the present through memory, the present also pre-imposes on the past by means of memory. It is worth noting that John Perry, a philosopher who has written widely on the relationship between memory and personal identity, believes that "a sufficient and necessary condition of my having participated in a past event is that I am able to remember it" (69). The one-way track memory is what Nietzsche calls the "inability to forget," a symptom of a sick person who has given in to past failures and discomforts, making the present unbearable and the future hopeless. What we find with the Joy Luck Club mothers is what Nietzsche calls "memory of the will," an active memory that is sustained by the will to survive (Nietzsche "Second Essay"). Suyuan told her refugee story in so many varied ways that her daughter does not know how to relate them to reality and can only take them as "a Chinese fairy tale" (12). These stories, in the form of memory, test Suyuan's ability to forget. These stories are her symptomatic records of a traumatized soul making a desperate effort to push back the memory of the tragic loss of a husband and two baby daughters during the war. The real memory was suppressed but did not go away; and Suyuan, as her second husband feels intuitively, "was killed by her own thoughts," which she could not even articulate to her husband and daughter (5).

Not only does Suyuan's early experience of extreme situations results in a defensive contraction of self, but also it transforms her relationship with her daughter into one of survival: a fear that she will lose her connection with her daughter, and that her experiences, thoughts, beliefs, and desires will have no future successors. The daughter may look like the mother, or even identify with her; and yet, the two are still worlds apart from each other. Perry makes a very important differentiation between "identification" and "identity," and points out, "Identity is not a necessary condition of identification. I can identify with the participant in events I did not do, and would not do, even if they were to be done" (76). Georges Rey, in his study of the existential unrepeatability of personal experience and identity, emphasizes the impossibility of passing on identity through the narrative of memory:

> There are . . . an alarmingly diverse number of ways in which one person might come to share the seeming memories of another: vivid stories, hallucinations. . . . All my and my grandfather's hopes to the contrary, he does not survive as me, no matter how much I seem to recollect (and even take as my own) the experiences of his life from having heard of them at his knees. This is partly because we were both alive when I heard and identified with them; and, for all our not inconsiderable mutual concern, none of it was (strictly) personal. I didn't thereafter enjoy any privileged access to his feelings and thoughts. (Rey 41)

Memory is not just a narrative, even though it does have to take a narrative form; it is more importantly an experiential relation between the past and the present, projecting a future as well. It is the difference of experiential networks between Suyuan Woo and her daughter that accounts for the daughter's resistance to the mother's nagging about hard work and persistence, as well as for her confusion about the mother's constant sense of crisis.

Hard work and persistence are with the mother—and most "diligent" Chinese immigrants—less self-sufficient virtues than means and conditions of survival. These qualities are desirable to her just because she learnt from her previous experiences that they are attributes of a "winner" in life, and she is going to treat them only as such. It is only on the usefulness of these qualities that she will base her self-approval for exercising them. Even though she knows pretty well that her daughter will never get a Ph.D., she keeps telling her friends and neighbors that Jing-mei Woo is working on it. This is less a lie or wishful thinking than an expression of her survival instinct: what the mother seeks from her friends and neighbors is not the kind of approval that applauds her daughter's personal qualities, but the conviction for herself that her daughter possesses the attributes of a survivor. It is too easy to advance diligence, frugality, or whatever as Chinese ethnic qualities. What is wrong in such a view is an essentialist interpretation of these qualities as *inherent* "Chinese" attributes, and a blindness to their special relations with a particular kind of ethnic memory.

The disposition for many first generation Chinese immigrants in America to see life as a constant test of survival, to the extent that it almost becomes ethnic symbolism, is a complex mentality. It is deeply rooted in China's past of hardship and numerous famines and wars. The word in Chinese that denotes "making a living in the world" is *qiusheng*—seeking survival, or *mousheng*—managing survival. The Chinese classics are full of wisdom on how to survive, whether it be Taoist escapism, Confucian doctrine of the mean, or Legalist political trickery. The lack of religion and of a systematic belief in an after-life in Chinese culture indicates the preoccupation with the urgency of surviving in the present world. The simultaneous contempt for business (and "the rich")[6] and love of money (in the form of thriftiness) support the view of money not as a measure of success but as a means of survival.

However, survival mentality in China has never become a symbol of nationality and ethnicity. It is part of the living conditions which have remained intact with little change throughout centuries; but it has never been mobilized and turned into what Werner Sollors, in his *The Inven-*

tion of Ethnicity, calls "kinship symbolism." Only when a Chinese person is uprooted from his or her own culture and transplanted into an alien one does he or she become aware of the fluidity, proteanness, and insecurity of his or her self. It is not until then that he or she feels the need to define himself or herself by a reference group, or even deliberately manages a certain image or presentation of self using the symbolism of survival. "Ethnicity," as Sollors aptly observes, "is not so much an ancient and deep-seated force surviving from the historical past. . . . It marks an acquired . . . sense of belonging that replaces visible, concrete communities whose kinship symbolism ethnicity may yet mobilize in order to appear more natural" (xiv). The newly acquired ethnic awareness of being Chinese in America and the sense of urgency about the individual's and the group's preservation and survival register the waning of the old sense of a durable public world, reassuring in its definiteness, continuity, and long-tested survival strategies.

Once the imagery of confinement, insecurity, alienation, and extreme situations takes hold of the imagination of an ethnic group, the temptation to extend this imagery to lesser forms of stress and hardship and to reinterpret every kind of adversity or difference in the light of survival proves almost irresistible. Things as trifling as the Chinese way of playing mah jong, which, according to the mothers in *The Joy Luck Club*, is different from and far superior to the Jewish mah jong, is jealously guarded as a matter of immense significance. The excessive concern with being "genuinely Chinese" announces the abandonment of efforts to adapt to a mixed and heterogeneous society in favor of mere ethnic survival.

Even at the mah jong table people have to face the agony of how to survive. "We used to play mah jong," explains Auntie An-mei to Jing-mei, "winner take all. But the same people were always winning, the same people always losing." This is what life has always been: there has to be someone who is a loser and a victim. But the San Francisco Joy Luck Club Aunties reformulate their mah jong game so that it becomes, symbolically at least, a game with no losers:

We got smart. Now we can all win and lose equally. We can have stock market luck. And we can play mah jong for fun, just for a few dollars, winner take all. Losers take home leftovers! (18)

The change in the mah jong game may appear insignificant. But it reflects the Club Aunties' view of the loser as a victim who fails to survive, and their belief that one should make every effort to defend oneself against the bruising experience of being a loser, even at a mah jong table. Such a view can alter the way competition and rivalry are experienced. Competition, whether it be in a chess game, in a piano performance, or for a college degree, now centers not so much on the desire to excel as on the struggle to avoid a crushing defeat. A willingness to risk everything in the pursuit of victory gives way to a cautious hoarding of the reserves necessary to sustain life over the long haul. For Lindo Jong, her daughter's chess championship is not just proof of her talent. It is more essentially her attribute of being "lucky" and being a winner. Worldly success has always carried with it a certain poignancy, an awareness that "you can't take it with you"; but among the Chinese, glory is more fleeting than ever, and those who win a game worry incessantly about losing it.

Lindo Jong gives her daughter Waverly her own talisman of luck— "a small tablet of red jade which held the sun's fire" (98)—in order to add to the latter's "invisible strength." Her daughter's chess battle becomes her own battle. But the worry and concern of her subtle survivalism is not appreciated by her daughter, who accuses her mother of using her to show off and trying to take all the credit. Lindo Jong's "all American made" daughter has a hard time understanding why her mother believes that "luck" and "tricks" are more valuable and more important than "skill" and "smartness." "You don't have to be so smart to win chess," Lindo Jong tells her daughter. "It is just tricks" (187).

Waverly Jong feels immobilized by her mother's "sneak attack" (191), and at first completely misses the disenchanted heroic style that underlies the "sneakiness" of her mother's attack. What she fails to see is that her mother's "sneakiness" is meant to prepare her for dealing with the unpredictable, in which she will constantly find herself faced with unstructured situations and the need to survive on her own. In contrast to the American strategies of survival that Waverly has been introduced to (such as upward mobility, security in legal protection, and active individual choice), Lindo Jong's survivalist strategy of "sneakiness" or "trickiness" is miserably nonheroic and shamefully "Chinese." Waverly fears and despises her mother, and resists her mother's teaching. Puzzled by her daughter's reaction, Lindo Jong confesses:

> I couldn't teach her about the Chinese character. How to obey parents and listen to your mother's mind. How not to show your own thoughts, to put your feelings behind your face so you can take advantage of hidden opportunities. Why easy things are not worth pursuing. How to know your own worth and polish it, never flashing it around like a cheap ring. Why Chinese thinking is best. (289)

The wearing of a mask is to Lindo Jong an heroic act—an act necessary for the survival of poor immigrants like herself, who feel "it's hard to keep your Chinese face in America" (294). Wearing a mask means the ability to suppress one's true feelings and emotions—even to deceive—in order to be allowed to live. She is not unaware of the debt that the mask wearer has to pay to human guile; but in her understanding there is no rage that rips the heart, no passion of combat which stresses the heroic deeds of ethnic rebellion. With many Chinese-Americans like Lindo Jong, survivalism has led to a cynical devaluation of heroism, and to a resignation that is tinged with a bitter sense of humor.

When they first arrived in America, Lindo Jong and An-mei Hsu worked in a fortune cookie factory, making Chinese sayings of fortune for American consumption. Lindo Jong was wondering what all this nonsense of Chinese fortunes was about. An-mei explained to her:

"American people think Chinese people write these sayings."

"But we never say such things!" [Lindo Jong] said. "These things don't make sense. These are not fortunes, they are bad instructions."

"No, miss," [An-mei] said, laughing, "it is our bad fortune to be here making these and somebody else's bad fortune to pay to get them." (299-300)

Lindo Jong knows that the Chinese wearing of the mask, just like those Chinese fortunes, can convince many Americans that they know and understand Chinese people. She also has an unusual insight into the risk that the mask wearer can become psychologically dependent upon the mask, even when the mask is not needed. Continued wearing of the mask makes it difficult for the wearer of the mask to be her real self. Maskedness has almost become the ethnic symbolism for Chinese-Americans like Lindo Jong, who thinks like a person of "two faces," being neither American nor Chinese (304).

In a self-consciously two-faced person like Lindo Jong we find a detached, bemused, ironic observer, who is almost fascinated by the fact that she has not a self that she can claim as "me." The sense of being an observer of one's own situation and that all things are not happening to "me" helps to protect "me" against pain and also to control expressions of outrage or rebellion.[7] Survivors have to learn to see themselves not as free subjects, but rather as the victims of circumstances, be they the current situation or prefixed fate or disposition.

Chinese Taoist culture helps to maintain this kind of victim mentality because it reinforces a passive if not fatalist attitude toward life. The influence of Taoism, in its popularized form, is obvious in how *yin-yang-wu-hsing* is used by the mothers in *The Joy Luck Club* as a physiotherapy that helps explain why the life of the unlucky people is what it is. In this popularized form of Taoism, human life is a constant struggle for a precarious balance between *yin* and *yang*, affected even by the placing of your bedroom mirror or the location of your condominium apartment. *Wu-hsing* (the five elements: water, fire, wood, metal, and earth), which were conceived by the Taoist masters as five fundamental phases of any process in space-time, become the mystical ingredients that determine every person's character flaw according to one's birth hour. "Too much fire and you had a bad temper. . . . Too much water and you flowed in too many directions" (19).

Rose Hsu Jordan, like her mother, An-mei, has too little wood, and as a consequence, she bends to other people's ideas. Her marriage with Ted breaks down because he is annoyed by her lack of decision. Measured by the *Wu-hsing* system, none of us has all the five character elements perfectly balanced, and therefore, every one of us is by nature flawed. This view of human imperfection may appear like the Greek idea of tragic flaw. But the Chinese view of character flaw has no interest in any unyielding defiance to fate. The wily Chinese wisdom and belief that heroes do not survive informs the disenchantment with conventional codes of defiance and heroism. While the Greek tragic heroes face their inevitable destruction with dignity and grace, the believers in *Wu-hsing* want to survive by amending the flaw through non-heroic small acts such as taking special names—the "rose" in Rose Hsu Jordan's name, for example, is supposed to add wood to her character.

Both Rose Hsu Jordan and her mother regard themselves as victims of circumstances, but, belonging to two different generations, they resort to different strategies in order to alleviate their fear of disaster. An-mei Hsu copes with everyday mishaps by preparing for the worst and by keeping faith in hope. Her faith in God, which she held for many years before her youngest boy was drowned, was less a religious belief for which she was ready to sacrifice herself than a survival strategy of keeping herself in hope. Although An-mei keeps telling her daughter to make her choice, or even to indulge in a fantasy revenge for the wrongs suffered by women, she is prepared to accept the worst thing that can happen to a woman: the fate of being a woman, "to desire nothing, to swallow other people's misery, to eat my own bitterness" (241).

An-mei's faith in God, or, after the death of her boy, in hope, is to her American-made daughter only a fatalist's self-created illusion. "[My mother] said it was faith that kept all these good things coming our way," Rose Hsu Jordan tells us with her tongue in cheek, "only I thought she said 'fate,' because she couldn't pronounce that 'th' sound in 'faith.'" Rose has to be tempered by her own suffering before she will discover that "maybe it was fate all along, that faith was just an illusion that somehow you're in control" (128).

Instead of relying completely on her mother's advice, Rose, devastated by her broken marriage, goes to her psychiatrist. Psychiatry, for Rose the young Chinese-American, has played the role of modern successor to religion. In psychiatry, the religious relief for souls has given way to "mental hygiene," and the search for salvation to the search for peace of mind. Rose tells her psychiatrist about her fantasy revenge against Ted, and feels like having "raced to the top of a big turning point in my life, a new me after just two weeks of psychotherapy." She expects an illuminating response from her psychiatrist. However, just like her mother was forsaken by God, Rose is let down by her mundane saver: "my psychiatrist just looked bored" (211). It is only after her frustrating experience with her psychiatrist that Rose feels an accidental connection of a shared fate between herself and her mother. The mother and daughter are co-victims of a common threatening force over which they have no control. It is when Rose, in her dream, sees her mother planting trees and bushes in the planter boxes, adding wood to both of them, that she lets us get a close view of a mother-daughter relation that is defined neither by blood tie nor by material service, a relation that is neither Chinese nor American, but Chinese-American.

This mother-daughter relationship with a unique ethnic character is what we discern not only in the Hsu family, but also in the families of Woos, Jongs, and St. Clairs. The family tie between the mother and daughter in each of these Chinese-American families is no longer what determines the Chinese daughter's obligation or the Chinese mother's authority. Family features shared by mother and daughter in those Chinese-American families are not something to be proud of, but rather something that causes embarrassment on one side or the other, and often on both sides. However, neither does this mother-daughter relationship rest, as is common in the American family, on material service. The cross-generation relationship rests on a special service the mother renders to the daughter: the mother prepares the daughter for the extreme situations of life, gives her psychic protection whenever possible, and introduces her to resources she needs to survive on her own. The mother does all this not in the capacity of a self-righteous mother, but as a co-victim who has managed to survive. The traditional role of a Chinese mother has been greatly curtailed in America. If formerly she represented an automatic authority, now she is unsure of herself, defensive, hesitant to impose her own standards on the young. With the mother's role changed, the daughter no longer identifies with her mother or internalizes her authority in the same way as in China, if indeed she recognizes her authority at all.

The loosened family tie and shaky continuity between the two generations represented in *The Joy Luck Club* account for the particular narrative form in which their life acts and events are told. These stories share no apparently recognizable pattern or fully integrated narrative structure. The character relations are suggested but never sufficiently interwoven or acted out as a coherent drama. Our attention is constantly called to the characteristics of fiction that are missing from the book. It is neither a novel nor a group of short stories. It consists of isolated acts and events, which remain scattered and disbanded. It has neither a major plot around which to drape the separate stories, nor a unitary exciting climax which guides the book to a final outcome.

Yet all these customary habitual ingredients have a place in *The Joy Luck Club*. The successions of events are fully timed and narrators of these events are carefully grouped in terms of theme as well as generation distribution (mothers and daughters). The book's sixteen stories are grouped into four sections: the two outer sections are stories by three mother-narrators, and Jing-mei Woo, who takes the place of her recently deceased mother; and the two inner sections are stories by four daughter-narrators. The stories in the first two sections are followed by successive denouements in the next two sections, leading to a series of revelations. All the energies set in motion in the first story of the book, which is told by the book's "framework" narrator, come to fruitful release in the book's last story told by the same narrator, Jing-mei Woo.

Just as the mah jong table is a linkage between the past and present for the Club Aunties, Jing-mei Woo, taking her mother's seat at the table, becomes the frame narrator linking the two generations of American Chinese, who are separated by age and cultural gaps and yet bound together by family ties and a continuity of ethnic heritage. It is Jing-mei Woo who tells the book's two frame stories, the first and the last. These two frame stories, ending with a family reunion in China, suggest strongly a journey of maturity, ethnic awakening, and return-to-home, not just for Jing-mei Woo, but metaphorically for all the daughters in the book. This experience is like a revelation—sudden unveiling of the authentic meaning of being "Chinese." The ecstatic character of this experience is well expressed by Jing-mei Woo:

> The minute our train leaves the Hong Kong border and enters Shenzhen, China, I feel different. I can feel the skin on my forehead tingling, my blood rushing through a new course. My mother was right. I am becoming Chinese. (306)

At this moment, she seems to come to a sudden realization that to be "Chinese" is a lofty realm of being that transcends all the experiential attributes she once associated with being a Chinese, when she was unable to understand why her mother said that a person born Chinese cannot help but feel and think Chinese:

> And when she said this, I saw myself transforming like a werewolf, a mutant tag of DNA suddenly triggered, replicating itself insidiously into a syndrome, a cluster of telltale Chinese behaviors, all those things my mother did to embarrass me—haggling with store owners, pecking her mouth with a toothpick in public, being color-blind to the fact that lemon yellow and pale pink are not good combinations for winter clothes.

But today I realize I've never really known what it means to be Chinese. I am thirty-six years old. My mother is dead and I am on a train, carrying with me her dreams of coming home. I am going to China. (306-7)

The book has, for other daughters, other moments of revelation like this one experienced by Jing-mei Woo, though they are of a more subtle nature and of less intensity. It is at these moments of revelation, often after their own sufferings in life, that the daughters come to realize the value and reason of their mothers' survival mentality and the disenchanted heroism of mask and endurance, and begin to hear the rich and multiple meanings in their mothers' stories instead of mere dead echoes of past acts and events. They become less resistant to identifying with their mothers and more receptive to the humble wisdom of the previous generations. The change from resistance to acquiescence signifies simultaneously the growth of a mature self and the ethnicization of experience.

The need to ethnicize their experience and to establish an identity is more real and more perplexing to the daughters than to the mothers, who, after all, are intimate with and secure in their Chinese cultural identity in an experiential sense, in a way their American-born daughters can never be. The daughters, unlike their mothers, are American not by choice, but by birth. Neither the Chinese nor the American culture is equipped to define them except in rather superficial terms. They can identify themselves for sure neither as Chinese nor American. Even when they feel their identity of "Americanness" is an estrangement from their mothers' past, there is no means of recovering the Chinese innocence, of returning to a state which their experiential existence has never allowed them. They are Chinese-Americans whose Chineseness is more meaningful in their relationship to white Americans than in their relationship to the Chinese culture they know little about. The return to their ethnic identity on the part of the daughters is represented in *The Joy Luck Club* as realizable on a level where a real split between the existential self and the ethnic self is alluded to by a narrative rivalry between "tale of the past" and "tale of the present." Not only are the contrast and discontinuity between the two types of tales metaphorical of the split of self, but also their organizing narrator, Jing-mei, is symbolic of the split self of the daughters' generation.

The ethnicization of experience does not automatically mean an ethnic identity. The ethnicized and mature self acquiesces to the ethnic affiliation that fixes its patterns and meanings, but at the very point of acquiescence, registers discomfort with such constraints. Indeed the strange blending of acquiescence and resistance accounts for the fact that the return to the motherland in *The Joy Luck Club* is temporary and disillusioning, no more than a "visit." Such a visit is at once an assertion of "going home" and a painful realization of "going home as a stranger."

Therefore, the significance of the book's frame device of return-to-home and its satisfaction of the reader's formal expectations should not disarm our critical query as to whether the ethnic self really represents a higher form of self or self-awareness. The book's frame device suggests the split between the true but unrecognized self and the false outer being whose sense of self and identity is determined by the need to adjust to the demands of a fundamentally alien society. Such a dualist view of self offers the reassuring but problematic concept of ethnic reality as that which is familiar and recuperated, and which, in the homeland, loyally awaits our return even though we turn from it. It assumes that the "inner" or "true" self is occupied in maintaining its identity by being transcendent, unembodied, and thus never to be discovered until the moment of epiphany. Not only does this cozy view of return to the authentic self suggest a split between the existential self and the ethnic self, but also a fixed hierarchy of them, with the changing and trapped existential self at the bottom, and the essential and free ethnic identity at the top. However, this hierarchy is unstable: the ethnic self, just like the existential self, is neither free nor self-sufficient, and therefore never an authentic or genuine self. Our ethnic experience, no less than our existential experience, depends on the mediation of others. We become aware of our ethnicity only when we are placed in juxtaposition with others, and when the priority of our other identities, such as individual, class, gender, and religious, give place to that of ethnicity. Like other kinds of identities, ethnic identity is not a fixed nature, or an autonomous, unified, self-generating quality. It is a self-awareness based on differentiation and contextualization. The self is not a given, but a creation; there is no transcendent self, ethnic or whatever else. Ethnic awareness is not a mysteriously inherited quality; it is a measurable facet of our existence, whose conditions and correlates are the only context in which we can understand how we reconstitute feelings and inner knowledge of our own ethnic being.

Notes

1. Philosophers dealing with memory are typically concerned with its representative function, as capable of bringing to our mind "images" (St. Augustine and others), "presentation" (Aristotle), "impressions" (Aristotle and others), "ideas" (Locke and Hume), and the "immediate" or "present" objects in memory (A. D. Woozley and others). See, for example, Aristotle, "On Memory and Reminiscence," in R. McKeon, ed., *The Basic Works of Aristotle* (New York, 1941). Augustine, *Confessions*. Many translations and editions. Book X, 8-19; John Locke, *An Essay Concerning Human Understanding*, 2 vols., ed. A. C. Fraser (Oxford, 1894), Book II, Ch. 10; David Hume, *A Treatise of Human Nature*, ed. L. A. Selby-Bigge (Oxford, 1888), Book I, Pt. I, Sec. 3 and Pt. III, Sec. 5; A. D. Woozley, *Theory of Knowledge* (London, 1949), Chs. 2-3. The psychological study of memory owes a substantial debt to Hermann Ebbinghaus, who single-handedly moved memory from the domain of the speculative philosopher to the province of the experimental scientist. In the two-volume *Practical Aspects of Memory: Current Research and Issues* (Chichester, England: John Wiley and Sons, 1988), M. M. Gruneberg, P. E. Morris, and R. N. Sykes put together a whole variety of approaches and methods that are used today in experimental psychological studies of memory, such as eyewitnessing, autobiographical memory, maintenance of knowledge, etc.

2. Aristotle, St. Augustine, John Locke, David Hume, etc., op. cit.

3. See for example, H. Markus, "Self-Schemata and Processing Information about

the Self," *Journal of Personality and Social Psychology* 35 (1977): 63-78; S. T. Fiske and S. E. Taylor, *Social Cognition* (Reading, MA: Addison-Wesley, 1984); B. R. Schlenker, "Self-Identification: Toward an Integration of the Private and Public Self," in R. F. Baumeister, ed., *Public Self and Private Self* (New York: Springer-Verlag, 1986), 21-62.

4. John Perry refers to this cognitive hermeneutic circle of memory, and the reciprocal reality between a person who remembers and the things that he remembers. He writes, "That my present apparent memory of a past event stands at the end of a causal chain of a certain kind leading from that event is not something I can directly perceive, but something believed because it fits into the simplest theory of the world as a whole which is available to me" (69).

5. This view was most representatively voiced by the nineteenth-century British philosopher Sir William Hamilton, who regarded memory as one of the undeniable conditions of consciousness. See, for instance, *Lectures on Metaphysics and Logic*, ed. H. L. Mansel and John Weitch (Edinburgh: W. Blackwood and Sons, 1859-1860), "Lecture XI," 205. Identity is explained as constituting in the assurance that our thinking ego, notwithstanding the ceaseless changes of state, is essentially the same thing. What such a view fails to see is that in remembering, a person not only records what has happened to him but also strives toward a restitution of his own ego—a construction of a continuous, integrated sense of his real existence in relation to time, nature and society, cause and effect.

6. The Chinese proverb *weifu buren* suggests the incompatibility between "being rich" and "being benevolent."

7. In today's mainland China, the wearing of a political mask is still practiced as a gesture of self-preservation and, hopefully, of potential resistance.

Works Cited

Nietzsche, Friedrich. *On The Genealogy of Morals*. Trans. Walter Kaufman and R. J. Hollingdale. New York: Vintage, 1967.

Perry, John. "The Importance of Being Identical," in Amelie Oksenberg Rorty, ed., *The Identities of Persons*. Berkeley: U of California P, 1976. 67-90.

Rey, Georges. "Survival," in Amelie Oksenberg Rorty, ed., *The Identities of Persons*. Berkeley: U of California P, 1976.

Sollors, Werner, ed. *The Invention of Ethnicity*. New York: Oxford UP, 1989.

Tan, Amy. *The Joy Luck Club*. New York: Ivy, 1989.

White, Hayden. *Tropics of Discourse: Essays in Cultural Criticism*. Baltimore: Johns Hopkins UP, 1978.

"Only Two Kinds of Daughters":
Inter-Monologue Dialogicity in *The Joy Luck Club*____

Stephen Souris

> "Only two kinds of daughters," she shouted in Chinese. "Those who are obedient and those who follow their own mind! Only one kind of daughter can live in this house. Obedient daughter!" (142)

> My mother and I never really understood one another. We translated each other's meanings and I seemed to hear less than what was said, while my mother heard more. (37)

> —Amy Tan, *The Joy Luck Club*

Amy Tan has said that she never intended *The Joy Luck Club* to be a novel. Instead, she thought of it as a collection of stories. But she did plan on having the stories cohere around a central theme, and she did plan the prefaces from the start, although they were written last ("Interview").[1] More importantly, her collection of first-person monologues participates in and contributes to a tradition of multiple monologue narratives. Since the precedent-setting experiments of Woolf and Faulkner— *The Waves, The Sound and the Fury, As I Lay Dying, Absalom, Absalom!*—a number of interesting novels written in the decentered, multiple monologue mode have been published. Louise Erdrich's *Tracks*, Peter Matthiessen's *Killing Mister Watson*, Louis Auchincloss's *The House of the Prophet*, and Kaye Gibbons's *A Virtuous Woman* are just a few of the contemporary examples of this compelling genre.[2]

Because of its decentered, multi-perspectival form, *The Joy Luck Club* invites analysis from critical perspectives that theorize and valorize fragmented, discontinuous texts and the possibilities of connection across segments. Mikhail Bakhtin may come to mind first because of his emphasis on and celebration of texts flaunting a diversity of fully valid and autonomous voices with relativistic and centrifugal consequences as well as counter-centrifugal tendencies such as the active intermingling of perspectives within single consciousnesses (what I call "intra-monologue dialogicity"). Tan's "novel" offers a heteroglot collection of very different, fully valid voices each presented from its own perspective, with relativistic and centrifugal implications.[3] Moreover, its unique theme—mothers from China and their American-born daughters struggling to understand each other—allows for a rich array of dialogized perspectives within single utterances: the Chinese, the American, and the Chinese-American, all three of which can be discerned, to varying degrees, in the monologues.[4]

My concern in this essay, however, will not be with the counter-centrifugal phenomenon of "intra-monologue dialogicity." Rather, it will be with what I call "inter-monologue dialogicity," or the potential for active intermingling of perspectives across utterances, with the site of the dialogicity located in the reader's experience of the narrative. Although Bakhtin has some provocative things to say about the dialogic potential of textual segments set side by side and even hints at the role a reader would have to play in establishing that dialogicity, his theory does not fully allow for a reader's moment-by-moment processing of a text. Wolfgang Iser picks up where Bakhtin leaves off regarding the counter-centrifugal dialogicity that can be said to exist between textual elements in a multiple narrator novel. It is with his narrative model that I propose to uncover and articulate the dialogic potential across monologues in *The Joy Luck Club*.[5]

* * *

Iser's phenomenologically rigorous model of the act of reading is ideally suited to the pursuit and articulation of inter-monologue dialogicity in narratives modeled more or less after *The Sound and the Fury*, *As I Lay Dying*, or *The Waves*. Although *The Act of Reading* is a classic text in the reader-response school, a brief summary of the main points of Iser's theory will establish the context for my analysis of the potentially interacting structures of *The Joy Luck Club*.

Like other reader-response critics, Iser emphasizes the active involvement of the reader in the creation of meaning. For Iser, reading is a "dynamic happening" (*Act*, 22) and is the product of a "dyadic interaction" (66) betwcen text and reader. "Meaning is an effect to be experienced," he asserts (10); it does not inhere in a literary work independent of the reading experience. For Iser, "literary texts initiate 'performances' of meaning rather than actually formulating meanings themselves" (27). Meaning for Iser is "text-guided though reader-produced" ("Interview," 71). What a reader encounters in processing a text are "instructions for the production of the signified" (*Act*, 65).

Iser's emphasis on the reader's active involvement with the text does not allow for the extreme subjectivism that Norman Holland and David Bleich allow for in their theories. As such, Iser's model is relatively conservative because it insists that all concretizations be "intersubjectively" valid: "The subjective processing of a text is generally still accessible to third parties, i.e., available for intersubjective analysis" (*Act*, 49). Indeed, the reason for restricting the creative activity of the reader is to allow for observations that can be agreed upon across subjectivities: "One task of a theory of aesthetic response is to facilitate intersubjective discussion of individual interpretations" (x). To that end, Iser distinguishes between "meaning" and "significance": "meaning" is what all readers who are properly following the "instructions for the production of the signified" should arrive at; "significance" concerns how a particular reader might apply that meaning to his or her own life. But the emphasis in Iser's model is always with the processing of textual elements rather than the production of a detachable message, as he indicates by asserting that "what is important to readers, critics, and authors alike is what literature does and not what it means" (53).

In calling for an "erotics of art" (following Sontag ["Indeterminacy," 1]), and in inviting the reader to "climb aboard" the text (*Implied*, 277), Iser emphasizes the moment-by-moment experience of what a text "does" to the reader. He refers to the reader's "wandering viewpoint" because of this emphasis on the temporal experience of a text. "The wandering viewpoint," he argues, "divides the text up into interacting structures, and these give rise to a grouping activity that is fundamental to the grasping of a text" (*Act*, 119). These interactive structures are conceptually apprehended as a gestalt. Any perspective of the moment—or "theme," in his terminology—is apprehended against the backdrop of a previous "theme," which becomes the "horizon." For Iser, responding to the textual prompts as "instructions for the production of the signified" amounts to actively recalling previous moments and allowing them to enter into significant combinations with present moments. Or, since his model allows for readers rereading, any present moment can be creatively paired up with a moment one remembers will be encountered later in the text. Constantly creating foreground/background *Gestalten*, an Iserian reader's experience of a text is very three-dimensional. But each theme/horizon concretization is temporary and may have to be modified as other *Gestalten* are experienced. Iser expresses this complex concept thusly: "The structure of theme and horizon constitutes the vital link between text and reader . . . because it actively involves the reader in the process of synthesizing an assembly of constantly shifting viewpoints, which not only modify one another, but also influence past and future syntheses in the reading process" (*Act*, 23). Iser illustrates the concept of constantly modifying one's concretizations by comparing the reading experience to a cybernetic feedback loop. Because of this experiential emphasis, he can assert that "the text can never be grasped as a whole, only as a series of changing viewpoints, each one restricted in itself and so necessitating further perspectives" (68).

"Gaps" or "blanks" (*Unbestimmtsheitsstellen*) provide the impetus for the creation of a theme/horizon gestalt by inviting the reader to respond to an interruption in the flow or exposition with a meaning-creating pairing. "Wherever there is an abrupt juxtaposition of segments there must automatically be a blank," he argues, "breaking the expected order of the text" (*Act*, 195). Iserian gaps have been explained as "conceptual spaces" between textual elements (Martin 261) that allow for reader ideation. According to Iser, "Gaps are bound to open up, and offer a free play of interpretation for the specific way in which the various views can be connected with one another. These gaps give the reader a chance to build his own bridges" ("Indeterminacy," 12). But gaps do not really allow for "free play"; the reader must engage in "intersubjectively" valid concretizations: "The structured blanks of the text stimulate the process of ideation to be performed by the reader on terms set by the text" (*Act*, 169). The concept of *Unbestimmtsheitsstellen*, or gaps, is Iser's central trope for figuring the active reader involvement required by the reading experience.

The final concept to summarize before applying Iser's phenomenologically precise model of the reading process to Tan's *Joy Luck Club* is negativity. For Iser, the depiction of anything unattractive or deformed automatically causes the reader to imagine a positive counterbalance. This is another kind of gap, then: deformity creates a space in which the active reader compensates for the unattractive depiction with the imagining of a more positive situation or character.

Iser's unusual sensitivity to the moment-by-moment construction of the text by a reader makes his theory especially relevant to fragmented texts. Indeed, he "valorizes the discontinuous work" that is full of gaps (Kuenzli 52). This can be seen in his comments on *Ulysses*, *The Sound and the Fury*, and *Humphrey Clinker* in *The Implied Reader* and *The Act of Reading*.

Reading *The Joy Luck Club* in the context of Iser's elaborately worked out theory and his remarks on fragmented, multi-perspectival texts requires paying attention to the way in which a reader's moment-by-moment processing of the text confers a centripetal coherence upon a potentially chaotic, centrifugal collection. We need to ask how the discontinuous nature of the narrative (the gaps between sections, in particular) impels the reader to establish *Gestalten* that are multiple, constantly shifting, and thematically suggestive. We need to look for ways in which initial constructions of foreground/background configurations have to be revised as additional text is encountered. And we need to ask where the line can be drawn between responses that are "intersubjectively" valid and those that range beyond what can be agreed upon intersubjectively.

The segmented presentation of *The Joy Luck Club* allows for many combinational possibilities. I will present some of the most salient *Gestalten*; other foreground/background pairings will, no doubt, suggest themselves based on the examples I offer.

* * *

One way *Gestalten* can be created is through juxtapositions of contiguous and non-contiguous monologues. With contiguously placed utterances that "speak to" each other, the side-by-side placement of monologues with common denominators, or, to use Bakhtin's term, "semantic convergence" (*Speech*, 124), constitutes an overt invitation to the reader to explore the dialogic potential between the monologues. In these cases, the gap between the sections, which always invites a reflective pause, ensures that a rereading reader will make the connection (although the reader still deserves credit for making the connection).

The first cluster of four monologues provides us with some examples of meaningful juxtapositions, both contiguous and non-contiguous.

In the opening monologue of the novel, Jing-mei (June) offers comments on both Ying-ying and An-mei that color our attitude toward those two. Of Ying-ying, she says that the aunt "seems to shrink even more every time I see her" (29). A few pages later, she adds to this unflattering picture by reporting what her mother thought of Ying-ying: "'Oh, I have a story,' says Auntie Ying loudly, startling everybody. Auntie Ying has always been the weird auntie, someone lost in her own world. My mother used to say, 'Auntie Ying is not hard of hearing. She is hard of listening'" (35). A few monologues later, we meet Ying-ying from her own point of view. Her account of the traumatic experience of falling off her family's boat and, more generally, growing up in a wealthy family without much contact with her mother, sets up a meaningful gestalt with Jing-mei's comments. On first reading, June's unappreciative comments prejudice us against Ying-ying as the "weird" one; when we read her own account of her childhood and pair that with Jing-mei's words, we realize Jing-mei's account is reductive. On the outside she may appear to be shrinking, and she may appear "hard of listening"; on the inside she has a story to tell that helps explain why she is the way she is. The experience of this gestalt, which shifts depending on one's position in the text (June's words as foreground, Ying-ying's monologue as background, or the latter's monologue as foreground, and June's unappreciative words as background), points out to the reader that greater understanding can lead to greater appreciation and tolerance.

June also comments on An-mei in an unappreciative manner, reporting what her mother has said of An-mei. This allows for the establishment of another theme/horizon configuration. "'She's not stupid,' said my mother on one occasion, 'but she has no spine. . . . Auntie An-mei runs this way and that,' said my mother, 'and she doesn't know why.' As I watch Auntie An-mei, I see a short bent woman in her seventies, with a heavy bosom and thin, shapeless legs. She has the flattened soft fingertips of an old woman" (30). When we meet An-mei in "Scar," immediately after June's opening monologue, we realize that her childhood helps explain why she appears to have no spine. Her moving account of her painful separation from her mother and the traumatic circumstances resulting in her throat scar establishes a context for her apparent spinelessness; it adds to the outer appearance of weakness a story that makes the reductive labeling inadequate to the human reality. This juxtaposition would be interesting even if An-mei herself said she did not have spine: the theme/horizon juxtaposition would make for a poignant realization in the reader's mind of the subjective, limited nature of understanding, with An-mei's terrible childhood, on the one hand, helping to explain why she behaves the way she does, and the unsympathetic, reductive pigeonholing by Suyuan, on the other, typifying the overly reductive manner in which we often sum people up.

The theme/horizon gestalt produced and experienced by the reader following the textual prompts is further enhanced, however, when it is remembered that An-mei thinks she herself does have spine, and that her daughter Rose is the one who is weak. Rose tells us in "Without Wood": "My mother once told me why I was so confused all the time. She said I was without wood. Born without wood so that I listened to too many people. She knew this, because once she had almost become this way" (191). June's mother, Suyuan, who was a bold woman, may have thought that An-mei lacked spine; An-mei, who is proud of having stood up for herself after her mother died, thinks that her daughter lacks "wood": what results is a vivid realization in the mind of the reader who is alert to the potential dialogicity between textual segments that some things are entirely relative.

Another kind of inter-monologue dialogicity in the first cluster of four monologues consists of a triptych of personality differences—the monologues of An-mei, Lindo, and Ying-ying. At the center of this trio of self-portraits is a remarkably bold and strong individual who managed to extract herself from a repressive situation cleverly and diplomatically so that everyone benefited. Lindo's resourcefulness and boldness is framed by two portraits of passivity and weakness: An-mei and Ying-ying are victims of their childhood circumstances. As we move from An-mei's "Scar" to Lindo's "Red Candle," we are impressed with the very different responses to repressive circumstances; as we move from Lindo's "Red Candle" to Ying-ying's "Moon Lady" we return to the perspective of a victim. One specific gestalt the reader is invited to create between Lindo's "Red Candle" and Ying-ying's "Moon Lady" revolves around the "semantic convergence" (using Bakhtin's phrase) of losing and finding oneself. Lindo tells us that she discovered her inner power through an epiphany:

I asked myself, What is true about a person? Would I change in the same way the river changes color but still be the same person? And then I saw the curtains blowing wildly, and outside rain was falling harder, causing everyone to scurry and shout. I smiled. And then I realized it was the first time I could see the power of the wind. I couldn't see the wind itself, but I could see it carried the water that filled the rivers and shaped the countryside. It caused men to yelp and dance.

I wiped my eyes and looked in the mirror. I was surprised at what I saw. I had on a beautiful red dress, but what I saw was even more valuable. I was strong. I was pure. I had genuine thoughts inside that no one could see, that no one could ever take away from me. I was like the wind.

I threw my head back and smiled proudly to myself. And then I draped the large embroidered red scarf over my face and covered these thoughts up. But underneath the scarf I still knew who I was. I made a promise to myself: I would always remember my parents' wishes, but I would never forget myself. (58)

This remarkable passage about self-discovery and self-assertion in the midst of repression can be set in dialogue with the concluding passage in Ying-ying's monologue following Lindo's, where Ying-ying tells us that the most important moment of her childhood was when she lost herself:

Now that I am old, moving every year closer to the end of my life, I . . . feel closer to the beginning. And I remember everything that happened that day [the day she fell into the water] because it has happened many times in my life. The same innocence, trust, and restlessness, the wonder, fear, and loneliness. How I lost myself.

I remember all these things. And tonight, on the fifteenth day of the eighth moon, I also remember what I asked the Moon Lady so long ago. I wished to be found. (83)

These contiguously placed monologues with a common denominator of finding or losing one's self enter into a dialogicity of difference with the reader as the agent and site of the dialogicity. The result is to enhance the range of personalities offered: the mothers, for all their similarities, are indeed very different, as comparisons such as the one just made establish. Tan succeeds in achieving a truly diverse and heteroglot range of mothers' perspectives in *The Joy Luck Club*.

Another example of a counter-centrifugal gestalt the reader is invited to create from contiguously placed monologues consists of a pairing of Lena's worries in "Rice Husband" with Waverly's worries in "Four Directions." In this third quartet of monologues, both Lena and Waverly express frustration over their meddlesome mothers. In "Rice Husband," Lena is apprehensive about her mother's visit, fearing that her mother will perceive that her relationship with Harold is flawed. Ying-ying has an unusual ability to sense trouble and even predict calamity.

> During our brief tour of the house, she's already found the flaws. . . . And it annoys me that all she sees are the bad parts. But then I look around and everything she's said is true. And this convinces me she can see what else is going on, between Harold and me. She knows what is going to happen to us. (151)

Knowing that there is something wrong with the rigid policy she and Harold follow of sharing all costs equally, she is afraid her mother will confront her with a truth she does not want to admit. Waverly, on the other hand, is worried that her mother will poison her relationship with Rich the way Lindo poisoned her marriage with her previous husband, Marvin (174). Lindo had effectively ruined the gift of a fur coat Rich had given Waverly: "Looking at the coat in the mirror, I couldn't fend off the strength of her will anymore, her ability to make me see black where there was once white, white where there was once black. The coat looked shabby, an imitation of romance" (169). Lindo has destroyed something that Waverly took pleasure in. Likewise, she is apprehensive that Lindo will undermine her love for Rich.

I already knew what she would do, how she would be quiet at first. Then she would say a word about something small, something she had noticed, and then another word, and another, each one flung out like a little piece of sand, one from this direction, another from behind, more and more, until his looks, his character, his soul would have eroded away. And even if I recognized her strategy, her sneak attack, I was afraid that some unseen speck of truth would fly into my eye, blur what I was seeing and transform him from the divine man I thought he was into someone quite mundane, mortally wounded with tiresome habits and irritating imperfections. (173-74)

Whereas Ying-ying will confront Lena with something Lena should deal with, Lindo will insidiously undermine the love Waverly has for Richard, thus poisoning her relationship. The gestalt that the text invites the reader to create from these contiguously placed monologues counters the centrifugal tendency of this decentered text by setting into an aesthetically meaningful dialogue these two very different kinds of apprehension. This linkage across monologues works to point out the difference between the two daughters—thus enhancing the heteroglot nature of the multi-voiced narrative—even as it creates coherence across fragments through the essential similarity.

In Bakhtinian terms, we might think of Lena's and Waverly's apprehensions as entering into a dialogic relationship of similarity. Bakhtin points out in *Problems of Dostoevsky's Poetics* that there can be a dialogicity between two speakers uttering the same words—"Life is good"—depending on the particular nuances each gives to the utterance from embodied and distinct reference points. Simple disagreement can be less dialogic than agreement, he points out (183-84).[6] We might say that Lena declares, "Mothers are meddlesome," and that Waverly concurs with "Mothers are meddlesome"; the reader is the agent and the site of the dialogic engagement of these two essentially similar, yet very different, complaints.

My final example of counter-centrifugal *Gestalten* created from contiguously placed monologues is the triptych of three mothers in the final cluster. An-mei's "Magpies," Ying-ying's "Waiting Between the Trees," and Lindo's "Double Face" all present the reader with a mother who wants desperately to reach out and establish a connection with her daughter—in spite of the disagreements and conflicts. Each mother hopes to establish a closer relationship by telling her a story. And each mother is shown with a story to tell. Each mother offers the second installment of her life story: An-mei tells what it was like living with her mother as Fourth Wife; Ying-ying describes her marriage in China, the murder of her child, and her marriage to her current husband; and Lindo tells about how she left China and came to the United States. In each case, however, it appears that the actual communication does not occur. Tan's multiple monologue novel seems to participate in the convention of having speakers speak into the void—or to the reader as audience. No actual communication between mothers and daughters occurs. Presented with these three monologues, the reader is invited to establish the connection between them. The dialogicity of similarity in this gestalt, where each theme of the moment can be set against one or both of the other monologues as the horizon, is a powerfully persuasive method of arguing on behalf of the mothers. No narrative voice need announce that mothers should be listened to; the narrative makes the reader poignantly aware of the distance between each mother and daughter by showing the unbridged gap between them and the potential for sharing and communication that is only partially realized. This triptych of well-meaning mothers who want to pass on something to their daughters is another example of how there can be dialogic potential between similar utterances (as in "Life is good," "Life is good") in a multiple narrator novel, with the reader's consciousness as the site of the inter-monologue dialogicity.[7]

So far, my discussion of the counter-centrifugal *Gestalten* created by the reader has focused on the pairing of "themes" (Iser's term for perspectives of the moment) that are already presented by the narrative in a relationship through simple contiguous juxtaposition. It is also possible to consider *Gestalten* that a reader's wandering viewpoint might create from "themes" that are not already set side by side. These juxta-positions might be called conceptual rather than contiguous (although even with side-by-side placement, the resulting gestalt must be a creation in the reader's mind and thus conceptual).

The pairings possible with monologues from Lena and Ying-ying are examples of the interesting *Gestalten* creatable from non-contiguous monologues. We might take Lena's "The Voice from the Wall" as a starting point. Her perspective on her mother is entirely unappreciative here; she has no understanding or sympathy—and how could she, since Ying-ying's past is never talked about ("My mother never talked about her life in China, but my father said he saved her from a terrible life there, some tragedy she could not speak about" [104]). She presents her mother as psychologically imbalanced. She thinks of her mother as a "Displaced Person," using a photograph taken after the scared woman was released from Angel Island Immigration Station to represent her personality:

> In this picture you can see why my mother looks displaced. She is clutch-ing a large clam-shaped bag, as though someone might steal this from her as well if she is less watchful. She has on an ankle-length Chinese dress. . . . In this outfit she looks as if she were neither coming from nor going to someplace. . . .
>
> My mother often looked this way, waiting for something to happen, wearing this scared look. Only later she lost the struggle to keep her eyes open. (105)

We realize that Ying-ying's troubled mental state must have impinged negatively on Lena as she grew up, and we sympathize with her for that. But as readers who are privileged to know the inner thoughts of every character, we can balance off that perspective with what we know from Ying-ying's "Moon Lady" monologue, where we learn about the childhood trauma that has clearly affected her personality. And from "The Voice from the Wall," we can look forward, as well, and set Lena's frustration with her mother's aberrational personality against "Waiting Between the Trees": in this moving monologue, Ying-ying reveals a side of herself that Lena would be surprised to learn about. The Ying-ying we meet here is completely unknown to her daughter.

> So I will tell Lena of my shame. That I was rich and pretty. I was too good for any one man. That I became abandoned goods. I will tell her that at eighteen the prettiness drained from my cheeks. That I thought of throwing myself in the lake like the other ladies of shame. And I will tell her of the baby I killed because I came to hate this man so much.
>
> I took this baby from my womb before it could be born. This was not a bad thing to do in China back then, to kill a baby before it is born. But even then, I thought it was bad, because my body flowed with terrible revenge as the juices of this man's firstborn son poured from me.
>
> When the nurses asked what they should do with the lifeless baby, I hurled a newspaper at them and said to wrap it like a fish and throw it in the lake. My daughter thinks I do not know what it means to not want a baby.
>
> When my daughter looks at me, she sees a small old lady. That is because she sees only with her outside eyes. She has no *chuming*, no inside knowing of things. If she had *chuming*, she would see a tiger lady. And she would have careful fear. (248)

This set of *Gestalten*—"Voices" and "Moon Lady," "Voices" and "Waiting"—points out the relativity theme that this multiple narrator novel, like many, proposes. The very structure and narrative mode of the novel suggest that we appreciate the subjective nature of perception: there is Lena's thinking of her mother as a Displaced Person and Ying-ying's thinking of herself as a "Tiger Woman." However, *The Joy Luck Club* differs from other radically decentered multiple narrator novels—such as *As I Lay Dying* and, more recently, Auchincloss's *The House of the Prophet* or Matthiessen's *Killing Mister Watson*—in that it does not insist on absolute epistemological relativism: the reader

---

who actively pairs momentary "themes" realizes that there is more to Ying-ying than Lena's "Displaced Person" label allows for; the reader senses the potential for dialogue between mother and daughter that fails to take place.

This repeated failure for mother and daughter to enter into meaningful exchange is effectively represented through another Lena/Ying-ying gestalt: the pairing of Lena's "Rice Husband" monologue with Ying-ying's "Waiting Between the Trees." In "Waiting," Ying-ying is apparently about to cause the unstable table to fall, sending the vase crashing to the floor. She hopes to attract her daughter's attention and get her to come into the room where Ying-ying can talk to her. Ying-ying clearly wants to use it as the occasion to tell Lena everything she has wanted to tell her and to pass on her *chi* to her daughter (252). But in "Rice Husband," five monologues prior to "Waiting," the vase has already crashed to the floor and mother and daughter have already had their moment together. From what Lena reports in "Rice Husband," nothing came of the encounter (165). Tan's use of the unstable table as a common denominator across the two monologues constitutes an effective exercise in triangulation, a common technique in multiple narrator novels to demonstrate (usually) the subjective nature of perception.[8]

Another example of triangulation that prompts the reader to create a gestalt pairing two monologues that have a common denominator occurs with An-mei's "Magpies" and Rose's "Without Wood." The common denominator inviting a pairing of the monologues is Rose's psychiatrist. This gestalt is an especially interesting one for the novel because of the way it foregrounds the distance between the traditionally minded Chinese mother living in the United States and the American-born daughter who has embraced many American ways. From the American perspective, it is normal and even stylish for Rose to see a psychiatrist; from the Chinese perspective, seeing a psychiatrist is incomprehensible—indeed, An-mei might even regard it as bringing shame upon the family.[9] An-mei's "Magpies" begins and ends with her complete dismissal of the idea of seeing a psychiatrist; she does not approve of Rose's seeing one. But this conceptual gestalt—"Without Wood" and "Magpies" on the issue of seeing a psychiatrist—is more interesting than just the representation of complete lack of understanding on the part of mother and daughter: Rose actually does stop seeing her shrink—and she's better off because of it. She stops talking to other people as well, which her mother recommended. After a prolonged period of isolation and sleep—three days—she emerges defiant, ready to take on Ted. She thus relies on her own inner strength and faces up to Ted, which is just what her mother wanted her to do. However, she reaches this point on her own, not by simply listening to her mother (her mother's alternative to seeing a psychiatrist is the daughter simply listening to the mother's advice [188]). And confronting Ted seems to have unleashed a realization at a deeper, psychic level about the abusive nature of her mother, as well. In her dream, her mother is planting weeds in her garden that are running wild.

Another example of how non-contiguous "themes" can be set into a gestalt through the active memory and conceptual pairing activity of an Iserian reader is the linkage of the moments of self-assertion throughout the novel. This involves a series of linkages, with several possible pairings, or even one mega-gestalt. Rose's self-assertion in "Without Wood" can be linked up with June's in "Two Kinds" (134), An-mei's in "Magpies" (where her self-assertion after the death of her mother is described [240]), and Lindo's in "The Red Candle" (where she describes the epiphany that led her to her ruse, as previously discussed [58]). Here we have another example of the dialogic potential of similar utterances: each of these women has had to assert herself in the face of some kind of oppression; in spite of their differences, they are united on this theme, but each has a different nuance to give to the statement, "I have had to assert myself."

Another way in which *The Joy Luck Club* invites through its discontinuous form the creative work of a reader pairing segments into order—conferring *Gestalten* in response to textual prompts—is with the four prefaces. They serve, much like the interludes in *The Waves*, as a universalizing backdrop against which to see the particularized mono-logues. Each monologue can be set against the preface, and each cluster can be taken as an Iserian "theme" set against the "horizon" of the respective preface. The prefaces also help the reader pick up on what Tan calls the "emotional curve" of each "quartet" ("Address").

The prelude to Part One, "Feathers From a Thousand *Li* Away," presents in fable-like form a nameless Chinese woman who emigrated to America with hopes that she'd have a daughter who would lead a better life than was possible for a woman in China.[10] The Chinese woman is full of good intentions and hopes for that daughter. But her relationship with her daughter is characterized by distance and lack of communication. The following four monologues reveal mothers who bemoan the distance to their daughters but who had good intentions. This prefatory piece, then, helps us organize the four very different opening mono-logues around that "emotional curve," which serves as a horizon against which the monologues can be apprehended.

The preface to Part Two, "The Twenty-six Malignant Gates," helps organize the way we think about the daughters' monologues in that section by suggesting that Chinese mothers can be overbearing in their attempts to protect and control their daughters, and that this will result in rebelliousness on the part of their daughters, as well as misfortune. This brief fable-like anecdote manages to encapsulate the dynamics of the monologues that follow and helps us organize the disparate elements of those monologues around the implied criticism of overprotective, overbearing mothers. If the first preface prepares us to be sympathetic towards the mothers, this second preface prepares us to be sympathetic towards the daughters as we read each monologue against that preface as a backdrop.

The preface to Part Three, "American Translation," also enters into a dialogic relationship with the monologues of that section through the gestalt-producing activity of the reader. Introducing another round of daughters' monologues, it presents us with a mother who appears to be overbearing in her desire for a grandchild. She insists that her daughter mount a mirror on the wall for good luck. The mother sees her grand-child in the mirror; the daughter sees only "her own reflection look-ing back at her" (147). Tan seems to be suggesting with this the theme of conflicting perspectives and the struggle between daughters and mothers—a theme that is seen in the monologues that follow. Mothers see one thing; daughters see something entirely different. But the meta-phor here is actually relevant only to the daughters' perspective: it sug-gests that mothers project their own subjective preferences upon what they see whereas daughters see objectively, which is itself a distorted notion. From the mothers' perspective, they see clearly and daughters distort reality. Because this preface is designed to make us sympathetic to the daughters, it is slanted towards them; the "emotional curve" is with the daughters.

A dialogic relationship also exists between the final fable-like pref-ace and the final four monologues when the gestalt-creating capacity of the reader is called upon. The preface gives shape to the monologues that follow by presenting a mother who has a grandchild and who is treated sympathetically: she is self-critical and hopeful for her daugh-ter, wishing that her daughter can learn "how to lose [her] innocence but not her hope" (213). Very sympathetic to the mother, this preface prepares us to organize the monologues we are about to encounter in a manner that is sympathetic to the mothers. Reading each monologue in this cluster against the backdrop of the fourth preface helps establish the thematic point.

The *Gestalten* the reader creates from the four prefatory pieces thus confer considerable order upon what might at first appear to be a dizzy-ing display of very different personalities, even with the common de-nominator of Chinese mothers and Chinese-American daughters. Like *The Waves*, *The Joy Luck Club* sets monologues against third-person interludes that function by suggesting a universal backdrop to the se-ries of individualized voices; unlike *The Waves*, however, which uses nature as the universal backdrop, *The Joy Luck Club* prefaces use name-less human figures and abstract situations to suggest general truths.

Although the narrative invites the reader to establish all sorts of specific pairings between contiguous and non-contiguous monologues, the fundamental *Gestalten*, of course, consist of pairings of mothers collectively and daughters collectively. The daughters complaining about their mothers can be gathered together as one gestalt, with each daughter set against another daughter or the rest of the daughters. Presenting the daughters together in the middle two quartets encourages this kind of pairing. The mothers complaining about their daughters can be gathered together as well, with each complaining mother set against any other or the group. The narrative's most basic gestalt is that of mothers apprehended against the backdrop of daughters, or daughters apprehended against the backdrop of mothers. Among the daughters and among the mothers there is a dialogicity of sameness that consists of a fundamental similarity with individual nuances.

The narrative steers the reader, however, towards a particular kind of gestalt consisting of mothers' and daughters' perspectives; we have more than just an array of different perspectives with combinational possibilities among them. The daughters' positions, however understandable and valid, are enclosed and framed by the mothers' positions; however unreasonable or narrow-minded the mothers may seem in their attempts to impose their wills on their daughters, the narrative's structure, which invites the reader to apprehend the daughters against the backdrop of mothers, gives the mothers the upper hand in the argument. The three mothers presented before Jing-mei's closing monologue acquire a critical mass; their voices add up to an overwhelming appeal to respect the life experience and wishes of the mothers. Amy Ling's observation that the book "more often takes a sympathetic stand toward the mother" (136) is a sound assessment because of the shape Tan gives the collection by allowing the mothers to have the final say.

The reader's processing of the four quartets over time necessitates changing initial assessments and thus illustrates Iser's concept of reading as a feedback loop requiring the revision of *Gestalten*. The Iserian reader's primary activity and response consists of creatively pairing different sections or moments into meaningful *Gestalten* and then revising initial constructions when new material is encountered. The clustering of monologues into quartets tempts the reader into certain judgments that must be revised as more of the text is encountered (upon an initial reading): the first cluster biases us towards the parents; the second and third clusters make us more sympathetic to the daughters; the final cluster ensures that the mothers get the upper hand in the debate, even though the daughters are given a very full hearing. The various foreground/background conceptual structures (and *Gestalten* from contiguously placed monologues are conceptual as well as *Gestalten* from non-contiguous monologues) can be created during an initial reading, or upon rereading (which allows one to reach forward as well as backwards from any present moment of reading).

Iser's concept of negativity, another kind of "gap," also applies to *The Joy Luck Club*. The reader is poignantly aware of the potential for greater communication and understanding, but only in the reader's mind is the dialogicity between positions uncovered and experienced. The mothers and daughters are speaking into a void, not to each other (I read the occasional use of the second person in some of the monologues as an aside to an imagined audience, not an actual audience). Thus the narrative form and the thematic point complement each other. The result of this depiction of failed communication is that the reader, through the process of "negativity," is motivated to imagine a healthier response. Although the narrative provides a solution to the dilemma in the final chapter, the reader's experience before the final chapter of the failure to communicate ensures that the reader will be motivated to avoid such incommunicative relationships in his or her own life.

* * *

At this point I would like to address the issue of closure in *The Joy Luck Club*. Although depicting in the final chapter an answer to the problem of non-communication demonstrated up to the ending may seem like the perfect way for Tan to conclude, I have had difficulty accepting what seemed to me to be an overly sentimental and facile resolution. I would like to present my initial assessment of this issue and then attempt to move beyond that resisting response with a more accepting reading of the ending. My purpose in presenting my own experience with the issue of closure in *The Joy Luck Club* is to foreground various issues that I believe are important for an understanding of Tan's book.

In my 1992 study of contemporary American multiple narrator novels, I summed up my discomfort with June's novel-ending monologue thusly:

> My sense, when viewing *The Joy Luck Club* in the context of other multiple narrator novels, is that the book is at odds with itself. The various monologues of mothers and daughters, monologues that foreground difference—indeed, that flaunt discrepancy, conflict and relativism—set in motion a centrifugality that cannot so easily be overcome. The happy ending . . . [is] not true to the heteroglot diversity actually revealed throughout the text. . . . In my experience of *The Joy Luck Club*, the Suyuan/Jing-mei reconciliation is not convincing, and there clearly is no final reconciliation between all the mothers and daughters. Thus, as I see it, the attempt to rein in the heteroglossia does not do justice to the resonating diversity; that diversity actually eludes subduing through the kind of reductive thematic reading [that the ending invites]. (277)

I then pointed out the similarity between my observation about closure in *The Joy Luck Club* and Dale Bauer's comment about the novels she analyzes in her *Feminist Dialogics*. In Bauer's Bakhtin-inspired uncovering of repressed heteroglossia, she observes that "while the plot resolutions give closure to the novels, the dialogue resists that closure" (10). I continued my attempt to articulate my discomfort with the ending by arguing that the process Iser terms "negativity" is sufficient to make the thematic point without a heavy-handed ending.

The reader's sense of the poignancy inherent in a situation where mothers and daughters do not communicate as fully as they might in itself implies a remedy, in itself motivates the reader to imagine a solution—one that would accommodate the needs of both mothers and daughters. . . . *The Joy Luck Club* interferes with the imagined affirmation by prodding the reader too much. It is one thing to show Waverly, at the close of "Four Directions," attempting to impose an artificial, superficial pleasantness on her deeply problematic relationship with her mother by thinking about taking her mother with her on her honeymoon: that reveals an interesting split within this particular consciousness; it is another matter to have Tan . . . [impose] a superficial sense of harmony at the end of the book that does not do justice to the actual diversity and conflict between the covers. The collection of stories is full of moral potential without the heavy-handed ending simply through its presentation of multiple voices, artistically organized. (284-85)

My having been immersed in Bakhtin, Iser, and Faulkner at the time contributed to my lack of appreciation for the way this novel ends. Bakhtin's take on the novel as a genre is one that privileges the flaunting of diverse perspectives that, while dialogized, are never resolved into harmonious agreement or simple synthesis. His insistence on "unfinalizability" led me to privilege open-ended multiple narrator novels over those with strong closure. Iser's model led me to privilege texts that allow the reader to establish the thematic point without having it boldly announced. And my reading of Faulkner's own multiple narrator novels likewise biased me. *As I Lay Dying*, for example, while providing a sense of ending, flaunts diversity and discrepancy across subjectivities; it revels in the diverse viewpoints and the isolated personalities. *The Sound and the Fury*, too, while offering closure, resists its own ending and the thematic answer it provides (through Dilsey) to the problem of the solipsistic ego epitomized by the Quentin and Jason monologues. Faulkner, as I read him, is more interested in the poetic potential of pathology than in offering any thematic proposition about life.

My effort to rethink my initial response to the strong sense of closure in *The Joy Luck Club* involves a number of considerations based on feedback about this response from other scholars and my own students.[11]

One of those considerations is gender. The "sentimental" ending of the novel may simply evoke different responses from male and female readers. With the kind of psychodynamic model of personality development that feminists like Nancy Chodorow offer (cf. *The Reproduction of Mothering*), it is possible to argue that women, who are more oriented to bonding and relationships than men (men emphasize separation and autonomy instead, according to this theory), are less likely to resist Tan's ending. My experience teaching the novel in an all-female classroom at Texas Woman's University was enlightening because no one found the ending to be sentimental or false.[12]

Perhaps the most useful approach to the issue of closure in *The Joy Luck Club* is a culturally grounded one. When Tan's contribution to the multiple narrator sub-genre is considered in the context of Asian values, the desire for an ending that brings the resonating diversity and conflicting positions to a tidy close is entirely understandable.

A culturally nuanced reading of the novel might begin with the fundamental orientation toward the group rather than the individual in Asian cultures generally, as stated in the following passage taken from the classic reference book cited earlier of Asian culture for American therapists whose client population includes Asian Americans:

American society has tended toward the ideals of the self-sufficient, self-reliant individual who is the master of his or her fate and chooses his or her own destiny. High value is placed on the ability to stand on your own two feet, or pull yourself up by your own bootstraps, or do your own thing. In contrast, Asian philosophies tend toward an acknowledgment that individuals become what they are because of the efforts of many things and many people. They are the products of their relationship to nature and other people. Thus, heavy emphasis is placed on the nature of the relationship among people, generally with the aim of maintaining harmony through proper conduct and attitudes. (McGoldrick et al. 213)

This general orientation toward the group is manifested in the emphasis on respecting and serving one's parents, not resisting them. "The greatest obligation of East Asians," according to McGoldrick and her colleagues, "is to their parents, who have brought them into the world and have cared for them when they were helpless. The debt that is owed can never be truly repaid; and no matter what parents may do the child is still obligated to give respect and obedience" (214)—an attitude that can be traced back to Confucius.

Another aspect of Asian cultures generally (East Asian in this particular case) that is pertinent to a culturally nuanced response to *The Joy Luck Club* has to do with shaming. McGoldrick and her co-authors explain that in these cultures, "shame and shaming are the mechanisms that traditionally help reinforce societal expectations and proper behavior" (214). Vacc and his colleagues explain more specifically that "control of the children [in Chinese and Japanese families] is maintained by fostering feelings of shame and guilt" (251). Without knowing this, it is more likely that the shaming behavior some of the mothers of *The Joy Luck Club* engage in to control their children will result in a reading that blames those mothers for inappropriate behavior. As a consequence of the misunderstanding, such a reader would not grant those mothers the sympathy for which they qualify.

Yet another aspect of Asian culture that contributes to a sensitive reading of Tan's novel is the close relationship between a mother and her children in Asian countries. McGoldrick and her co-authors explain it thusly:

The traditional role of the mother must also be understood and respected within the context of her role expectations within the family. Issues involving the children reflect upon her self-esteem as a mother. We must remember that in the traditional family, the children are primarily her responsibility, as well as her resource for the future. Frequently, issues around perceived dependence of children and overprotection of the mother are raised by American therapists who are unfamiliar with traditional family dynamics of Asian families. Therapists do not always understand that within the family mutual interdependence is stressed and expected. This is not to say that individuation does not occur or is not promoted, but it is constantly tinged with the subconscious knowledge of the relationships and obligations between the individual and other family members. (224)

Although *The Joy Luck Club* gives equal time to the position of daughters who resist or resent a domineering mother, an American reader is less likely to grant those mothers their due without understanding that Asian mothers normally behave in a more heavy-handed manner than their American counterparts.

The final point I wish to make about Asian cultures that contributes to a balanced response to both the mothers and the daughters in *The Joy Luck Club* is that Asian families in America tend to place extraordinary emphasis on the importance of education for their children. Vacc and his co-authors explain it thusly:

The pressure to succeed academically among Asians is very strong. From early childhood, outstanding achievement is emphasized because it is a source of pride for the entire family. . . . Reflecting the emphasis on education is the finding that college enrollment rates for Chinese and Japanese between the ages of 18 and 24 and the percentage completing college is higher than for any other group in the United States. Parental expectations for achievement can be an additional stress factor in young Asian-Americans. (253)

This information is important for a sensitive response to both Jing-mei and Suyuan, who calls her daughter a "college drop-off" (37). It is in the context of explaining her dropping out of college that Jing-mei tells us: "My mother and I never really understood one another. We translated each other's meanings and I seemed to hear less than what was said, while my mother heard more" (37).

With this background information in mind, it is easier to understand the thematic readings of Tan's novel that do not focus on the differences between mothers and the differences between daughters as much as upon the similarities. In this culture-specific context, Tan's attempt to rein in the reverberating heteroglossia has a compelling logic.

The readings of *The Joy Luck Club* offered by Amy Ling and Elaine Kim are undertaken within this context. They emphasize the mother/ daughter gestalt discussed earlier and the importance of the broader dynamic between mothers and daughters that this gestalt suggests; Ling and Kim are not as focused on individual personalities as a reader coming from Faulkner, Bakhtin, and Iser would be. Ling argues that "though the mothers all have different names and individual stories, they seem interchangeable in that the role of mother supersedes all other roles and is performed with the utmost seriousness and determination. All the mothers in *The Joy Luck Club* are strong, powerful women" (138). Kim likewise argues that "one of the triumphs of the book is that it is easy to lose track of the individual women's voices: the reader might turn distractedly to the table of contents, trying to pair the mothers and daughters or to differentiate among them, only to discover the point that none of this matters in the least" (82). Ling's reading privileges the mothers' perspectives and argues that the narrative endorses their position more than the daughters' resisting positions. Her reading of the novel is that it "more often takes a sympathetic stand toward the mother" (136). Ling further argues that in spite of the battles described, the daughters eventually acquiesce: "The daughters' battles for independence from powerful commanding mothers is fierce, but eventually, as in [*The Woman Warrior*], a reconciliation is reached. The daughters realize that the mothers have always had the daughters' own best interests at heart" (139-40). Ling has no problem with Jing-mei's "act of filial obedience" closing the narrative (141). Her concluding remarks clearly indicate her acceptance of the ending as a perfectly appropriate one; she does not resist the narrative's attempt to counterbalance the conflicting voices with its ending: "[The novel] ends on a note of resolution and reconciliation. The struggles, the battles, are over, and when the dust settles what was formerly considered a hated bondage is revealed to be a cherished bond." Thematizing the novel, she interprets its message thusly:

> To be truly mature, to achieve a balance in the between-world condition then . . . one cannot cling solely to the new American ways and reject the old Chinese ways, for that is the way of the child. One must reconcile the two and make one's peace with the old. If the old ways cannot be incorporated into the new life, if they do not "mix" as Lindo Jong put it, then they must nonetheless be respected and preserved in the pictures on one's walls, in the memories in one's head, in the stories that one writes down. (141)

Bonnie TuSmith, in her recent study of the importance of community in American ethnic literatures, *All My Relatives* (1993), offers a reading of the battling positions of the narrative that also privileges the mothers' perspective. She interprets the passage describing the Polaroid shot of the three sisters as follows: "This composite image of three daughters who, together, make up one mother reflects the novel's communal subtext, which works as a counterpoint to the textual surface of individualistic strife between mothers and daughters" (68). More specifically, she suggests that the narrative argues against the daughters' individualistic voices and for the establishment of harmony with the mothers:

> The novel opens with Jing-mei's assuming her mother's role at the mahjongg table of the Joy Luck Club. Her "substitute" role is recalled in the conclusion when she is in China and taking her mother's place once again. This literary frame alone suggests that, although the mother-daughter power struggle appears individualistic on the surface, there is a different message embedded in the text. (68)

The culturally based, heavily thematic readings that TuSmith and Ling offer thus emphasize the overall *Gestalten* of mothers set against daughters and daughters set against mothers with a nod towards the position of the mothers. Ling emphasizes the importance of the daughters respecting and acknowledging the position of the mothers; TuSmith offers a more complex surface versus deep structure analysis that sees the conflicting perspectives as merely a surface phenomenon and the difference-transcending communalism as a more fundamental underlying impulse.

* * *

Although my own earlier reading was not sufficiently cognizant of cultural factors—such as the emphasis in Chinese-American cultures on group and family orientation, respect for parents, shaming by parents for control of children, dependent relationships, and education of children—a reading of *The Joy Luck Club* that fully accounts for its complexity perhaps requires taking a middle-ground position: the narrative, with its overall structure (framing) and thematic conclusion, suggests resolution and reconciliation, but the actual collection of voices cannot with complete accuracy be reduced to a thematic reading.[13] If one imagines Tan writing with her mother looking on (and from what she has said about her relationship with her mother, this seems accurate ["Address"]), there should be no surprise that the novel argues for something while at the same time resisting it through the very presentation of a heteroglot array of individual voices.

In either case, a Bakhtin-inspired and Iser-based reading of *The Joy Luck Club* is possible and contributes to a moment-by-moment uncovering and articulation of the counter-centrifugal dialogicity in the collection of monologues. An Iserian reading locates the various points of difference and agreement across monologues and establishes the connections between them. As Bakhtin suggests, the dialogicity can be of agreement as well as disagreement; to use his example, "Life is good" and "Life is good" can resonate through slightly different accents given to the basic proposition. "Mothers are oppressive" and "Mothers are oppressive"—or "daughters should show respect" and "daughters should show respect"—can likewise resonate across monologues by having a different accentuation with each speaker.

Whether or not one agrees that the novel genuinely achieves a resolution and reconciliation (that might be an objective "meaning" versus subjective "significance" issue, in Iserian terms), an Iserian reading focuses on the moment-by-moment experience of the dialogicity of difference and agreement across monologues. On a first reading, during a rereading, or standing back after reading and selectively meditating on the assemblage, there are several ways the segments enter into a dialogic relationship through the active agency of the reader responding in a controlled way to textual prompts. Meaningful connections can be established between contiguous monologues, non-contiguous monologues, moments within monologues or entire monologues, prefaces and post-preface monologues, and quartets (such as the mothers' quartets framing the daughters' quartets). We might say that the fundamental Iserian gap in this text is the conceptual space between daughters and mothers, between one generation and the other. The primary objective "meaning" that obtains at the site of the dialogicity—the reader's consciousness—is one of unrealized potential. That, in itself, argues, through Iserian negativity, for children and parents to try to listen better and communicate more. By writing a multiple narrator novel with an argumentative edge to it—a thematic thrust that extends beyond an assertion of the relativity of perception—Tan makes a distinct contribution to the genre of the multiple first-person monologue novel.

From *MELUS* 19, 2 (Summer 1994): 99-123. Copyright © 1994 by *MELUS: The Journal of the Society for the Study of the Multi-Ethnic Literature of the United States*. Reprinted here with the permission of *MELUS*.

Notes

1. During a conversation I had with Tan after she gave a talk at the University of Wisconsin-Madison, she told me that the galleys that went out to reviewers had the word "stories" printed along with the title, but when the reviews came back with the book referred to as a "novel," the publisher wanted "stories" changed to "novel." She and her publisher compromised: neither word appeared in association with the title (Interview).

2. Tan has referred to Erdrich and Gibbons as friends ("Amy Tan" 9). That both Erdrich and Gibbons are writers of very interesting multiple narrator novels helps establish a novelistic context for *The Joy Luck Club*.

3. Although I believe a close reading of *The Joy Luck Club* reveals carefully delineated personalities and a compellingly structured puzzle of monologues, some reviewers throw up their hands at the considerable interpretive task the novel presents to its reader. For example, Carole Angier writes: "*The Joy Luck Club* is over-schematic. We move too often from one corner of the table to another to remember or care enough about each. And at the same time it is over-significant. In the end it gives you indigestion, as if you've eaten too many Chinese fortune cookies" (35). Charlotte Painter experiences difficulty distinguishing between narrators and accepting the multiple first-person technique: "The voices, in unrelieved first person, resemble one another too closely. . . . I wish Tan had taken charge with an authorial voice, given that the book's theme, the author's overriding obsession, is so constant throughout" (17). The multiple monologue novel, one might argue, is so distinct a narrative form that any evaluative statement attempted by a reviewer is likely to reveal the predispositions of the evaluator.

4. Susan Stanford Friedman made this clear to me.

5. For a discussion of the relevance of Bakhtin for a study of inter-monologue dialogicity in multiple narrator novels, see the Bakhtin chapter in my 1992 dissertation, "Recent American Multiple Narrator Novels: A Bakhtinian/Iserian Analysis."

6. Gary Saul Morson and Caryl Emerson, in their *Mikhail Bakhtin: Creation of a Prosaics*, discuss this kind of dialogicity (131-32).

7. Tan's clustering of mothers and daughters, which allows for the kind of triptych of mothers discussed here (and in the first quartet), is one of the major differences between the novel and the film based on the novel. By strictly pairing mothers and daughters so that the narration consists of an alternation between a mother and that mother's daughter, the film's presentation gains a certain clarity at the expense of some of the kinds of aesthetic implications I am discussing.

8. An example of triangulation in *As I Lay Dying* would be the use of the river as a common denominator across monologues. In contrast to Faulkner, Kaye Gibbons uses triangulation in her A *Virtuous Woman* to establish similarity and unity.

The acute failure of Lena and Ying-ying to communicate is effectively suggested by the way Tan shows the family interacting via mistranslations: interpreting for Lena what his wife says, the father makes things up; when Lena translates from Chinese into English for her father's benefit, she offers false translations; and when she brings home official communications from school, Lena intentionally mistranslates them for her mother.

9. As discussed in *Ethnicity and Family Therapy* (McGoldrick et al.), Asian Americans traditionally underuse psychiatric resources because they are unfamiliar with Western treatment interventions for mental health; they tend to think one is either normal or "crazy"; they tend to solve problems within the family; and they regard seeking help outside the family as bringing disgrace upon the family (221-22). (See also Nicholas Vacc et al., *Experiencing and Counseling Multicultural and Diverse Populations*, 255.)

10. Tan wrote "Feathers From a Thousand *Li* Away" after writing everything else ("Address").

11. I wish to acknowledge here the audience response to my paper on *The Joy Luck Club* at the 1992 "'Other Voices': American Women Writers of Color" conference in Ocean City, Maryland; student comments in my English 3153 course, "Ethnic American Literature," at Texas Woman's University; and the suggestions of my University of Wisconsin-Madison dissertation committee, especially Susan Stanford Friedman.

12. One exchange between two female students was especially significant. One student said to another: "I love this book; I told my husband he should read it." The other responded: "If he ever read the book, do you think he'd 'get it'?" "Probably not," replied the first.

13. Although Malini Johar Schueller is sensitive to the conflicts between mothers and daughters that cannot be easily overcome, she oversimplifies the novel in stating that the final quartet consists of "four narratives of mothers and daughters coming to an understanding" (82). Nancy Willard, likewise, is too reductive in stating: "Amy Tan's special accomplishment in this novel is not her ability to show us how mothers and daughters hurt each other, but how they love and ultimately forgive each other" (12).

Works Cited

Angier, Carole. "Chinese Customs." *The New Statesman and Society*, June 30, 1989: 35.

Auchincloss, Louis. *The House of the Prophet*. Boston: Houghton Mifflin, 1980.

Bakhtin, Mikhail. *Problems of Dostoevsky's Poetics*. Trans. Caryl Emerson. Minneapolis: U of Minnesota P, 1984.

_____. *Speech Genres and Other Late Essays*. Trans. Vern McGee. Austin: U of Texas P, 1986.

Bauer, Dale. *Feminist Dialogics: A Theory of Failed Community*. Albany: State U of New York P, 1988.

Chodorow, Nancy. *The Reproduction of Mothering: Psychoanalysis and the Sociology of Gender*. Berkeley: U of California P, 1978.

Erdrich, Louise. *Tracks*. New York: Harper & Row, 1988.

Faulkner, William. *As I Lay Dying*. New York: Random House, 1930.

Gibbons, Kaye. *A Virtuous Woman*. New York: Random House, 1989.

Iser, Wolfgang. *The Act of Reading: A Theory of Aesthetic Response*. Baltimore: Johns Hopkins UP, 1978.

_____. *The Implied Reader: Patterns of Communication in Prose Fiction from Bunyan to Beckett*. Baltimore: Johns Hopkins UP, 1974.

_____. "Indeterminacy and the Reader's Response in Prose Fiction." *Aspects of Narrative*. Ed. J. Hillis Miller. New York: Columbia UP, 1971.

_____. "Interview: Wolfgang Iser." *Diacritics* 10 (1980): 57-74.

Kim, Elaine. "'Such Opposite Creatures': Men and Women in Asian American Literature." *Michigan Quarterly Review* 29 (1990): 68-93.

Kuenzli, Rudolf. "The Intersubjective Structure of the Reading Process: A Communication-Oriented Theory of Literature." *Diacritics 10* (1980): 47-56.

Ling, Amy. *Between Worlds: Women Writers of Chinese Ancestry*. New York: Pergamon, 1990.

Martin, Wallace. [Untitled review article.] *Criticism* 21 (1979): 260-62.

Matthiessen, Peter. *Killing Mister Watson*. New York: Random House, 1990.

McGoldrick, Monica, John K. Pearce, and Joseph Giordano, eds. *Ethnicity and Family Therapy*. New York: Guilford P, 1982.

Morson, Gary Saul, and Caryl Emerson. *Mikhail Bakhtin: Creation of a Prosaics*. Stanford: Stanford UP, 1990.

Painter, Charlotte. "In Search of a Voice." *San Francisco Review of Books 14* (Summer 1989): 15-17.

Schueller, Malini Johar. "Theorizing Ethnicity and Subjectivity: Maxine Hong Kingston's *Tripmaster Monkey* and Amy Tan's *The Joy Luck Club*." *Genders* 15 (Winter 1992): 72-85.

Souris, Stephen. "Recent American Multiple Narrator Novels: A Bakhtinian/Iserian Analysis." Diss. U of Wisconsin-Madison, 1992.

Tan, Amy. Address. Chinese-American Student Association. University of Wisconsin-Madison. Madison, 11 April 1991.

_____. "Amy Tan on Amy Tan and *The Joy Luck Club*." *California State Library Foundation Bulletin* 31 (April 1990): 1-10.

_____. *The Joy Luck Club*. New York: Putnam's, 1989.

_____. Personal interview. 11 April 1991.

TuSmith, Bonnie. *All My Relatives: Community in Contemporary Ethnic American Literatures*. Ann Arbor: U of Michigan P, 1993.

Vacc, Nicholas A., Joe Wittmer, and Susan B. DeVaney, eds. *Experiencing and Counseling Multicultural and Diverse Populations*. 2nd ed. Muncie, IN: Accelerated Developments, 1988.

Willard, Nancy. "Tiger Spirits." *Women's Review of Books* 6 (10-11) (July 1989): 12.

Woolf, Virginia. *The Waves*. New York: Harcourt Brace, 1931.

Mothers and Daughters_____

Esther Mikyung Ghymn

The images of Asian American mothers and daughters as drawn by Kingston and Tan are so similar that it seems they have created a new set of stereotypes. Strikingly different from the familiar Madame Butterflies and Suzy Wongs, the new images of dragons, tigers, swans, shadows, bones, and stairs are the newly created metaphors for Asian American mothers and daughters. As Tan remarks to Emory Davis, "It's the images that are so important to me. That's where the mystery of the writing and the beauty of the story is" (Davis, Vol. 1, No. 1, p. 9). These new images define the Asian American woman as seen by the major Asian American women writers.

For Kingston and Tan the right image is not necessarily a realistic one, but one which fits into the moral of their stories and provides the right perspective. The right balance in form and message is achieved when the daughters realize that they are not alone in the universe; that the ties to their mothers and grandmothers will always keep them in balance; that life does not change from generation to generation despite shifts in space and time; that, in a sense, all characters are stereotypes in a universe where "each and all are the same." As in the last line of Emerson's "Each and All" ("I yielded myself to the perfect whole"), the mothers and daughters in *The Woman Warrior* and *The Joy Luck Club* finally realize that they are all part of each other.

I

The Woman Warrior is a complex narrative of varied voices, songs, and images. It is a book about Anju's quest for self-identity. Born in Stockton, California, to an old Chinese couple, Anju finds it difficult to communicate at home and at school. Although born in the year of the dragon like her mother, she is at first characterized as quiet and fearful. These traits are not usually associated with those born with the most favorable zodiac sign. In China the dragon symbolizes strength and wisdom, and such traits are transformed into images and words such as "dragon," "brave," and "warrior" throughout the book. Thus, Anju's weaker qualities are inevitably replaced by images of inherent strength when she realizes true selfhood at the end of the novel.

Anju hates herself at school because she hates to talk. Her low self-image makes her hate the sound of her own voice: "It spoils my day with self-disgust when I hear my broken voice coming skittering out into the open. It makes people wince to hear it" (*The Woman Warrior*, p. 191). Her low self-esteem is heightened by her assumption that her mother thinks her ugly. Her mother does not give her the recognition that she craves. When Anju tells her mother, "I got straight A's, Mama," her mother replies, "let me tell you a true story about a girl who saved her village" (*The Woman Warrior*, p. 54). Communication between mother and daughter is at best difficult. When Anju tries to tell her mother about "three hundred things," her mother says, "Senseless babblings every night. I wish you would stop. Go away and work. Whispering, whispering, making no sense. Madness, I don't feel like hearing your craziness" (*The Woman Warrior*, p. 233). Her mother wants Anju to go to a typing school: "learn to type if you want to be an American girl." Anju refuses because she wants to do something better. She shouts to her parents, "I'm smart. I can do all kinds of things. I know how to get A's, and they say I could be a scientist or a mathematician if I want. I can make a living and take care of myself" (*The Woman Warrior*, p. 234).

Anju retreats and fantasizes about becoming a woman warrior. She wants to know how she can storm across the States and fight her own battles. She wonders how she can use this ancient warrior example in her contemporary life. But Anju is afraid to act. Kingston characterizes this fear by using ghostly images. Anju and her family see real people as ghosts. To them there are white ghosts, black ghosts, and Mexican ghosts. Feelings of fear are conceptualized into images of ghosts and shadows. Kingston typically uses contrasting images, as the images of fear balance images of strength mentioned earlier. These images are parallel and interrelated, creating contrasting rhythms in this surrealistic novel form.

All Anju knows about China is what she has seen in the movies and what she has heard from her mother. What she has heard from her mother is the tale of the legendary Fa Mu Lan and the tale of the forgotten No Name Woman. Fa Mu Lan is a woman warrior who takes the place of her father in battle. As such, she is the metaphorical center of this novel and an extended metaphor of a sense of continuity in Asian women's lives. On the other hand, the No Name Woman is a disgrace, for an unmarried pregnant woman is considered very shameful in China. She commits suicide by drowning herself in the family well when the villagers come to punish her. Kingston's strategy is to create such contrasting characters clothed in different images.

These tales, however, make it difficult for the confused daughter to find her own identity. In frustration, Anju addresses the reader: "Chinese-Americans, when you try to understand what things in you are Chinese, how do you separate what is peculiar to childhood, to poverty, insanities, one family, your mother who marked your growing with stories from what is Chinese? What is Chinese tradition and what is the movies?" (*The Woman Warrior*, p. 6). Anju analyzes herself as she compares herself to Fa Mu Lan and the No Name Aunt. The shifting back and forth from her imagination to reality enables the narrative to sublimate the distinction between them. In real life her mother, Brave Orchid, and Aunt Moon Orchid also serve as models. Brave Orchid is a strong woman who earned a medical degree in China but who struggles in the States with her husband at the steaming laundry day after day to feed their six children. Moon Orchid, on the other hand, is weak. She eventually ends up in a mental asylum as she is unable to cope with her disappointments in life which culminate in being rejected by her husband. Should Anju become strong like Fa Mu Lan and Brave Orchid, or should she become weak like the No Name Aunt and Moon Orchid? At the end Anju chooses the stronger models.

When mother and daughter cannot speak the same language to explain adequately the reasons and feelings behind the words, frustration is inevitable. The first words of the book are, "'You must not tell anyone,' my mother said, 'what I am about to tell you'" (*The Woman Warrior*, p. 3). Anju thinks her mother wants to silence her so much that (in her fantasy) she cuts out her own tongue. The daughter, not understanding the real meaning behind her mother's broken English, screams, "And I don't want to listen to any more of your stories; they have no logic. They scramble me up. . . . You can't stop me from talking. You tried to cut off my tongue, but it didn't work" (*The Woman Warrior*, p. 235). Here Anju does not understand her mother's desire or her reply when she says, "I cut it to make you talk more, not less, you dummy!" (*The Woman Warrior*, p. 235). Although this remark is confusing, it reveals that the mother has a plan to motivate her daughter. Anju, in the meantime, struggles toward self-understanding.

The use of words is a major unifying thread that sews the novel together. "You must not tell anyone . . . what I am about to tell you" (*The Woman Warrior*, p. 3). The mother's admonition reflects her determination to control Anju. Anju resents and resists such control. She blames her mother for her own quietness, saying that her mother cut out her tongue. Although she hates quietness, Anju is unable to break out of it. Thus, going to school becomes a dreadful burden. In the first years of school she colors everything black to symbolize her dread. She notices that other Chinese girls also do not talk very much at school, so she associates being Chinese with silence. In particular there is one girl whom she hates for her quietness. This hatred erupts into violence when Anju beats her up one day.

On the other hand, Kingston wants to make it clear to the reader that speaking is properly associated with strength. For example, when the woman warrior prepares for battle, her father carves words of revenge on her back. Such pain is endured because it is only through such carving that the warrior becomes empowered to act. Each Chinese character etched in blood is worthy of a fighting warrior. The warrior says,

"When I could sit up again, my mother brought two mirrors, and I saw my back covered entirely with words in red and black files, like an army, like my army" (*The Woman Warrior*, p. 42). It is as if the words empower her to act. Thus, words signify empowerment.

The mother/daughter relationship evolves through various stages until it reaches a reconciliation. As a child Anju follows her mother around the house singing the song of the woman warrior. The chanting makes her believe that she will also grow up to be a warrior. It seems that the singing is a source of inspiration and communication. Night after night the mother tells stories of the woman warrior. Perhaps the reason for telling the stories is that they give the mother a feeling of hope and power. As Nancy Walker points out, "Fantasy of the 'woman warrior' in Kingston's book, are [*sic*] at least empowering because they allow the characters to escape imaginatively the boundaries of their lives as 'young women'—they permit images of freedom and power denied by the characters' immediate social context" (Walker, p. 115). Perhaps as a mother working in a laundry after earning a medical degree she needs to have a dream to instill in her daughter. Thus Brave Orchid inspires her daughter through songs and words.

It is also through words and singing that mother and daughter reconcile. As a child, Anju remembers how she followed her mother around the house singing about Fa Mu Lan and her victories in battle. At the end she joins her mother in singing about Poetess T'sai. "She brought her songs back from the savage lands, and one of the three that has passed down to us is 'Eighteen Stanzas for a Barbarian Reed Pipe,' a song that Chinese sing to their own instruments. It translated well" (*The Woman Warrior*, p. 243). This episode parallels Brave Orchid's situation, for like the poetess, Brave Orchid is in a foreign land. Her story is translated by Anju, who becomes the narrator of these stories.

Reconciliation occurs at the end when Anju and her mother tell a story together. "Here is a story my mother told me, not when I was young, but recently, when I told her I also talk story. The beginning is hers, the ending mine" (*The Woman Warrior*, p. 240). It seems that as the narrator grows older she also comes to "talk story." The book begins with the mother talking and ends with the daughter speaking. Suzanne Juhasz points out that "at the core of the relationship between daughter and mother is identification" (Juhasz, p. 176). As Kingston says, "[critics] read the beginning and can't understand that things are resolved by the end. There is a lot of resolution—the mother and daughter come out okay, you know. But it's the price of a lifetime of struggle" (Yalom, *Women Writers of the West Coast*, p. 14). Temporal displacement is replaced by generational continuity. By joining their voices they find their place in the community and continuity of women's spirits.

In Kingston's novel the cycle of mother and daughter conflict and recovery plays itself out poignantly. At the end Anju achieves a balanced and peaceful state of mind as she reconciles herself to her mother. For an Asian American girl who has grown up ashamed of herself and her Chinese heritage, this is a very positive conclusion, for many second-generation Chinese Americans reject their parents and their culture for the white majority culture and values. By selecting old Chinese legendary heroines as her role models and joining her mother in the singing, Anju clearly values herself as a Chinese American woman. *The Woman Warrior* is therefore a triumph not only for the individual woman but also for the Chinese heritage. This line from grandmother to granddaughter can be linear but also circular. Understanding of self produces understanding of mother, family, and society. Layer after layer of confusion is peeled off to arrive at the core of understanding.

These layers of confusion are structurally and aesthetically powerful as they underscore the struggles between mother and daughter. Although the novel seems disjointed at first glance, as I mentioned earlier, there is a definite pattern to Kingston's artistry. Marilyn Yalom argues that *The Woman Warrior* is an example of "modern aesthetics" with its various stylistic techniques (Yalom, "Postmodern Autobiography," p. 112). Like music, variation upon variation makes the work more exquisite. Joan Lidoff also comments on the complexity of Kingston's work: "In Kingston we don't get a single account of an incident; we are given alternative conjectures about the same 'fact.' . . . Memory and conjecture bracket all tellings of the past: fantasy is as real as incident, and any event has multiple interpretations" (Lidoff, p. 119). Indeed, to peel the outer layers of meanings is like untying a very complicated knot. However, if one looks closely there is a definite pattern or backbone to the novel, as parallel characters contrast with or complement each other. As mentioned earlier, for example, Fa Mu Lan and Brave Orchid are both depicted as strong characters. On the other hand, the No Name Woman and Moon Orchid are portrayed as similarly weak. The parallels between warrior and mother and the two aunts especially unify the book.

There are also decisive chapter endings which often point to the theme of mothers and daughters. The last paragraph in each of the five chapters helps the reader to arrive at each chapter's meaning. For example, at the end of chapter one, "No Name Woman," Anju writes, "My aunt haunts me—her ghost drawn to me because now, after fifty years of neglect, I alone devote pages of paper to her, though not origamied into houses and clothes" (*The Woman Warrior*, p. 19). Again, at the end of chapter two, "White Tigers," Anju remarks, "The reporting is the vengeance—not the beheading, not the gutting, but the words" (*The Woman Warrior*, p. 63). And again at the end of chapter three, "Shaman," Anju reflects, "I am really a Dragon, as she is a Dragon. Both of us born in dragon years" (*The Woman Warrior*, p. 127). This identification with her mother moves the novel towards final reconciliation between mother and daughter.

Mother and daughter both battle with real and imagined ghosts. Ghosts exist in old China as they do in Stockton, California. The use of ghosts also helps to unify the novel, for ghostly images are embedded throughout. The No Name Woman has become a ghost who has to fight other ghosts for food. As the dead aunt has no one to remember her on her memorial day, she must steal from other ghosts' tables. This allusion refers to the Asian tradition of preparing a special meal for one's dead relatives. As everyone is ashamed of the No Name Woman, no one would honor her on her memorial day by serving a special meal. Ghosts also represent fear. Like background music, the use of ghosts makes the reader understand the sense of fear which drives Anju to quiet and drives her aunt to insanity. The subtitle of the book is "Memoirs of a Girlhood among Ghosts." Thus, images of ghosts—black ghosts, Mexican ghosts, and white ghosts—exist everywhere for Anju and her mother. The weaving of such images reinforces fear of the unknown throughout the novel.

For the Chinese American daughter, one must understand and accept one's own mother to find out about oneself. Barker-Nunn points out that in China individuals are insignificant by themselves. Only in the context of their families do the women find significance. And it is not only the immediate family but the long line of women that goes back even to ancestors. To reinforce this point, Kingston repeats circular images. "The round moon cakes and round doorways, the round tables of graduated size that fit one roundness inside another, round windows and rice bowls—these talismans had lost their power to warn this family of the law: a family must be whole, faithfully keeping the descent line by having sons to feed the old and the dead, who in turn look after the family" (*The Woman Warrior*, p. 15). The repeated use of the word "round" and its synonyms underlines the concept of continuity. For the Chinese lineage triumphs over individualism, unity defeats isolation. Anju realizes this point at the end and stops struggling. As a Chinese American she finally accepts the harmonious Chinese view of the universe and joins her mother in singing ancient tales. The emphasis is on collectivity as the voices of mother and daughter form a duet echoing the multiple voices of mothers, aunts, and sisters in the past. Kingston's telling reasserts the spirit of the women and their need to be articulate and to be heard. Matrilineal ancestry becomes life giving.

The title *The Woman Warrior* is therefore the central image of the book, an image which represents strong women like Brave Orchid.

Kingston's work is not only about Fa Mu Lan but the concept of the woman warrior. The archetype of the woman warrior is an extended metaphor of a cultural ancestor. Anju realizes that she herself can be a word warrior; indeed, it is only by speaking and writing that she can become such a warrior. Anju's singing is an affirmation of her understanding. As one unravels all the threads in this novel it is clear that the moral fable is a call to action. One should use the power of the spoken or written word to overcome her own weaknesses. As Kingston says to Yalom, "The daughter becomes the inheritor of the mother's oral tradition, which subsequently becomes a written tradition. . . . I went through a time when I did not talk to people. It's still happening to me but not so severely. I'm all right now but I do know people who never came out of it" (Yalom, *Women Writers of the West Coast*, p. 17). As I note in *The Shapes and Styles of Asian American Prose Fiction*, "Kingston's moral fable is existentialist in the most basic sense. Her call is for the reader to pick up his or her sword of knowledge" (Ghymn, p. 113). By carrying on the oral tradition, one is linked to the community of women and ancestral spirits. Community triumphs over individuality. This is an appropriate conclusion, as it fits the Chinese philosophy of life.[1]

II

In *The Joy Luck Club*, the relationship between mothers and daughters starts with imbalance and finally ends with a definite balance. In this book, as in *The Woman Warrior*, the structure is the key through which the messages are to be deciphered. The daughters searching for their mothers' real pasts finally arrive at their own identities. The confusion or anger that they feel towards their mothers while growing up is dissolved. Tan explains that the key to the structure of her novel is finding the right balance: "The basic one in the book is a question about balance. Where is the part of balance that we're searching for in our lives? What throws our lives off balance and how can one restore balance?" (Davis, Vol. 1, No. 2, p. 7). As with Anju, the daughters in *The Joy Luck Club* have to find their own understanding through all the conflicts they have with their mothers. Tan says in an interview, "Part of my writing the book was to help me discover what I knew about my mother and what I knew about myself" (Henderson, p. 22). This understanding is achieved when, like Anju, the daughters in *The Joy Luck Club* realize the sameness in themselves and their mothers. Together mothers and daughters create a satisfying wholeness from generation to generation.

The first page of *The Joy Luck Club* lists the characters. Interestingly, the names of the mothers and daughters are set opposite each other as if the book were a chess game. Indeed, chess is an appropriate analogy for Tan's strategy. In a chess game when a pawn reaches the other side of the board she becomes a queen; likewise, daughters have to travel through many conflicts to achieve independence and self-understanding. Like such canonical figures as Ishmael and Huckleberry Finn, daughters have to journey into the unknown to find their own identities. To these second-generation Chinese American women Emerson's "Know Thyself" is the motivating energy.

Images of doubles, ghosts, and shadows misdirect the daughters' journeys. The use of the double is an especially prominent structural device. The word "two" and its synonyms are used several times in chapter titles: "Half and Half," "Two Kinds," "Double Face," and "A Pair of Tickets." Like Humbert and Quilty in *Lolita*, the characters serve as doubles for other characters. Images of ghosts and shadows fit that purpose as well. The total image pattern is that of a fable, which is typically defined as "a brief tale, either in prose or verse, told to point a moral. The characters are most frequently animals, but people and inanimate objects are sometimes the central figures" (Holman and Harmon, p. 197). Tan admits that she wanted to write such a fable. "In fairy tales and fables there's often a moral attached. I didn't want to have something that was exactly the moral but I wanted to have something that was equivalent because I see an ending as a release of some type, and for me releases are always emotional" (Davis, Vol. 1, No. 1, p. 8). The "equivalent" in *The Joy Luck Club* is a growing up lesson, and fairy-tale elements can be found throughout Kingston's and Tan's works.

In a comic book the violence seems amusing rather than frightening. Likewise the overall comic tone of *The Joy Luck Club* subdues the violent details of some of the scenes. Just as we can laugh rather than shudder when we watch Mickey Mouse or Donald Duck smash each other, so can we read Tan's novel. The flat characters are surrounded by mysterious forces, filled with fairy-tale elements of ghosts, animals, and magical objects. I believe that Tan deliberately used flat characters because she was writing a fable. Tan says, "When she [my mother] read the stories, the ones set in China, she laughed. She didn't see that they were anything like herself. There was one story in particular, 'The Moon Lady,' that has nothing to do with her life. She did not live in that area, she never went out on a boat during the moon festival, she never fell into the water, and she never saw a shadow play" (Davis, Vol. 1, No. 2, p. 6). Thus we cannot really believe the stories that the mothers tell about themselves in *The Joy Luck Club*. Real people do not cut their mothers' flesh and cook it. Why then does Tan create such scenes? I think that she does so to make the stories more mysterious and entertaining. At one point Davis asks, "So the struggle in the writing process is to find the right image. The one that works for that story?" Tan replies, "The one that is the most mysterious" (Davis, Vol. 1, No. 1, p. 9). The mysterious images make Tan's story a modern fairy tale. In the last section, the queen mother of "The Queen Mother of the Western Skies" is a fairy. Like Cinderella's fairy godmother, the queen mother provides essential wisdom. In the book's first section, "Feathers from a Thousand *Li* Away," Tan presents the stories of Jing-mei Woo and three mothers, An-mei Hsu, Lindo Jong, and Ying-ying St. Clair. Jing-mei Woo's mother has already died, so Jing-mei speaks in her place. Jing-mei remembers that her mother's story is like that of a fairy tale. "I never thought my mother's Kweilin story was anything but a Chinese fairy tale" (*The Joy Luck Club*, p. 25). This statement seems to apply not only to Jing-mei's story but to all the mothers' stories.

The American-born daughter dismisses China as puzzling, Chinese customs and clothes as mysterious. Jing-mei Woo says, "These clothes were too fancy for real Chinese people, I thought, and too strange for American parties" (*The Joy Luck Club*, p. 28). To the daughters, the mothers are part of an unknown world, a world complicated by their own imaginations. "I imagined Joy Luck was a shameful Chinese custom, like the secret gathering of the Ku Klux Klan or the tom-tom dances of TV Indians preparing for war" (*The Joy Luck Club*, p. 28). Indeed, the mothers' worlds as seen by the daughters are unreal. "I used to dismiss her criticisms as just more of her Chinese superstitions, beliefs that conveniently fit the circumstances" (*The Joy Luck Club*, p. 31), Jing-mei reflects. "These kinds of explanations made me feel my mother and I spoke two different languages, which we did" (*The Joy Luck Club*, p. 33). Limited in American perception, language, and customs, the mothers can't understand that their daughters don't understand them. They say in unison, "Imagine, a daughter not knowing her own mother!" (*The Joy Luck Club*, p. 40). This is an ironical statement because it reveals the lack of understanding the mothers have towards their daughters in presuming that the daughters should understand them despite cultural and generational differences. Jing-mei starts to see things a little differently when she says, "And then it occurs to me. They are frightened. In me, they see their own daughters, just as ignorant, just as unmindful of all the truths and hopes they have brought to America. They see daughters who grow impatient when their mothers talk in Chinese, who think they are stupid when they explain things in fractured English" (*The Joy Luck Club*, pp. 40-41). Interestingly, the mothers see their daughters as "ignorant" and the daughters think their mothers are "stupid." As Marie Wunsch points out, "When conflicts arise the mothers and daughters seem only players in a world so personal, so foreign to the other, that any understanding of the other is impossible" (Wunsch, p. 139). To the daughters, the mothers are embarrassing, confusing, and humiliating; to the mothers, the daughters are rebellious, unyielding, and stubborn.

The four short prologues that introduce the four main chapters advance Tan's moral intentions by clarifying this generational conflict. The prologues suggest that Tan was deeply influenced by her father, a Baptist minister. "He would tell these stories and I realize one of the things that was so amazing was that he could keep them simple so that they would reach everybody. He had an absolute belief in what these stories had to mean" (Davis, Vol. 1, No. 1, p. 6). Tan follows in her father's footsteps in using the form of the fable. The first prologue's fable is that of a mother bringing a swan to the States. Unlike Hans Christian Andersen's ugly duckling who becomes a beautiful swan, this Chinese swan is already grown. "She cooed to the swan: 'In America I will have a daughter just like me. . . . Over there nobody will look down on her, because I will make her speak only perfect American English. And over there she will always be too full to swallow any sorrow!'" (*The Joy Luck Club*, p. 17). The swan is taken away by the customs officials. In this section the irony of the mothers' lack of American customs is revealed in a humorous way as Tan sets out to convey in English Chinese rhythms and idiomatic intonations.

In the second prologue, "The Twenty-six Malignant Gates," the mother warns her daughter by quoting from an old Chinese book: "Do not ride your bicycle around the corner." The daughter replies, "You can't tell me because you don't know! You don't know anything!" (*The Joy Luck Club*, p. 87). The girl runs outside, jumps on her bicycle, and falls before she reaches the corner. The message of this section is that the mother is always right. This juxtaposition of old Chinese proverbs with American reality, continued throughout the book, is without question purposeful. In this section the four daughters tell their own childhood stories. Waverly Jong becomes a national chess player by her ninth birthday, much to the delight of her proud mother. Waverly does not, however, feel equally proud of her mother. When Waverly talks back to her mother, her mother shouts, "'Embarrass you be my daughter?' Her voice was cracking with anger. 'That's not what I meant. That's not what I said'" (*The Joy Luck Club*, p. 99). Waverly's conversation with her mother reveals her growing resentment and also demonstrates the crucial misunderstandings between mothers and daughters.

As portrayed in this prologue the other daughters are no less anxious. Lena St. Clair is confused by what is real and what is unreal. She fantasizes about her neighbors, a mother and daughter whose loud voices often come through the thin walls. She sees the girl pull out a sharp sword and tell her mother, "Then you must die the death of a thousand cuts. It is the only way to save you." After this ordeal the mother says that she has "perfect understanding" (*The Joy Luck Club*, p. 115). The neighbor and her daughter act as doubles for Lena and her mother. Fighting voices, echoing through the walls, make Lena fantasize.

Rose Hsu Jordan's childhood is darkened by the death of her younger brother, Bing, for which she feels responsible: "I knew it was my fault. I hadn't watched him closely enough" (*The Joy Luck Club*, pp. 126-127). Jing-mei Woo also feels that she is to blame for her mother's disappointment. Her mother wants her to be a concert pianist, but Jing-mei feels that she will never make it: "It was not the only disappointment my mother felt in me. In the years that followed, I failed her so many times, each time asserting my own will, my right to fall short of expectations. I didn't get straight A's. I didn't become class president. I didn't get into Stanford. I dropped out of college" (*The Joy Luck Club*, p. 142). Her feelings of guilt, rejection, and doubt haunt Jing-mei.

In the third prologue, "American Translation," the daughters are all grown up. Two have married Caucasian husbands despite their mothers' protests. However, their marriages do not go well. Lena and Harold are constantly battling about different budgets and thinking of divorce. Rose Hsu and Ted are in the process of getting a divorce. Rose says, "Over the years, I learned to choose from the best opinions. Chinese people had Chinese opinions. American people had American opinions. And in almost every case, the American version was much better. It was only later that I discovered there was a serious flaw with the American version. There were too many choices, so it was easy to get confused and pick the wrong thing" (*The Joy Luck Club*, p. 191). Waverly Jong is not as unfortunate. She is dating Rich, a Caucasian, and although Rich and her mother have their misunderstandings, all three plan to visit China together. Jing-mei, still single, even achieves self-understanding. She thinks of her mother, who has died: "And she's the only person I could have asked, to tell me about life's importance, to help me understand my grief" (*The Joy Luck Club*, p. 197).

How does the third prologue correlate with the stories in this section? In the prologue, a daughter asks, "What is peach blossom luck?" "The mother smiled, mischief in her eyes. 'It is in here,' she said, pointing to the mirror. 'Look inside. Tell me, am I not right? In this mirror is my future grandchild, already sitting on my lap next spring.' And the daughter looked—and *haule*! There it was: her own reflection looking back at her" (*The Joy Luck Club*, p. 147). The use of the mirror is like that in "Cinderella" when the stepmother asks the mirror, "who is the fairest of them all?" The reflections of mother, daughter, and grand-child appear much the same and the daughters are revealed as the "American translations" of the mothers.

In the last prologue, "Queen Mother of the Western Skies," the grandmother tells the baby, "Thank you, Little Queen. Then you must teach my daughter this same lesson. How to lose your innocence but not your hope. How to laugh forever" (*The Joy Luck Club*, p. 213). The word "lesson" reinforces the fable elements while the word "laugh" adds a comic touch. The mother talks to the baby who has lived for-ever. The grandmother and baby seem to be one, just as the mother and daughter seem to be identical. The idea of wholeness again reminds us of "Each and All," in which Emerson writes about the transcendent unity of the many and the one.

In this section the mothers unveil their pasts in China, but they are unreliable narrators. Their stories are unrealistic and exaggerated, mixed with the supernatural. As Janet Burroway notes, the unreliable narrator has become one of the most popular characters in modern fiction but "is far from a newcomer to literature and in fact predates fiction. Every drama contains characters who speak for themselves and present their own cases and from whom we are partly or wholly distanced in one area of value or another" (Burroway, p. 274). Tan chooses to make this section the most unrealistic, perhaps because the material is the most unfamiliar to her. For example, An-mei Hsu tells her daughter, "This is how a daughter honors her mother. It is *shou* so deep it is in your bones. The pain of the flesh is nothing. The pain you must forget. Because sometimes that is the only way to remember what is in your bones. You must peel off your skin, and that of your mother, and her mother before her. Until there is nothing. No scar, no skin, no flesh" (*The Joy Luck Club*, p. 48). The idea of peeling her mother's flesh and cooking it is unrealistic, of course. This violent scene is like Kingston's in *The Woman Warrior* when Fa Mu Lan's mother cuts the warrior's back with a knife engraving the list of wrongs to be avenged. Yet unlike apparently comparable scenes in *The Silence of the Lambs*, say, these scenes are not gruesome, but magical.

Limited by their cultural experiences, the mothers think and speak alike. One mother can easily substitute for another and both seem to be characterized as mere Chinese-American abstractions. Ying-ying St. Clair says, "I think this to myself even though I love my daughter. She and I have shared the same body. There is a part of her mind that is part of mine. But when she was born, she sprang from me like a slippery fish" (*The Joy Luck Club*, p. 242). Lindo Jong says, "And now I have to fight back my feelings. These two faces, I think, so much the same! The same happiness, the same sadness, the same good fortune, the same faults" (*The Joy Luck Club*, p. 256). An-mei Hsu says, "And even though I taught my daughter the opposite, still she came out the same way! Maybe it is because when she was born to me and she was born a girl. And I was born to my mother and I was born a girl. All of us are like stairs, one step after another, going up and down, but all going the same way" (*The Joy Luck Club*, p. 215). Likewise, Anju in *The Woman Warrior* describes her mother looking out of her Chinese medical school graduation photo: "She stares straight as if she could see me and past me to her grandchildren and grandchildren's grandchildren" (*The Woman Warrior*, p. 68). The identification that the mothers feel with their daughters is not based on common interests or thoughts but on biological factors. Jing-mei Woo, a seeming spokeswoman for the daughters' side, also admits, "And now I also see what part of me is Chinese. It is so obvious. It is my family. It is in our blood. . . . Together we look like our mother. Her same eyes, her same mouth, open in surprise to see, at last, her long-cherished wish" (*The Joy Luck Club*, p. 288). Reconciliation occurs when mothers and daughters realize the unbreakable bonds between them.

Indeed, the sameness of the daughters and mothers is the novel's central image. Thus the images of the mothers are conventionalized. The mothers do not appear as real women and some of their traits are especially exaggerated. It is true that there are moments of realistic portrayal, but these moments are intertwined with fantasies such as the women carrying swans and a woman cooking a mother's flesh. While the daughters are characterized realistically, the mothers are depicted as unreal. Despite this difference, the mothers and daughters are described as physically alike as the central image takes precedence over realistic portrayal.

Although the activities described are gruesome, the audience does not feel disgust but a mild, amused shudder, because the treatment of these scenes seems to be in the tradition of the comic novel. As Booth points out, "In much of the great comic fiction, for example, our amusement depends on the author's telling us in advance that the characters' troubles are temporary and their concern ridiculously exaggerated" (Booth, *The Rhetoric of Fiction*, p. 175). Tan herself notes, "So with the stories in *The Joy Luck Club*, I often began with a frame, which was 'the reason' for telling the story" (Davis, p. 10). Thus, it would be inaccurate for anyone to see these images as those of real mothers struggling in the United States, though we do get glimpses of reality. In a way there is an element of "faking," as Frank Chin points out in *The Big Aiiieeeee*: "Kingston, Hwang, and Tan are the first writers of any race, and certainly the first writers of Asian ancestry, to so boldly fake the best-known works from the most universally known body of Asian literature and lore in history" (p. 3). However, the fairy-tale elements in the stories make the serious and sad relationships interesting and light. Creating a light touch to handle heavy materials, the authors are able to amuse and entertain the reader even as they write about confusion and painful relationships.

In *The Joy Luck Club* four separate mother/daughter relationships are explored, but the struggles are really variations of each other. The mothers tell from their own points of view their stories in China while the daughters recount their stories of growing up. The four mothers seem to speak in similar voices, making it difficult for the reader to distinguish among them. Likewise, although the episodes are different, the daughters also seem to speak in similar tones. The daughters resist their mothers but somehow always seem vulnerable to their mothers' opinions. As Waverly says, "In her hands I always became the pawn. I could only run away. And she was the queen, able to move in all directions, relentless in her pursuit, always able to find my weakest spots" (*The Joy Luck Club*, p. 180). As in a chess game the daughter runs away until she reaches the far end of the board and then becomes a queen herself by being able to identify with her mother.

Realistically speaking, there is a wide gap between first-generation mothers and second-generation daughters. As Patricia Lin suggests, "The polarity between traditional Chinese and American values is felt with particular keenness by American-born Chinese women. Unlike their mothers, such women face conflicting demands from two opposing cultures. While American-born daughters are familiar with the cultural nuances of Chinese life, their dilemmas frequently stem from having to vacillate between 'Chinese-ness' and 'American-ness.' Their Chinese-born mothers, in contrast, are less plagued by the complexities of being Chinese, American, and woman" (Lin, p. 41). Jing-mei makes much the same point: "These kinds of explanations made me feel my mother and I spoke two different languages, which we did" (*The Joy Luck Club*, pp. 33-34). Despite their differences, however, the mothers and daughters are portrayed as equals. In fact, in *The Woman Warrior* both the mother and daughter are said to be dragons. In *The Joy Luck Club* Lena St. Clair as well as her mother, Ying-ying St. Clair, are born in the year of the tiger. Ying-ying St. Clair states, "I was born in the year of the Tiger. It was a very bad year to be born, a very good year to be a Tiger. . . . The bad spirit stayed in the world for four years. But I came from a spirit even stronger, and I lived. This is what my mother told me when I was old enough to know why I was so heart-strong in my ways. Then she told me why a tiger is gold and black. It has two ways. The gold side leaps with its fierce heart. The black side stands still with cunning, hiding its gold between trees, seeing and not being seen, waiting patiently for things to come" (*The Joy Luck Club*, p. 248). "Two ways" again underlines the idea of the double. The mother like a tiger is strong and shrewd. Her survival and character are attributed to being born in the year of the tiger. Literally, these animals are part of the Chinese zodiac; metaphorically, the image contributes to the work's fairy-tale atmosphere.

In China, women born in the year of the tiger or the dragon are considered too strong to be desirable mates. Women born in the year of the rabbit or pig are said to have gentler personalities, so they are selected before women born in the year of the tiger or dragon. It is interesting that Kingston and Tan have reversed the culture-bound stereotypes of femininity. But then they are looking through American eyes. To them, strength, fierceness, and power are positive signs.

As depicted by Tan, the battle between mother and daughter is especially fierce because both possess equal strength. Both mother and daughter are depicted as tigers. The mother uses her experience to control the daughter but the daughter resists such control even if it is from her own mother. The daughters continue to resist until they realize the truth about the universe. The universe is one and harmonious. Thus both mothers and daughters are winners and losers. The opposing sides of nature complement and balance each other. Both yin and yang enforce the recurring pattern of life. Their combat does not end in a victor or victim; the daughters are not better or worse than their mothers. Holbrook explains this relationship in psychological terms: "The problem of woman is thus the problem of life and its secret. Woman can create us—by reflecting us—and enable us to seek meaning in existence; or, she can leave us without a created identity and in a condition of meaninglessness. No wonder she is feared and hated, as well as respected and loved" (Holbrook, p. 62). This explanation clarifies Waverly's reaction when she sees her mother lying quietly on the sofa. "And then I was seized with a fear that she looked like this because she was dead. I had wished her out of my life, and she had acquiesced, floating out of her body to escape my terrible hatred" (*The Joy Luck Club*, p. 180). Waverly is relieved to find her mother just sleeping. When Lindo Jong awakens and calls her daughter by a childhood name, "Meimei-ah," Waverly's anger dissolves and she feels "as if someone had unplugged me and the current running through me had stopped" (*The Joy Luck Club*, p. 181). Likewise, Anju feels as if a "weight lifted from me" when her mother calls her "Little Dog," an endearing term from childhood (*The Woman Warrior*, p. 127). And as in all fairy tales the stories end on a positive note when the daughters realize the truth about their world.

Motivated by ambition and fear, the mothers try to control their daughters. As Helen Bannan says,

> immigrant women fought to survive, to preserve what they considered to be the essence of their cultural origins, and to pass on both survival skills and cultural traditions to their daughters. When the women of the second generation chose American survival over ethnic tradition, they sometimes brought the war home, but they were often following battle strategies for which their mothers had, perhaps unwillingly, performed the reconnaissance. (Bannan, p. 165)

Therefore, as Barker-Nunn notes,

> These painful episodes are a result of the difficulty mother and daughter have separating from one another; this is the darker side of connection. The daughters' resentment springs from what they see as a lack of willingness on their mothers' part to see them as they are, to accept them as having lives both different and separate from those of their own. (Barker-Nunn, p. 59)

The degree to which the daughters' growing identities depend upon their unquestioning acceptance of their mothers is central to the novel's conclusion.

Tan invokes truly widespread, if not universal, patterns. According to Simone de Beauvoir, "real conflicts arise when the girl grows older; as we have seen, she wishes to establish her independence from her mother. This seems to the mother a mark of hateful ingratitude; she tries obstinately to checkmate the girl's will to escape; she cannot bear to have her double become an other. . . . Whether a loving or a hostile mother, the independence of her child dashes her hopes. She is doubly jealous: of the world, which takes her daughter from her, and of her daughter, who in conquering a part of the world robs her of it" (Beauvoir, p. 519). Perhaps this is the reason why Tan's mothers attempt to control their daughters' lives.

Tan's mothers are very ambitious for their daughters. Jing-mei remembers her mother wanting her to be like Shirley Temple and starting her on a series of piano lessons despite Jing-mei's protests. At a talent show, she "played this strange jumble through two repeats, the sour notes staying with me all the way to the end" (*The Joy Luck Club*, p. 139). But it is the expression on her mother's face that truly affects her. "But my mother's expression was what devastated me: a quiet, blank look that said she had lost everything" (*The Joy Luck Club*, p. 140). Jing-mei does care deeply what her mother thinks of her. She feels that her mother has indeed lost everything and is haunted by a sense of failure. She explains, "And for all those years, we never talked about the disaster at the recital or my terrible accusations afterward at the piano bench. All that remained unchecked, like a betrayal that was now unspeakable. So I never found a way to ask her why she had hoped for something so large that failure was inevitable" (*The Joy Luck Club*, p. 142). In exasperation she shouts at her mother, "You want me to be someone that I'm not! . . . I'll never be the kind of daughter you want me to be." The insensitive mother retorts, "Only two kinds of daughters. . . . Those who are obedient and those who follow their own mind!" "Then I wish I wasn't your daughter. I wish you weren't my mother," Jing-mei replies (*The Joy Luck Club*, p. 142). Real communication is blocked by language problems. The mother's inability to speak English well denies her the opportunity to explain her true thoughts and feelings to her daughter. In broken English the mother tries to teach her daughter by using her knowledge of old Chinese proverbs and chants. Frustration breaks out on both sides, and the scene ends with shouting and ultimatums.

The ambition of Waverly Jong's mother is to make her daughter a champion chess player. "And my mother loved to show me off, like one of my many trophies she polished. She used to discuss my games as if she had devised the strategies" (*The Joy Luck Club*, p. 170). However, one day Waverly must respond, "I hated the way she tried to take all the credit. And one day I told her so, shouting at her on Stockton Street, in the middle of a crowd of people. I told her she didn't know anything, so she shouldn't show off. She should shut up" (*The Joy Luck Club*, p. 170). Her mother's loud Chinese voice cracking with broken English words is embarrassing. The mother doesn't behave the way a white mother behaves, not knowing any better, so she is a source of humiliation for the daughter. Likewise, a daughter telling her mother "to shut up" is a disgrace for the mother. And yet the mothers have a strong hold over the daughters. Waverly feels that "in her hands, I always became the pawn. I could only run away. And she was the queen, able to move in all directions, relentless in her pursuit, always able to find my weakest spots" (*The Joy Luck Club*, p. 180). Entrapped in her sensitivities, the daughter struggles and rebels.

Despite the daughters' rebellions, their sense of guilt, need for approval, and desire for reassurance tie them to their mothers' judgments. Yet their fears of being rejected make them hesitate. An-mei Hsu hesitates about explaining her divorce to her mother. Waverly Jong wants desperately for her mother to approve her white boyfriend, Rich. She tells him, however, that her mother doesn't think anyone is good enough for her. When Waverly shows her mother her present from Rich, a mink coat, her mother replies, "This is not so good." "It is just leftover strips. And the fur is too short, no long hairs" (*The Joy Luck Club*, p. 169). Waverly observes, "My mother knows how to hit a nerve. And the pain I feel is worse than any other kind of misery. Because what she does always comes as a shock, exactly like an electric jolt, that grounds itself permanently in my memory. I still remember the first time I felt it" (*The Joy Luck Club*, p. 170).

Just as the daughters hesitate, so too the mothers wait to reveal their pasts. Ying-ying St. Clair states, "My daughter does not know that I was married to this man so long ago, twenty years before she was even born" (*The Joy Luck Club*, p. 246). Jing-mei Woo's mother dies before revealing her whole past to her. Jing-mei goes on a quest to find out more about her dead mother and to find her lost sisters. This lack of communication and honesty between daughter and mother is one of the major sources of conflict and misunderstanding. Only when the mothers start to reveal their true natures do the daughters begin to understand their mothers and themselves. Ying-ying St. Clair says, "All these years I kept my true nature hidden, running along like a small shadow so nobody could catch me. And because I moved so secretly now my daughter does not see me. She sees a list of things to buy, her checkbook out of balance, her ashtray sitting crooked on a straight table. And I want to tell her this: We are lost, she and I, unseen and not seeing, unheard and not hearing, unknown by others" (*The Joy Luck Club*, p. 67). The longer the mothers wait, the deeper become the misunderstandings.

Reconciliation occurs after a series of reversals and recognitions. The daughters realize that the mothers are just as sensitive as they are, that their mothers can be hurt just as they themselves are hurt. Waverly feels torn: "Oh, her strength! Her weakness!—both pulling me apart. My mind was flying one way, my heart another. I sat down on the sofa next to her, the two of us stricken by the other" (*The Joy Luck Club*, p. 181). At one point Lindo Jong says to her daughter, "Yes, but you said it just to be mean, to hurt me, to . . . ." And when her daughter responds with more abuse, she is horrified. "So you think your mother is this bad. You think I have a secret meaning. But it is you who has this meaning. Ai-ya! She thinks I am this bad!" (*The Joy Luck Club*, p. 181). And just as Waverly feels acutely her mother's remarks, so any rude remarks that Waverly makes give Lindo sharp pain. As Ling points out, "Tan's implication is clear: we all take our mothers (and motherlands) for granted. They are just there, like air or water, impossible really to know or understand because we are so intimate, and more often than not they have seemed a force to struggle against" (Ling, *Between Worlds*, p. 136).

Ying-ying believes that by revealing the secrets of her past she can help her daughter. "Now I must tell my daughter everything. . . . I will gather together my past and look. I will see a thing that has already happened. The pain that cut my spirit loose. I will hold that pain in my hand until it becomes hard and shiny, more clear. And then my fierceness can come back, my golden side, my black side. I will use this sharp pain to penetrate my daughter's tough skin and cut her tiger spirit loose. She will fight me, because this is the nature of two tigers. But I will win and give her my spirit because this is the way a mother loves her daughter" (*The Joy Luck Club*, p. 252). And when Lindo and Waverly Jong are at the beauty parlor, the mother thinks, "And now I have to fight back my feelings. These two faces, I think, so much the same! The same happiness, the same sadness, the same good fortune, the same faults" (*The Joy Luck Club*, p. 256). Likewise the daughter sees her mother as so weak and frail that she comes to a new understanding. "I saw what I had been fighting for: It was for me, a scared child, who had run away a long time ago to what I had imagined was a safer place. And hiding in this place, behind my invisible barriers, I knew what lay on the other side: Her side attacks. Her secret weapons. Her uncanny ability to find my weakest spots. But in the brief instant that I had peered over the barriers I could finally see what was really there: an old woman, a wok for her armor, a knitting needle for her sword, getting a little crabby as she waited patiently for her daughter to invite her in" (*The Joy Luck Club*, pp. 183-84). The clash of these wills is finally stilled in a moment's revelation.

At the end, when Jing-mei goes to China to find her two lost sisters, she is all but overcome: "And now I see [my mother] again, two of her, waving, and in one hand there is a photo, the Polaroid I sent them. As soon as I get beyond the gate, we run toward each other, all three of us embracing, all hesitations and expectations forgotten. 'Mama, Mama,' we all murmur, as if she is among us" (*The Joy Luck Club*, p. 287). Eager yet hesitant, happy but somewhat shy, Jing-mei embraces her lost sisters. When Jing-mei looks at the Polaroid picture of herself and her two Chinese sisters, she realizes their perfect likeness: "The gray-green surface changes to the bright colors of our three images, sharpening and deepening all at once. . . . Together we look like our mother. Her same eyes, her same mouth, open in surprise to see, at last, her long-cherished wish" (*The Joy Luck Club*, p. 288). The dim shadowy images give way to the sharply focused features underlined by the similar bone structures. These images of likeness break down the walls of resistance. As Holbrook notes, "The symbolic use of faces and eyes is found in fairy tales, as well as in the fantasies of C. S. Lewis, George MacDonald, Lewis Carroll, and others. Symbolism of the mother's body, of birth, and of play may also be found—associated with existence and development" (Holbrook, p. 64). This development is achieved when Jing-mei's search for the mother ends by finding her sisters.

Jing-mei's need to find her own identity is realized when she meets her sisters. Pearson notes that "women writers in particular emphasize the female hero's need, following her liberation from male definition, for reconciliation with the mother. They also emphasize how inextricably bound together are the search for the mother and the search for the self" (Pearson and Pope, p. 197). The image of the mother superimposed on the sisters' reflections brings about this revelation. As Lazarre says, "It is the process of quiet, loving, insistent identification, the repeated testifying of one to the other that says, I am the same as you, that unlocks the doors and unravels the tangles" (Pearson and Pope, p. 203). Mirror images reflect the unbreakable bonds between mother and daughter.

Jing-mei's journey correlates with Holbrook's explanation of how fantasies work in stories by writers like C. S. Lewis and George MacDonald. "There is a journey, and during the journey something crucial has to be sought in the bleak world and brought back to restore meaning. This often is something shiny, magical, fruitful or potent. This quest is symbolic of the need of the individual who cannot complete mourning to find the dead mother—in the world of death—and to obtain from her the completion of reflection, thus restoring meaning to life. The loss has left the individual aware of the lack of meaning in his existence, consequent upon the insufficiency of the mother's creative reflection. Therefore, the individual must find her . . . or her magic attributes . . . to complete the existential process" (Holbrook, p. 65). When Jing-mei sees herself in the photo, which serves as a magical mirror, she is restored. And the restoration she achieves is mirrored in the fates of her sisters, both Chinese and American.

Kingston's and Tan's images are more figurative and original than those of other, more conventional writers who tend to offer traditional images of the loving mother and dutiful daughter. Kingston's and Tan's images are more memorable and revealing of the problems of first-generation Asian American mothers and their daughters. In *The Woman Warrior* and *The Joy Luck Club*, however, real separation never occurs, although the mother-daughter bond is problematic. Although at various times there is a tug of war, the bond between mothers and daughters is never broken. This concept fits in perfectly with the Chinese view of the universe. In the end the American-born daughters accept and affirm their Chinese heritage. In both *The Woman Warrior* and *The Joy Luck Club* resolution occurs when the daughters accept their mothers. They realize that despite differences of environment and culture they share a deep and unchanging bond with their mothers. Kingston's and Tan's philosophies truly fit Emerson's in "Each and All." Like the speaker in the last line of this poem, the mothers and daughters in *The Woman Warrior* and *The Joy Luck Club* finally yield themselves to the perfect whole.

Note

1. For a more detailed discussion of these unifying devices, see my book *The Shapes and Styles of Asian American Prose Fiction*, pp. 91-115.

Works Cited

Bannan, Helen M. "Warrior Woman: Immigrant Mothers in the Works of the Daughters." *Women's Studies* 6 (1979): 165-77.

Barker-Nunn, Jeanne. "Telling the Mother's Story: History and Connection in the Autobiographies of Maxine Hong Kingston and Kim Chernin." *Women's Studies* 14 (1987): 55-63.

Beauvoir, Simone de. *The Second Sex.* New York: Vintage, 1989.

Booth, Wayne C. *The Rhetoric of Fiction.* Chicago: University of Chicago Press, 1961.

Burroway, Janet. *Writing Fiction: A Guide to Narrative Craft.* 3d ed. New York: HarperCollins, 1992.

Chin, Frank. "Come All Ye Asian American Writers of the Real and the Fake." *The Big Aiiieeeee: An Anthology of Chinese American and Japanese American Literature.* Ed. Jeffery Paul Chan et al. New York: Meridian, 1991.

Davis, Emory. "The Adventures of Amy Tan." *Professional Writer.* Ed. James N. Frey. Vol. 1, No. 1. September 1, 1991.

_____. "Further Adventures of Amy Tan." *Professional Writer*. Ed. James N. Frey. Vol. 1, No. 2. October 15, 1991.

Ghymn, Esther Mikyung. *The Shapes and Styles of Asian American Prose Fiction*. New York: Peter Lang Publishing, 1992.

Henderson, Katherine Usher. "Amy Tan." *A Voice of One's Own*. Ed. Mickey Pearlman and Katherine Usher Henderson. Boston: Houghton Mifflin, 1990.

Holbrook, David. *Images of Women in Literature*. New York: New York University Press, 1989.

Holman, C. Hugh, and William Harmon. *A Handbook to Literature*. New York: Macmillan, 1986.

Juhasz, Suzanne. "Maxine Hong Kingston: Narrative Technique and Female Identity." *Contemporary American Women Writers*. Ed. Catherine Rainwater and William J. Scheick. Lexington: University Press of Kentucky, 1985.

Kingston, Maxine Hong. *The Woman Warrior*. New York: Random House, 1976.

Lidoff, Joan. "Autobiography in a Different Voice: *The Woman Warrior* and the Question of Genre." *Approaches to Teaching Kingston's "The Woman Warrior."* Ed. Shirley Geok-lin Lim. New York: MLA, 1991. 116-20.

Lin, Patricia. "Use of Media and Other Resources to Situate *The Woman Warrior*." *Approaches to Teaching Kingston's "The Woman Warrior."* Ed. Shirley Geok-lin Lim. New York: MLA, 1991. 37-43.

Ling, Amy. *Between Worlds: Women Writers of Chinese Ancestry*. New York: Pergamon Press, 1990.

Pearson, Carol, and Katherine Pope. *The Female Hero*. New York: R. R. Bowker, 1981.

Tan, Amy. *The Joy Luck Club*. New York: Putnam & Sons, 1989.

Walker, Nancy A. *Feminist Alternatives*. Jackson: University Press of Mississippi, 1990.

Wunsch, Marie Ann. "Walls of Jade: Images of Men, Women, and Family in Second Generation Asian-American Fiction and Autobiography." Unpublished dissertation, University of Hawaii, 1977.

Yalom, Marilyn. "*The Woman Warrior* as Postmodern Autobiography." *Approaches to Teaching Kingston's "The Woman Warrior."* Ed. Shirley Geok-lin Lim. New York: MLA, 1991. 108-15.

_____. *Women Writers of the West Coast*. Santa Barbara, CA: Capra Press, 1983.

Voice, Mind, Self:
Mother-Daughter Relationships in Amy Tan's
The Joy Luck Club and *The Kitchen God's Wife*_____

M. Marie Booth Foster

In *The Joy Luck Club* and *The Kitchen God's Wife*, Amy Tan uses stories from her own history and myth to explore the voices of mothers and daughters of Chinese ancestry. Each woman tells a story indicative of the uniqueness of her voice. Mary Field Belensky, in *Women's Ways of Knowing*, argues that voice is "more than an academic shorthand for a person's point of view. . . . it is a metaphor that can apply to many aspects of women's experience and development. . . . Women repeatedly used the metaphor of voice to depict their intellectual and ethical development; . . . the development of a sense of voice, mind, and self were intricately intertwined" (18). In Tan's fiction, the daughters' sense of self is intricately linked to an ability to speak and be heard by their mothers. Similarly, the mothers experience growth as they broaden communication lines with their daughters. Tan's women are very much like the women Belensky portrays in *Women's Ways of Knowing*: "In describing their lives, women commonly talked about voice and silence: 'speaking up,' 'speaking out,' 'being silenced,' 'not being heard,' 'really listening,' 'really talking,' 'words as weapons,' 'feeling deaf and dumb,' 'having no words,' 'saying what you mean,' 'listening to be heard'" (18). Until Tan's women connect as mothers and daughters, they experience strong feelings of isolation, a sense of disenfranchisement and fragmentation. These feelings often are a result of male domination, as Margery Wolf and Roxanne Witke describe in *Women in Chinese Society* (1-11).

A photo that is in part a pictorial history of Tan's foremothers is the inspiration for many of her portrayals of women. Tan writes in "Lost Lives of Women" of a picture of her mother, grandmother, aunts, cousins:

When I first saw this photo as a child, I thought it was exotic and remote, of a far-away time and place, with people who had no connection to my American life. Look at their bound feet! Look at that funny lady with the plucked forehead. The solemn little girl was in fact, my mother. And leaning against the rock is my grandmother, Jingmei. . . . This is also a picture of secrets and tragedies. . . . This is the picture I see when I write. These are the secrets I was supposed to keep. These are the women who never let me forget why stories need to be told. (90)

In her remembrances, Tan presents Chinese American women who are forging identities beyond the pictures of concubinage and bound feet, women encountering new dragons, many of which are derived from being "hyphenated" American females. She views mother-daughter relationships in the same vein as Kathie Carlson, who argues, "This relationship is the birthplace of a woman's ego identity, her sense of security in the world, her feelings about herself, her body and other women. From her mother, a woman receives her first impression of how to be a woman" (xi).

The Joy Luck Club and *The Kitchen God's Wife* are studies in balance—balancing hyphenation and the roles of daughter, wife, mother, sister, career woman. In achieving balance, voice is important: in order to achieve voice, hyphenated women must engage in self-exploration, recognition and appreciation of their culture(s), and they must know their histories. The quest for voice becomes an archetypal journey for all of the women. The mothers come to the United States and have to adapt to a new culture, to redefine voice and self. The daughters' journeys become rites of passage; before they can find voice or define self they must acknowledge the history and myth of their mothers—"herstories" of life in China, passage to the United States, and assimilation. And each must come to grips with being her mother's daughter.

The Joy Luck Club is a series of stories by and about narrators whose lives are interconnected as a result of friendship and membership in the Joy Luck Club: Suyuan and Jing-mei Woo, An-mei Hsu and Rose Hsu

Jordan, Lindo and Waverly Jong, and Ying-ying and Lena St. Clair. The stories illuminate the multiplicity of experiences of Chinese women who are struggling to fashion a voice for themselves in a culture where women are conditioned to be silent. The stories are narrated by seven of the eight women in the group—four daughters and three mothers; one mother has recently died of a cerebral aneurysm. Jing-mei, nicknamed June, must be her mother's voice. The book is divided into four sections: Feathers from a Thousand *Li* Away, The Twenty-six Malignant Gates, American Translation, and Queen Mother of the Western Skies. Each chapter is prefaced with an introductory thematic tale or myth, all of which tend to stress the advice given by mothers.

Tan tells her mother's stories, the secret ones she began to tell after the death of Tan's father and brother in *The Kitchen God's Wife*. Patti Doten notes that Tan's mother told stories of her marriage to another man in China and of three daughters left behind when she came to the United States in 1949 (14), a story that is in part remembered in *The Joy Luck Club* with An-mei's saga. In *The Kitchen God's Wife*, a mother and daughter, Winnie Louie and Pearl Louie Brandt, share their stories, revealing the secrets that hide mind and self—and history—and veil and mask their voices. Winnie Louie's tale is of the loss of her mother as a young girl, marriage to a sadistic man who sexually abused her, children stillborn or dying young, a patriarchal society that allowed little room for escape from domestic violence (especially against the backdrop of war), and her flight to America and the love of a "good man." Daughter Pearl Louie Brandt's secrets include her pain upon the loss of her father and the unpredictable disease, multiple sclerosis, that inhibits her body and her life.

Tan's characters are of necessity storytellers and even historians, empowered by relating what they know about their beginnings and the insufficiencies of their present lives. Storytelling—relating memories—allows for review, analysis, and sometimes understanding of ancestry and thus themselves. The storytelling, however, is inundated with ambivalences and contradictions which, as Suzanna Danuta Walters argues, often take the form of blame in mother-daughter relationships (1).

Voice balances—or imbalances—voice as Chinese American mothers and daughters narrate their sagas. Because both mothers and daughters share the telling, the biases of a singular point of view are alleviated. Marianne Hirsch writes, "The story of female development, both in fiction and theory, needs to be written in the voice of mothers as well as in that of daughters. . . . Only in combining both voices, in finding a double voice that would yield a multiple female consciousness, can we begin to envision ways to live 'life afresh'" (161). Tan's fiction presents ambivalences and contradictions in the complicated interactions of mothers' and daughters' voices.

Regardless of how much the daughters try to deny it, it is through their mothers that they find their voice, their mind, their selfhood. Voice finds its form in the process of interaction, even if that interaction is conflict. "Recognition by the daughter that her voice is not entirely her own" comes in time and with experiences (one of the five interconnecting themes referred to by Nan Bauer Maglin in *The Literature of Matrilineage* as a recurring theme in such literature [258]). The experiences in review perhaps allow the daughters to know just how much they are dependent upon their mothers in their journey to voice. The mothers do not let them forget their own importance as the daughters attempt to achieve self-importance.

As Jing-mei "June" Woo tells her story and that of her deceased mother, the importance of the mother and daughter voices resonating, growing out of and being strengthened by each other, is apparent in her state of confusion and lack of direction and success. Perhaps her name is symbolic of her confusion: she is the only daughter with both a Chinese and an American name. As she recalls life with her mother, Jing-mei/June relates that she is constantly told by her mother, Suyuan Woo, that she does not try and therefore cannot achieve success. June's journey to voice and balance requires self-discovery—which must begin with knowing her mother. June has to use memories as a guide instead of her mother, whose tale she tells and whose saga she must complete. She must meet the ending to the tale of life in China and daughters left behind that her mother has told her over and over again, a story that she thought was a dark fairy tale.

The dark tale is of a previous life that includes a husband and daughters. Suyuan's first husband, an officer with the Kuomintang, takes her to Kweilin, a place she has dreamed of visiting. It has become a war refuge, no longer idyllic. Suyuan Woo and three other officers' wives start the Joy Luck Club to take their minds off the terrible smells of too many people in the city and the screams of humans and animals in pain. They attempt to raise their spirits with mah jong, jokes, and food.

Warned of impending danger, June's mother leaves the city with her two babies and her most valuable possessions. On the road to Chungking, she abandons first the wheelbarrow in which she has been carrying her babies and her goods, then more goods. Finally, her body weakened by fatigue and dysentery, she leaves the babies with jewelry to provide for them until they can be brought to her family. America does not make Suyuan forget the daughters she left as she fled. June Woo secretly views her mother's story as a fairy tale because the ending always changed. Perhaps herein lies the cause of their conflict: neither mother nor daughter listens to be heard, so each complains of not being heard. June Woo's disinterest and lack of knowledge of her mother's history exacerbate her own voicelessness, her lack of wholeness.

At a mah jong table where, appropriately, June takes her mother's place, she is requested by her mother's friends to go to China and meet the daughters of her mother. Thus her journey to voice continues and begins: it is a journey started at birth, but it is only now that she starts to recognize that she needs to know about her mother in order to achieve self-knowledge. She is to tell her sisters about their mother. The mothers' worst fears are realized when June asks what she can possibly tell her mother's daughters. The mothers see their daughters in June's response, daughters who get irritated when their mothers speak in Chinese or explain things in broken English.

Although it startles her mother's friends, June's question is a valid one for a daughter whose relationship with her mother was defined by distance that developed slowly and grew. According to June, she and her mother never understood each other. She says they translated each other's meanings: she seemed to hear less than what was said, and her mother heard more. It is a complaint leveled by mothers and daughters throughout *The Joy Luck Club* and later in *The Kitchen God's Wife*. Both women want to be heard, but do not listen to be heard. They must come to understand that a voice is not a voice unless there is someone there to hear it.

Jing-mei is no longer sitting at the mah jong table but is en route to China when she summons up memories of her mother that will empower her to tell the daughters her mother's story. In the title story and in the short story "A Pair of Tickets," she occupies her mother's place in the storytelling, much as she occupies it at the mah jong table, and she is concerned with the responsibilities left by her mother. In her own stories, "Two Kinds" and "Best Quality," she is concerned with her selves: Jing-mei and June—the Chinese and the American, her mother's expectations and her belief in herself. Her stories are quest stories, described by Susan Koppelman in *Between Mothers and Daughters* as "a daughter's search for understanding" of her mother and herself (xxii). As June makes soup for her father, she sees the stray cat that she thought her mother had killed, since she had not seen it for some time. She makes motions to scare the cat and then recognizes the motions as her mother's; the cat reacts to her just as he had to her mother. She is reminded that she is her mother's daughter.

According to Judith Arcana in *Our Mothers' Daughters*, "we hold the belief that mothers love their daughters by definition and we fear any signal from our own mother that this love, which includes acceptance, affection, admiration and approval does not exist or is incomplete" (5). It does not matter to Jing-mei that she is not her mother's only disappointment (she says her mother always seemed displeased with everyone). Jing-mei recalls that something was not in balance and that something always needed improving for her mother. The friends

---

do not seem to care; with all of her faults, she is their friend. Perhaps it is a "daughter's" expectations that June uses to judge her mother. Suyuan tells the rebellious June that she can be the best at anything as she attempts to mold her child into a piano-playing prodigy. She tells June she's not the best because she's not trying. After the request by the Joy Luck Club mothers June, in really listening to the voice of her mother as reserved in her memory, discovers that she might have been able to demonstrate ability had she tried: "for unlike my mother I did not believe I could be anything I wanted to be. I could only be me" (154). But she does not recognize that the "me" is the one who has made every attempt to escape development. The pendant her late mother gave her is symbolic. It was given to her as her life's importance. The latter part of the message is in Chinese, the voice of wisdom versus the provider of American circumstances.

In archetypal journeys, there is always a god or goddess who supports the "traveler" along his or her way. In *The Kitchen God's Wife*, Lady Sorrowfree is created by Winnie Louie, mother of Pearl, when the Kitchen God is determined by her to be an unfit god for her daughter's altar, inherited from an adopted aunt. The Kitchen God is unfit primarily because he became a god despite his mistreatment of his good wife. A porcelain figurine is taken from a storeroom where she has been placed as a "mistake" and is made into a goddess for Pearl, Lady Sorrowfree. Note Winnie's celebration of Lady Sorrowfree:

> I heard she once had many hardships in her life. . . . But her smile is genuine, wise, and innocent at the same time. And her hand, see how she just raised it. That means she is about to speak, or maybe she is telling you to speak. She is ready to listen. She understands English. You should tell her everything. . . . But sometimes, when you are afraid, you can talk to her. She will listen. She will wash away everything sad with her tears. She will use her stick to chase away everything bad. See her name: Lady Sorrowfree, happiness winning over bitterness, no regrets in this world. (414-415)

Perhaps Tan's mothers want to be like Lady Sorrowfree; they are in a sense goddesses whose altars their daughters are invited to come to for nurturance, compassion, empathy, inspiration, and direction. They are driven by the feeling of need to support those daughters, to give to them "the swan" brought from China—symbolic of their her-stories and wisdom, and the advantages of America, like the mother in the preface to the first round of stories. In the tale, all that is left of the mother's swan that she has brought from China after it is taken by customs officials is one feather; the mother wants to tell her daughter that the feather may look worthless, but it comes from her homeland and carries with it all good intentions. But she waits to tell her in perfect English, in essence keeping secrets. The mothers think that everything is possible for the daughters if the mothers will it. The daughters may come willingly to the altar or may rebelliously deny the sagacity of their mothers.

The mothers struggle to tell their daughters the consequences of not listening to them. The mother in the tale prefacing the section "Twenty-six Malignant Gates" tells her daughter not to ride her bike around the corner where she cannot see her because she will fall down and cry. The daughter questions how her mother knows, and she tells her that it is written in the book *Twenty-six Malignant Gates* that evil things can happen when a child goes outside the protection of the house. The daughter wants evidence, but her mother tells her that it is written in Chinese. When her mother does not tell her all twenty-six of the Malignant Gates, the girl runs out of the house and around the corner and falls, the consequence of not listening to her mother. Rebellion causes conflict—a conflict Lady Sorrowfree would not have to endure. June Woo and Waverly Jong seem to be daughters who thrive on the conflict that results from rebellion and sometimes even the need to win their mother's approval. June trudges off every day to piano lessons taught by an old man who is hard of hearing. Defying her mother, she learns very little, as she reveals at a piano recital to which her mother has invited all of her friends. June notes the blank look on her mother's face that says she has lost everything. Waverly wins at chess, which pleases her mother, but out of defiance she stops playing until she discovers that she really enjoyed her mother's approval. As an adult she wants her mother to approve of the man who will be her second husband; mother and daughter assume the positions of chess players.

Tan's mothers frequently preach that children are to make their mothers proud so that they can brag about them to other mothers. The mothers engage in fierce competition with each other. Suyuan Woo brags about her daughter even after June's poorly performed piano recital. All of the mothers find fault with their daughters, but this is something revealed to the daughters, not to the community.

Much as Lindo Jong credits herself with daughter Waverly's ability to play chess, she blames herself for Waverly's faults as a person and assumes failures in raising her daughter: "It is my fault she is this way—selfish. I wanted my children to have the best combination: American circumstances and Chinese character. How could I know these things do not mix?" (289). Waverly knows how American circumstances work, but Lindo can't teach her about Chinese character: "How to obey parents and listen to your mother's mind. How not to show your own thoughts, to put your feelings behind your face so you can take advantage of hidden opportunities. . . . Why Chinese thinking is best" (289). What she gets is a daughter who wants to be Chinese because it is fashionable, a daughter who likes to speak back and question what she says, and a daughter to whom promises mean nothing. Nonetheless, she is a daughter of whom Lindo is proud.

Lindo Jong is cunning, shrewd, resourceful; Waverly Jong is her mother's daughter. Waverly manages to irritate her mother when she resists parental guidance. Judith Arcana posits that "some daughters spend all or most of their energy trying futilely to be as different from their mothers as possible in behavior, appearance, relations with friends, lovers, children, husbands" (9). Waverly is a strategist in getting her brother to teach her to play chess, in winning at chess, in gaining her mother's forgiveness when she is rude and getting her mother's acceptance of the man she plans to marry. Lindo proudly reminds Waverly that she has inherited her ability to win from her.

In literature that focuses on mother/daughter relationships, feminists see "context—historical time and social and cultural group" as important (Rosinsky, 285). Lindo relates in "The Red Candle" that she once sacrificed her life to keep her parents' promise; she married as arranged. Chinese tradition permits Lindo's parents to give her to Huang Tai for her son—to determine her fate—but Lindo takes control of her destiny. On the day of her wedding, as she prepares for the ceremony, she schemes her way out of the planned marriage and into America, where "nobody says you have to keep the circumstances somebody else gives to you" (289).

It takes determination to achieve voice and selfhood, to take control of one's mind and one's life from another, making one's self heard, overcoming silence. Lindo does not resign herself to her circumstances in China. Waverly reveals that she learns some of her strategies from her mother: "I was six when my mother taught me the art of invisible strength. It was a strategy for winning arguments, respect from others, and eventually, though neither of us knew it at the time, chess games" (89). Therein lies Lindo's contribution to her daughter's voice.

Lindo uses the same brand of ingenuity to play a life chess game with and to teach her daughter. Adrienne Rich writes in *Of Woman Born*: "Probably there is nothing in human nature more resonant with charges than the flow of energy between two biologically alike bodies, one which has lain in amniotic bliss inside the other, one which has labored to give birth to the other. The materials are there for the deepest mutuality and the most painful estrangement" (226). Lindo has to contend with a headstrong daughter: "'Finish your coffee,' I told her yesterday. 'Don't throw your blessings away.' 'Don't be old-fashioned, Ma,' she told me, finishing her coffee down the sink. 'I'm my own person.' And I think, how can she be her own person? When did I give her up?" (290).

Waverly is champion of the chess game, but she is no match for her mother in a life chess game. She knows her chances of winning in a contest against her mother, who taught her to be strong like the wind. Waverly learns during the "chess years" that her mother was a champion strategist. Though she is a tax attorney able to bully even the Internal Revenue Service, she fears the wrath of her mother if she is told to mind her business: "Well, I don't know if it's explicitly stated in the law, but you can't ever tell a Chinese mother to shut up. You could be charged as an accessory to your own murder" (191). What Waverly perceives as an impending battle for her mother's approval of her fiancé is nothing more than the opportunity for her mother and her to communicate with each other. She strategically plans to win her mother's approval of her fiancé, Rick, just as if she is playing a game of chess. She is afraid to tell her mother that they are going to be married because she is afraid that her mother will not approve. The conversation ends with her recognition that her mother also needs to be heard and with her mother's unstated approval of her fiancé. Waverly Jong recognizes her mother's strategies in their verbal jousts, but she also recognizes that, just like her, her mother is in search of something. What she sees is an old woman waiting to be invited into her daughter's life. Like the other mothers, Lindo views herself as standing outside her daughter's life—a most undesirable place.

Sometimes Tan's mothers find it necessary to intrude in order to teach the daughters to save themselves; they criticize, manage, and manipulate with an iron fist. An-mei Hsu and Ying-ying St. Clair play this role. "My mother once told me why I was so confused all the time," says Rose Hsu during her first story, "Without Wood" (212). "She said that I was without wood. Born without wood so that I listened to too many people. She knew this because she had almost become this way" (212). Suyuan Woo tells June Woo that such weaknesses are present in the mother, An-mei Hsu: "Each person is made of five elements. . . . Too little wood and you bend too quickly to listen to other people's ideas, unable to stand on your own. This was like my Auntie An-mei" (19). Rose's mother tells her that she must stand tall and listen to her mother standing next to her. If she bends to listen to strangers, she'll grow weak and be destroyed. Rose Hsu is in the process of divorce from a husband who has labeled her indecisive and useless as a marriage partner. She is guilty of allowing her husband to mold her. He does not want her to be a partner in family decisions until he makes a mistake in his practice as a plastic surgeon. Then he complains that she is unable to make decisions: he is dissatisfied with his creation. Finding it difficult to accept divorce, she confusedly runs to her friends and a psychiatrist seeking guidance.

Over and over again her mother tells her to count on a mother because a mother is best and knows what is inside of her daughter. "A psyche-atricks will only make you hulihudu, make you heimongmong" (210). The psychiatrist leaves her confused, as her mother predicts. She becomes even more confused as she tells each of her friends and her psychiatrist a different story. Her mother advises her to stand up to her husband, to speak up. She assumes the role of Lady Sorrowfree. When Rose does as her mother advises, she notices that her husband seems scared and confused. She stands up to him and forces him to retreat. She is her mother's daughter. She listens to her mother and finds her voice—her self.

Like the other mothers, An-mei demonstrates some of the qualities of "Lady Sorrowfree." An-mei is concerned that her daughter sees herself as having no options. A psychologist's explanation is "to the extent that women perceive themselves as having no choice, they correspondingly excuse themselves from the responsibility that decision entails" (Gilligan, 67). An-mei was "raised the Chinese way": "I was taught to desire nothing, to swallow other people's misery, to eat my own bitterness" (241). She uses the tale of the magpies to indicate that one can either make the choice to be in charge of one's life or continue to let others be in control. For thousands of years magpies came to the fields of a group of peasants just after they had sown their seeds and watered them with their tears. The magpies ate the seeds and drank the tears. Then one day the peasants decided to end their suffering and silence. They clapped their hands and banged sticks together, making noise that startled and confused the magpies. This continued for days until the magpies died of hunger and exhaustion from waiting for the noise to stop so that they could land and eat. The sounds from the hands and sticks were their voices. Her daughter should face her tormentor.

An-mei tells stories of her pain, a pain she does not wish her daughter to endure. Memory is, in part, voices calling out to her, reminding her of what she has endured and of a relationship wished for: "it was her voice that confused me," "a familiar sound from a forgotten dream," "she cried with a wailing voice," "voices praising," "voices murmuring," "my mother's voice went away" (41-45). The voices of her mother confused her. She was a young girl in need of a mother's clear voice that would strengthen her circumstances and her context. The voices remind her, in "Scar," of wounds that heal but leave their imprint and of the importance of taking control out of the hands of those who have the ability to devour their victims, as in the story "Magpies." A scar resulting from a severe burn from a pot of boiling soup reminds her of when her mother was considered a ghost: her mother was dead to her family because she became a rich merchant's concubine. With time the scar "became pale and shiny and I had no memory of my mother. That is the way it is with a wound. The wound begins to close in on itself, to protect what is hurting so much. And once it is closed, you no longer see what is underneath, what started the pain" (40). It is also the way of persons attempting to assimilate—the wounds of getting to America, the wounds of hyphenation, close in on themselves and then it is difficult to see where it all began.

An-mei remembers the scar and the pain when her mother returns to her grandmother Poppo's deathbed. Upon the death of Poppo, she leaves with her mother, who shortly afterward commits suicide. Poppo tells An-mei that when a person loses face, it's like dropping a necklace down a well: the only way you can get it back is to jump in after it. From her mother An-mei learns that tears cannot wash away sorrows; they only feed someone else's joy. Her mother tells her to swallow her own tears.

An-mei knows strength and she knows forgetting. Perhaps that is why her daughter tells the story of her loss. It is Rose Hsu who tells the story of her brother's drowning and her mother's faith that he would be found. She refuses to believe that he is dead; without any driving lessons, she steers the car to the ocean side to search once more for him. After her son Bing's death, An-mei places the Bible that she has always carried to the First Chinese Baptist Church under a short table leg as a way of correcting the imbalances of life. She gives her daughter advice on how to correct imbalances in her life. The tale prefacing the section "Queen Mother of the Western Skies" is also a fitting message for Rose Hsu. A woman playing with her granddaughter wonders at the baby's happiness and laughter, remembering that she was once carefree before she shed her innocence and began to look critically and suspiciously at everything. She asks the babbling child if it is Syi Wang, Queen Mother of the Western Skies, come back to provide her with some answers: "Then you must teach my daughter this same lesson. How to lose your innocence but not your hope. How to laugh forever" (159).

Like all the other daughters, Lena must recognize and respect the characteristics of Lady Sorrowfree that are inherent in her mother, Ying-ying. Ying-ying describes her daughter as being devoid of wisdom. Lena laughs at her mother when she says "arty-tecky" (architecture) to her sister-in-law. Ying-ying admits that she should have slapped Lena more as a child for disrespect. Though Ying-ying serves as Lena's goddess, Lena initially does not view her mother as capable of advice on balance. Ying-ying's telling of her story is very important to seeing her in a true mothering role; her daughter's first story makes one think that the mother is mentally unbalanced.

Evelyn Reed in *Woman's Evolution* writes: "A mother's victimization does not merely humiliate her, it mutilates her daughter who watches her for clues as to what it means to be a woman. Like the traditional foot-bound Chinese woman, she passes on her affliction. The mother's self-hatred and low expectations are binding rags for the psyche of the daughter" (293). Ying-ying, whose name means "Clear Reflection," becomes a ghost. As a young girl she liked to unbraid her hair and wear it loose. She recalls a scolding from her mother, who once told her that she was like the lady ghosts at the bottom of the lake. Her daughter is unaware of her mother's previous marriage to a man in China twenty years before Lena's birth. Ying-ying falls in love with him because he strokes her cheek and tells her that she has tiger eyes, that they gather fire in the day and shine golden at night. Her husband opts to run off with another woman during her pregnancy, and she aborts the baby because she has come to hate her husband with a passion. Ying-ying tells Lena that she was born a tiger in a year when babies were dying, and because she was strong she survived. After ten years of reclusive living with cousins in the country, she goes to the city to live and work. There she meets Lena's father, an American she marries after being courted for four years, and continues to be a ghost. Ying-ying says that she willingly gave up her spirit.

In Ying-ying's first story, "The Moon Lady," when she sees her daughter lounging by the pool she realizes that they are lost, invisible creatures. Neither, at this point, recognizes the importance of "listening harder to the silence beneath their voices" (Maglin, 260). Their being lost reminds her of the family outing to Tai Lake as a child, when she falls into the lake, is rescued, and is put on shore only to discover that the moon lady she has been anxiously awaiting to tell her secret wish is male. The experience is so traumatic that she forgets her wish. Now that she is old and is watching her daughter, she remembers that she had wished to be found. And now she wishes for her daughter to be found—to find herself.

Lena, as a young girl, sees her mother being devoured by her fears until she becomes a ghost. Ying-ying believes that she is already a ghost. She does not want her daughter to become a ghost like her, "an unseen spirit" (285). Ying-ying begins life carefree. She is loved almost to a fault by her mother and her nursemaid, Amah. She is spoiled by her family's riches and wasteful. When she unties her hair and floats through the house, her mother tells her that she resembles the "lady ghosts . . . ladies who drowned in shame and floated in living people's houses with their hair undone to show everlasting despair" (276). She knows despair when the north wind that she thinks has blown her luck chills her heart by blowing her first husband past her to other women.

Lena, Ying-ying's daughter, is a partner in a marriage where she has a voice in the rules; but when the game is played, she loses her turn many times. Carolyn See argues that "in the name of feminism and right thinking, this husband is taking Lena for every cent she's got, but she's so demoralized, so 'out of balance' in the Chinese sense, that she can't do a thing about it" (11). In the introductory anecdote to the section "American Translation," a mother warns her daughter that she cannot put mirrors at the foot of the bed because all of her marriage happiness will bounce back and tumble the opposite way. Her mother takes from her bag a mirror that she plans to give the daughter as a wedding gift so that it faces the other mirror. The mirrors then reflect the happiness of the daughter. Lena's mother, as does Rose's mother, provides her with the mirror to balance her happiness; the mirror is a mother's advice or wisdom. It is Lena's mother's credo that a woman is out of balance if something goes against her nature. She does not want to be like her mother, but her mother foresees that she too will become a ghost; her husband will transform her according to his desires. Ying-ying recalls that she became "Betty" and was given a new date of birth by a husband who never learned to speak her language. Her review of her own story makes her know that she must influence her daughter's "story" that is in the making. Lena sees herself with her husband in the midst of problems so deep that she can't see where the bottom is. In the guise of a functional relationship is a dysfunctional one. Her mother predicts that the house will break into pieces. When a too-large vase on a too-weak table crashes to the floor, Lena admits that she knew it would happen. Her mother asks her why she did not take steps to keep the house from falling, meaning her marriage as well as the vase.

The goddess role becomes all-important to Ying-ying as she becomes more determined to prevent her daughter from becoming a ghost. She fights the daughter that she has raised, "watching from another shore" and "accept[ing] her American ways" (286). After she uses the sharp pain of what she knows to "penetrate [her] daughter's tough skin and cut the tiger spirit loose," she waits for her to come into the room, like a tiger waiting between the trees, and pounces. Ying-ying wins the fight and gives her daughter her spirit, "because this is the way a mother loves her daughter" (286). Lady Sorrowfree helps her "charge" achieve voice.

From the daughter with too much water, to the mother and daughter with too much wood, to the tiger ghosts and just plain ghosts, to the chess queens, Tan's women in *The Joy Luck Club* find themselves capable of forging their own identities, moving beyond passivity to assertiveness—speaking up. They are a piece of the portrait that represents Amy Tan's family history—her own story included; they are, in composite, her family's secrets and tragedies. Tan is unlike some Asian American writers who have had to try to piece together and sort out the meaning of the past from shreds of stories overheard or faded photographs. As in her stories, her mother tells her the stories and explains the photographs. Bell Gale Chevigny writes that "women writing about other women will symbolically reflect their internalized relations with their mothers and in some measure re-create them" (80). From Tan's own accounts, her interaction with her mother is reflected in her fiction.

Tan's women with their American husbands attempt often without knowing it to balance East and West, the past and the future of their lives. A level of transcendence is apparent in the storytelling, as it is in *The Kitchen God's Wife*. Mothers and daughters must gain from the storytelling in order to have healthy relationships with each other.

In *The Kitchen God's Wife*, Winnie Louie and her daughter Pearl Louie Brandt are both keepers of secrets that accent the distance that characterizes their relationship. Pearl thinks after a trip to her mother's home: "Mile after mile, all of it familiar, yet not this distance that separates us, me from my mother" (57). She is unsure of how this distance was created. Winnie says of their relationship: "That is how she is. That is how I am. Always careful to be polite, always trying not to bump into each other, just like strangers" (82). When their secrets begin to weigh down their friends who have known them for years, who threaten to tell each of the other's secrets, Winnie Louie decides that it is time for revelation. The process of the revelation is ritual: "recitation of the relationship between mother and daughter," "assessment of the relationship," and "the projection of the future into the relationship" (Koppelman, xxvii). At the same time revelation is a journey to voice, the voice that they must have with each other. Again, voice is a metaphor for speaking up, being heard, listening to be heard. No longer will stories begin as Pearl's does: "Whenever my mother talks to me, she begins the conversation as if we were already in the middle of an argument" (11). That they argue or are in conflict is not problematic; it is the "talks to" that should be replaced with "talks with." As much as Pearl needs to know her mother's secrets, Winnie Louie needs to tell them in order to build a relationship that is nurturing for both mother and daughter.

Pearl's secret is multiple sclerosis. At first she does not tell her mother because she fears her mother's theories on her illness. What becomes her secret is the anger she feels toward her father, the inner turmoil that began with his dying and death. Sometimes the mother's voice drowns the voice of the daughter as she attempts to control or explain every aspect of the daughter's existence. "If I had not lost my mother so young, I would not have listened to Old Aunt," says Winnie Louie (65) as she begins her story. These might also be the words of her daughter, though Pearl's loss of mother was not a physical loss. The opportunity for the resonating of mother and daughter voices seems to be the difference between balance and imbalance. American circumstances are to be blamed for the distance; the need to keep secrets grows out of the perceived necessity of assimilation and clean slates. Because her mother was not there, Winnie "listened to Old Aunt" (65).

Winnie Louie's dark secret begins with her mother, who disappeared without telling her why; she still awaits some appearance by her mother to explain. Her mother's story is also hers: an arranged marriage—in her mother's case, to curb her rebelliousness; realization that she has a lesser place in marriage than purported; and a daughter as the single lasting joy derived from the marriage. The difference is that Winnie's mother escaped, to be heard from no more.

Winnie's family abides by all of the customs in giving her hand in marriage to Wen Fu: "Getting married in those days was like buying real estate. Here you see a house you want to live in, you find a real estate agent. Back in China, you saw a rich family with a daughter, you found a go-between who knew how to make a good business deal" (134). Winnie tells her daughter, "If asked how I felt when they told me I would marry Wen Fu, I can only say this: It was like being told I had won a big prize. And it was also like being told my head was going to be chopped off. Something between those two feelings" (136). Winnie experiences very little mercy in her marriage to the monstrous Wen Fu.

Wen Fu serves as an officer in the Chinese army, so during World War II they move about China with other air force officers and their wives. Throughout the marriage, Winnie knows abuse and witnesses the death of her babies. She tries to free herself from the tyranny of the marriage, but her husband enjoys abusing her too much to let her go. Her story is a long one, a lifetime of sorrow, death, marriage, imprisonment, lost children, lost friends and family. Jimmie Louie saves her life by helping her to escape Wen Fu and to come to the United States. She loves Jimmie Louie and marries him. The darkest part of her secret she reveals to Pearl almost nonchalantly: Pearl is the daughter of the tyrant Wen Fu.

The daughter asks her mother: "Tell me again . . . why you had to keep it a secret." The mother answers: "Because then you would know. . . . You would know how weak I was. You would think I was a bad mother" (398). Winnie's actions and response are not unexpected. She is every mother who wants her daughter to think of her as having lived a blemish-free existence. She is every mother who forgets that her daughter is living life and knows blemishes. Secrets revealed, the women begin to talk. No longer does Winnie have to think that the year her second husband, Jimmie Louie, died was "when everyone stopped listening to me" (81). Pearl knows her mother's story and can respect her more, not less, for her endurance. She is then able to see a woman molded by her experiences and her secrets—a woman who has lived with two lives. With the tiptoeing around ended, the distance dissipates. By sharing their secrets, they help each other to achieve voice. The gift of Lady Sorrowfree is symbolic of their bonding; this goddess has all of the characteristics of the nurturing, caring, listening mother. Her imperfections lie in her creation; experiences make her. She has none of the characteristics of the Kitchen God.

The story of the Kitchen God and his wife angers Winnie Louie; she looks at the god as a bad man who was rewarded for admitting that he was a bad man. As the story goes, a wealthy farmer, Zhang, who had a good wife who saw to it that his farm flourished, brought home a pretty woman and made his wife cook for her. The pretty woman ran his wife off without any objection from the farmer. She helped him use up all of his riches foolishly and left him a beggar. He was discovered hungry and suffering by a servant who took him home to care for him. When he saw his wife, whose home it was, he attempted to hide in the kitchen fireplace; his wife could not save him. The Jade Emperor, because Zhang admitted he was wrong, made him Kitchen God with the duty to watch over people's behavior. Winnie tells Pearl that people give generously to the Kitchen God to keep him happy in the hopes that he will give a good report to the Jade Emperor. Winnie thinks that he is not the god for her daughter. How can one trust a god who would cheat on his wife? How can he be a good judge of behavior? The wife is the good one. She finds another god for her daughter's altar, Lady Sorrowfree. After all, she has already given her a father.

Even as Winnie tells her story, one senses that the women are unaware of the strength of the bond between them that partly originates in the biological connection and partly in their womanness. Storytelling/revealing secrets gives both of them the opportunity for review; Winnie Louie tells Pearl that she has taught her lessons with love, that she has combined all of the love that she had for the three she lost during the war and all of those that she did not allow to be born and has given it to Pearl. She speaks of her desire "to believe in something good" (152), her lost hope and innocence: "So I let those other babies die. In my heart I was being kind. . . . I was a young woman then. I had no more hope left, no trust, no innocence" (312). In telling her story, she does not ask for sympathy or forgiveness; she simply wants to be free of the pain that "comes from keeping everything inside, waiting until it is too late" (88).

Perhaps this goddess, Lady Sorrowfree, to whom they burn incense will cause them never to forget the importance of voice and listening. On the heels of listening there is balance as both Winnie and Pearl tell their secrets and are brought closer by them. East and West, mother and daughter, are bonded for the better. Arcana notes that "mother/daughter sisterhood is the consciousness we must seek to make this basic woman bond loving and fruitful, powerful and deep" (34). It ensures that women do not smother each other and squelch the voice of the other or cause each other to retreat into silence.

In exploring the problems of mother-daughter voices in relationships, Tan unveils some of the problems of biculturalism—of Chinese ancestry and American circumstances. She presents daughters who do not know their mothers' "importance" and thus cannot know their own; most seem never to have been told or even cared to hear their mothers' history. Until they do, they can never achieve voice. They assimilate; they marry American men and put on American faces. They adapt. In the meantime, their mothers sit like Lady Sorrowfree on her altar, waiting to listen. The daughters' journeys to voice are completed only after they come to the altars of their Chinese mothers.

Works Cited and Consulted

Arcana, Judith. *Our Mothers' Daughters*. Berkeley: Shameless Hussy Press, 1979.

Belensky, Mary Field, et al. *Women's Ways of Knowing*. New York: Basic Books, 1986.

Blicksilver, Edith. *The Ethnic American Woman: Problems, Protests, Lifestyle*. Dubuque, Ia.: Kendall/Hunt Publishing, 1978.

Carlson, Kathie. *In Her Image: The Unhealed Daughter's Search for Her Mother*. Boston: Shambhala, 1990.

Chevigny, Bell Gale. "Daughters Writing: Toward a Theory of Women's Biography." *Feminist Studies* 9 (1983): 79-102.

Chodorow, Nancy. *Feminism and Psychoanalytic Theory*. New Haven: Yale University Press, 1989.

Doten, Patti. "Sharing Her Mother's Secrets." *Boston Globe*, June 21, 1991, E9-14.

Friday, Nancy. *My Mother/My Self*. New York: Delacorte Press, 1977.

Gardiner, Judith Kegan. "Mind Mother: Psychoanalysis and Feminism." In *Making a Difference: Feminist Literary Criticism*, ed. Gayle Greene and Coppélia Kahn, 113-145. New York: Methuen, 1985.

Gilligan, Carol. *In a Different Voice*. Cambridge, Mass.: Harvard University Press, 1982.

Hirsch, Marianne. *The Mother-Daughter Plot: Narrative, Psychoanalysis, Feminism*. Bloomington: Indiana University Press, 1989.

Hirsch, Marianne, and Evelyn Fox Feller. *Conflicts in Feminism*. New York: Routledge, 1990.

Kim, Elaine H. *Asian American Literature: An Introduction to the Writings and Their Social Context*. Philadelphia: Temple University Press, 1982.

Koppelman, Susan. *Between Mothers and Daughters, Stories across a Generation*. New York: Feminist Press at the City University of New York, 1985.

Maglin, Nan Bauer. "The Literature of Matrilineage." In *The Lost Tradition: Mothers and Daughters in Literature*, ed. Cathy N. Davidson and E. M. Broner, 257-267. New York: Frederick Ungar, 1980.

Marbella, Jean. "Amy Tan: Luck but Not Joy." *Baltimore Sun*, June 30, 1991, E-11.

"Mother with a Past." *Maclean's* (July 15, 1991): 47.

Reed, Evelyn. *Woman's Evolution*. New York: Pathfinder Press, 1975.

Rich, Adrienne. *Of Woman Born: Motherhood as Experience and Institution*. New York: Norton, 1976, 1986.

Rosinsky, Natalie M. "Mothers and Daughters: Another Minority Group." In *The*

Lost Tradition: Mothers and Daughters in Literature, ed. Cathy N. Davidson and E. M. Broner, 281-303. New York: Frederick Ungar, 1980.

See, Carolyn. "Drowning in America, Starving in China." *Los Angeles Times Book Review*, March 12, 1989, 1, 11.

Spence, Jonathan D. *The Search for Modern China.* New York: W. W. Norton, 1990.

Tan, Amy. *The Joy Luck Club.* New York: Ivy Books, 1989.

_____. *The Kitchen God's Wife.* New York: G. P. Putnam's Sons, 1991.

_____. "Lost Lives of Women." *Life* (April 1991), 90-91.

Walters, Suzanna Danuta. *Lives Together/Worlds Apart: Mothers and Daughters in Popular Culture.* Berkeley: University of California Press, 1992.

Wolf, Margery, and Roxanne Witke. *Women in Chinese Society.* Stanford: Stanford University Press, 1975.

Yamada, Mitsuye. "Invisibility Is an Unnatural Disaster: Reflections of an Asian American Woman." In *This Bridge Called My Back: Writings of Radical Women of Color*, ed. Cherríe Moraga and Gloria Anzaldúa, 35-40. Latham, N.Y.: Kitchen Table/Women of Color Press, 1982.

Feng Shui, Astrology, and the Five Elements:
Traditional Chinese Belief in
Amy Tan's *The Joy Luck Club*_____

Patricia L. Hamilton

A persistent thematic concern in Amy Tan's *The Joy Luck Club* is the quest for identity. Tan represents the discovery process as arduous and fraught with peril. Each of the eight main characters faces the task of defining herself in the midst of great personal loss or interpersonal conflict. Lindo Jong recalls in "The Red Candle" that her early marriage into a family that did not want her shaped her character and caused her to vow never to forget who she was. Ying-ying St. Clair's story "Waiting Between the Trees" chronicles how betrayal, loss, and displacement caused her to become a "ghost." Rose Hsu Jordan recounts her effort to regain a sense of self and assert it against her philandering husband in "Without Wood." Framing all the other stories are a pair of linked narratives by Jing-mei Woo that describe her trip to China at the behest of her Joy Luck Club "aunties." The journey encompasses Jing-mei's attempts not only to understand her mother's tragic personal history but also to come to terms with her own familial and ethnic identity. In all the stories, whether narrated by the Chinese-born mothers or their American-born daughters, assertions of self are shaped by the cultural context surrounding them. However, there is a fundamental asymmetry in the mothers' and daughters' understanding of each other's native cultures. The mothers draw on a broad experiential base for their knowledge of American patterns of thought and behavior, but the daughters have only fragmentary, secondhand knowledge of China derived from their mothers' oral histories and from proverbs, traditions, and folktales.[1] Incomplete cultural knowledge impedes understanding on both sides, but it particularly inhibits the daughters from appreciating the delicate negotiations their mothers have performed to sustain their identities across two cultures.

Language takes on a metonymic relation to culture in Tan's portrayal of the gap between the mothers and daughters in *The Joy Luck Club*. Jing-mei, recalling that she talked to her mother Suyuan in English and that her mother answered back in Chinese, concludes that they "never really understood one another": "We translated each other's meanings and I seemed to hear less than what was said, while my mother heard more" (37). What is needed for any accurate translation of meanings is not only receptiveness and language proficiency but also the ability to supply implied or missing context. The daughters' inability to understand the cultural referents behind their mothers' words is nowhere more apparent than when the mothers are trying to inculcate traditional Chinese values and beliefs in their children. The mothers inherited from their families a centuries-old spiritual framework, which, combined with rigid social constraints regarding class and gender, made the world into an ordered place for them. Personal misfortune and the effects of war have tested the women's allegiance to traditional ideas, at times challenging them to violate convention in order to survive. But the very fact of their survival is in large measure attributable to their belief that people can affect their own destinies. In the face of crisis the mothers adhere to ancient Chinese practices by which they try to manipulate fate to their advantage. Their beliefs and values are unexpectedly reinforced by the democratic social fabric and capitalist economy they encounter in their adopted country. Having immigrated from a land where women were allowed almost no personal freedom, all the Joy Luck mothers share the belief along with Suyuan Woo that "you could be anything you wanted to be in America" (132).

Ironically, the same spirit of individualism that seems so liberating to the older women makes their daughters resistant to maternal advice and criticism. Born into a culture in which a multiplicity of religious beliefs flourishes and the individual is permitted, even encouraged, to challenge tradition and authority, the younger women are reluctant to accept their mothers' values without question. Jing-mei confesses that she used to dismiss her mother's criticisms as "just more of her Chinese superstitions, beliefs that conveniently fit the circumstances" (31). Furthermore, the daughters experience themselves socially as a recognizable ethnic minority and want to eradicate the sense of "difference" they feel among their peers. They endeavor to dissociate themselves from their mothers' broken English and Chinese mannerisms,[2] and they reject as nonsense the fragments of traditional lore their mothers try to pass along to them. However, cut adrift from any spiritual moorings, the younger women are overwhelmed by the number of choices that their materialistic culture offers and are insecure about their ability to perform satisfactorily in multiple roles ranging from dutiful Chinese daughter to successful American career woman. When it dawns on Jing-mei that the aunties see that "joy and luck do not mean the same to their daughters, that to these closed American-born minds 'joy luck' is not a word, it does not exist," she realizes that there is a profound difference in how the two generations understand fate, hope, and personal responsibility. Devoid of a worldview that endows reality with unified meaning, the daughters "will bear grandchildren born without any connecting hope passed from generation to generation" (41).

Tan uses the contrast between the mothers' and daughters' beliefs and values to show the difficulties first-generation immigrants face in transmitting their native culture to their offspring. Ultimately, Tan endorses the mothers' traditional Chinese worldview because it offers the possibility of choice and action in a world where paralysis is frequently a threat. However, readers who are not specialists in Chinese cosmology share the same problematic relation to the text as the daughters do to their mothers' native culture: they cannot always accurately translate meanings where the context is implied but not stated. Bits of traditional lore crop up in nearly every story, but divorced from a broader cultural context, they are likely to be seen as mere brushstrokes of local color or authentic detail. Readers may be tempted to accept at face value the daughters' pronouncements that their mothers' beliefs are no more than superstitious nonsense. To ensure that readers do not hear less than what Tan is actually saying about the mothers' belief systems and their identities, references to Chinese cosmology in the text require explication and elaboration.

Astrology is probably the element of traditional Chinese belief that is most familiar to Westerners. According to the Chinese astrological system, a person's character is determined by the year of his or her birth. Personality traits are categorized according to a twelve-year calendrical cycle based on the Chinese zodiac. Each year of the cycle is associated with a different animal, as in "the year of the dog." According to one legend, in the sixth century B.C. Buddha invited all the animals in creation to come to him, but only twelve showed up: the Rat, Ox, Tiger, Rabbit, Dragon, Snake, Horse, Ram, Monkey, Cock, Dog, and Pig. Buddha rewarded each animal with a year bearing its personality traits (Scott). In addition to animals, years are associated with one of the Five Elements: Wood, Fire, Earth, Metal, and Water. Metal years end in zero or one on the lunar calendar; Water years end in two or three; Wood years end in four or five; Fire years end in six or seven; and Earth years end in eight or nine. Thus, depending on the year in which one is born, one might be a Fire Dragon, a Water Dragon, and so on. The entire animal-and-element cycle takes sixty years to complete.

Tan draws on astrology in *The Joy Luck Club* in order to shape character and conflict. Lindo Jong, born in 1918, is a Horse, "destined to be obstinate and frank to the point of tactlessness," according to her daughter Waverly (167). Other adjectives that describe the Horse include diligent, poised, quick, eloquent, ambitious, powerful, and ruthless (Rossbach 168). At one point or another in the four Jong narratives, Lindo manifests all of these qualities, confirming her identity as a Horse. In accordance with tradition, Lindo's first husband is selected by his birth year as being a compatible partner for her. The matchmaker in "The Red Candle" tells Lindo's mother and mother-in-law: "An earth horse for an earth sheep. This is the best marriage combination" (50). At Lindo's wedding ceremony the matchmaker reinforces her point by speaking about "birthdates and harmony and fertility" (59). In addition to determining compatibility, birth years can be used to predict personality clashes. Waverly notes of her mother Lindo, "She and I make a bad combination, because I'm a Rabbit, born in 1951, supposedly sensitive, with tendencies toward being thin-skinned and skittery at the first sign of criticism" (167). Lindo's friend Suyuan Woo, born in 1915, is also a Rabbit. No doubt the Joy Luck aunties have this in mind when they note that Suyuan "died just like a rabbit: quickly and with unfinished business left behind" (19). The friction between Horse and Rabbit mentioned by Waverly suggests why Lindo and Suyuan were not only best friends but also "arch enemies who spent a lifetime comparing their children" (37).[3]

Adherents of Chinese astrology contend that auspicious dates for important events can be calculated according to predictable fluctuations of *ch'i*, the positive life force, which is believed to vary according to the time of day, the season, and the lunar calendar. Thus, the matchmaker chooses "a lucky day, the fifteenth day of the eighth moon," for Lindo's wedding (57). Later, Lindo picks "an auspicious day, the third day of the third month," to stage her scheme to free herself from her marriage. Unlucky dates can be calculated as well. Rose Hsu Jordan recalls that her mother An-mei had a "superstition" that "children were predisposed to certain dangers on certain days, all depending on their Chinese birthdate. It was explained in a little Chinese book called *The Twenty-Six Malignant Gates*" (124). The problem for An-mei is how to translate the Chinese dates into American ones. Since the lunar calendar traditionally used in China is based on moon cycles, the number of days in a year varies. Lindo similarly faces the problem of translating dates when she wants to immigrate to San Francisco, but her Peking friend assures her that May 11, 1918 is the equivalent of her birthdate, "three months after the Chinese lunar new year" (258). Accuracy on this point would allow Lindo to calculate auspicious dates according to the Gregorian calendar used in the West. In a broader sense, Lindo's desire for exactness is a strategy for preserving her identity in a new culture.

Tan uses astrology to greatest effect in the life history of Ying-ying

St. Clair, who does not fare at all well in the matter of translated dates or preserved identity. Ying-ying is a Tiger, born in 1914, "a very bad year to be born, a very good year to be a Tiger" (248). Tigers are typically passionate, courageous, charismatic, independent, and active, but they can also be undisciplined, vain, rash, and disrespectful (Jackson; Rossbach 167). Tiger traits are central to Ying-ying's character. As a teenager she is wild, stubborn, and vain. As a four-year-old in "The Moon Lady," she loves to run and shout, and she possesses a "restless nature" (72). According to Ruth Youngblood, "As youngsters [Tigers] are difficult to control, and if unchecked, can dominate their parents completely." Ying-ying's Amah tries to tame her into conformity to traditional Chinese gender roles: "Haven't I taught you—that it is wrong to think of your own needs? A girl can never ask, only listen" (70). Ying-ying's mother, too, admonishes her to curb her natural tendencies: "A boy can run and chase dragonflies, because that is his nature. But a girl should stand still" (72). By yielding to the social constraints placed on her gender and "standing perfectly still," Ying-ying discovers her shadow, the dark side of her nature that she learns to wield after her first husband leaves her.

Long before adulthood, however, Ying-ying experiences a trauma regarding her identity. Stripped of her bloodied Tiger outfit at the Moon Festival, she tumbles into Tai Lake and is separated from her family for several hours. Ying-ying's physical experience of being lost parallels her family's suppression of her active nature and curtailment of her freedom. Whenever she wears her hair loose, for example, her mother warns her that she will become like "the lady ghosts at the bottom of the lake" whose undone hair shows "their everlasting despair" (243). After Ying-ying falls into the lake, her braid becomes "unfurled," and as she drifts along in the fishing boat that picks her up, she fears that she is "lost forever" (79). When one of the fishermen surmises that she is a beggar girl, she thinks: "Maybe this was true. I had turned into a beggar girl, lost without my family" (80). Later she watches the Moon Lady telling her tragic story in a shadow play staged for the festival: "I understood her grief. In one small moment, we had both lost the world, and there was no way to get it back" (81). Even though Ying-ying is eventually rescued, she is afraid that her being found by her family is an illusion, "a wish granted that could not be trusted" (82). The temporary loss of her sense of security and belonging is so disturbing that her perception of her identity is forever altered. She is never able to believe her family has found "the same girl" (82).

Ying-ying's traumatic childhood experience prefigures the profound emotional loss and identity confusion she experiences as an adult. Looking back on her experience at the Moon Festival, she reflects that "it has happened many times in my life. The same innocence, trust, and restlessness, the wonder, fear, and loneliness. How I lost myself" (83). As an adult she is stripped of her Tiger nature once again when she immigrates to America. Since there is no immigration category for "the Chinese wife of a Caucasian citizen," Ying-ying is declared a "Displaced Person" (104). Then her husband proudly renames her "Betty St. Clair" without seeming to realize he is effacing her Chinese identity in doing so. The final stroke is his mistakenly writing the wrong year of birth on her immigration papers. As Ying-ying's daughter Lena puts it, "With the sweep of a pen, my mother lost her name and became a Dragon instead of a Tiger" (104). Unwittingly, Clifford St. Clair erases all signs of Ying-ying's former identity and, more importantly, symbolically denies her Tiger nature.

The belief that personality and character are determined by zodiacal influences imposes predictable and regular patterns onto what might otherwise seem random and arbitrary, thereby minimizing uncertainty and anxiety. In this light, the anchor for identity that astrology offers Ying-ying is beneficial. Over the years she comes to understand what her mother once explained about her Tiger nature: "She told me why a tiger is gold and black. It has two ways. The gold side leaps with its fierce heart. The black side stands still with cunning, hiding its gold between trees, seeing and not being seen, waiting patiently for things to come" (248). The certainty that these qualities are her birthright eventually guides Ying-ying into renouncing her habitual passivity. The catalyst for this decision is her perception that her daughter Lena needs to have her own "tiger spirit" cut loose. She wants Lena to develop fierceness and cunning so that she will not become a "ghost" like her mother or remain trapped in a marriage to a selfish man who undermines her worth. Ying-ying expects resistance from Lena, but because of the strength of her belief system, she is confident about the outcome: "She will fight me, because this is the nature of two tigers. But I will win and give her my spirit, because this the way a mother loves her daughter" (252). Tan uses the Chinese zodiacal Tiger as a potent emblem of the way culturally determined beliefs and expectations shape personal identity.

Another element of Chinese cosmology that Tan employs in *The Joy Luck Club* is *wu-hsing*, or the Five Elements, mentioned above in conjunction with astrology.[4] The theory of the Five Elements was developed by Tsou Yen about 325 B.C. As Holmes Welch notes, Tsou Yen "believed that the physical processes of the universe were due to the interaction of the five elements of earth, wood, metal, fire, and water" (96). According to eminent French sinologist Henri Maspero, theories such as the Five Elements, the Three Powers, and *yin* and *yang* all sought to "explain how the world proceeded all by itself through the play of transcendental, impersonal forces alone, without any intervention by one or more conscious wills" (55). Derek Walters specifies how the Five Elements are considered to "stimulate and shape all natural and human activity":

The Wood Element symbolizes all life, femininity, creativity, and organic material; Fire is the Element of energy and intelligence; Earth, the Element of stability, endurance and the earth itself; Metal, in addition to its material sense, also encompasses competitiveness, business acumen, and masculinity; while Water is the Element of all that flows—oil and alcohol as well as water itself, consequently also symbolizing transport and communication. (29)

The Elements correspond to certain organs of the body and physical ailments as well as to particular geometric shapes. An extended array of correspondences includes seasons, directions, numbers, colors, tastes, and smells (Lam 32). In the physical landscape the Elements can be placed in a productive order, in which each Element will generate and stimulate the one succeeding it, or a destructive order, in which Elements in close proximity are considered harmful. To avoid negative effects, a "controlling" Element can mediate between two elements positioned in their destructive order.

Suyuan Woo subscribes to a traditional application of the theory of the Five Elements in what Jing-mei calls her mother's "own version of organic chemistry" (31). As Ben Xu has observed, the Five Elements are "the mystical ingredients that determine every person's character flaw according to one's birth hour." *Wu-hsing* theory posits that "none of us has all the five character elements perfectly balanced, and therefore, every one of us is by nature flawed" (Xu 12). Accordingly, Suyuan believes that too much Fire causes a bad temper while too much Water makes someone flow in too many directions. Too little Wood results in one bending "too quickly to listen to other people's ideas, unable to stand on [one's] own" (31). Jing-mei, who does not understand how Suyuan's pronouncements tie to a larger belief system, associates her mother's theories with displeasure and criticism: "Something was always missing. Something always needed improving. Something was not in balance. This one or that had too much of one element, not enough of another."

According to *wu-hsing* theory, flaws can be amended and balance attained by symbolically adding the element a person lacks. Xu points out that "the 'rose' in Rose Hsu Jordan's name, for example, is supposed to add wood to her character" (12). Conversely, elements can be removed to create an imbalance. When Lindo Jong does not become pregnant in her first marriage, the matchmaker tells her mother-in-law: "A woman can have sons only if she is deficient in one of the elements. Your daughter-in-law was born with enough wood, fire, water, and earth, and she was deficient in metal, which was a good sign. But when she was married, you loaded her down with gold bracelets and decorations and now she has all the elements, including metal. She's too balanced to have babies" (63). Although Lindo knows that the direct cause of her failure to become pregnant is not her having too much metal but rather her husband's refusal to sleep with her, she accepts the matchmaker's reasoning about the Five Elements. Years later Lindo comments: "See the gold metal I can now wear. I gave birth to your brothers and then your father gave me these two bracelets. Then I had you [Waverly]" (66). The implication here is that the gender of Lindo's male children corresponds to her natural deficiency in Metal. Adding Metal back into her composition through the bracelets causes her next child to be female.

More significantly, Lindo, like Suyuan, believes that the Elements affect character traits: "After the gold was removed from my body, I felt lighter, more free. They say this is what happens if you lack metal. You begin to think as an independent person" (63). Tan suggests that Lindo's natural "imbalance" is key to her true identity, the self that she promises never to forget. As a girl she had determined to honor the marriage contract made by her parents, even if it meant sacrificing her sense of identity. But on her wedding day she wonders "why [her] destiny had been decided, why [she] should have an unhappy life so someone else could have a happy one" (58). Once Lindo's gold and jewelry are repossessed by her mother-in-law to help her become fertile, Lindo begins to plot her escape from the marriage. Her feeling lighter and more free without Metal corresponds to her assertion of her true identity. Destiny is not so narrowly determined that she cannot use her natural qualities as a Horse—quickness, eloquence, ruthlessness—to free herself from her false position in the marriage. Because Lindo has secretly blown out the matchmaker's red candle on her wedding night, she has in effect rewritten her fate without breaking her parents' promise. Rather than restricting her identity, her belief in astrology and *wuhsing* gives her a secure base from which to express it.

As with astrology, Tan uses the theory of the Five Elements not only for characterization but also for the development of conflict in *The Joy Luck Club*. "Without Wood" deals with the disastrous effects of Rose Hsu Jordan's not having enough Wood in her personality, at least according to her mother An-mei's diagnosis. An-mei herself has inspired "a lifelong stream of criticism" from Suyuan Woo, apparently for bending too easily to others' ideas, the flaw of those who lack Wood (30-31). An-mei admits to having listened to too many people when she was young. She almost succumbed to her family's urgings to forget her mother, and later she was nearly seduced by the pearl necklace offered to her by her mother's rival. Experience has shown An-mei that people try to influence others for selfish reasons. To protect her daughter from opportunists, An-mei tells Rose that she must listen to her mother if she wants to grow "strong and straight." If she listens to others she will grow "crooked and weak." But Rose comments, "By the time she told me this, it was too late. I had already begun to bend" (191).

Rose attributes her compliant nature to the strict disciplinary measures of an elementary school teacher and to the influences of American culture: "Chinese people had Chinese opinions. American people had American opinions. And in almost every case, the American version was much better" (191). Not until much later does she realize that in the "American version" there are "too many choices," so that it is "easy to get confused and pick the wrong thing." Rose, emotionally paralyzed at fourteen by a sense that she is responsible for the death of her four-year-old brother, grows into an adult who not only listens to others but lets them take responsibility for her so that she may avoid committing another fatal error. Her husband, Ted, makes all the decisions in their marriage until a mistake of his own brings on a malpractice suit and shakes his self-confidence. When Ted abruptly demands a divorce, Rose's lack of Wood manifests itself: "I had been talking to too many people, my friends, everybody it seems, except Ted" (188). She tells a "different story" about the situation to Waverly, Lena, and her psychiatrist, each of whom offers a different response. An-mei chides Rose for not wanting to discuss Ted with her, but Rose is reluctant to do so because she fears that An-mei will tell her she must preserve her marriage, even though there is "absolutely nothing left to save" (117).

Contrary to Rose's expectations, her mother is less concerned that she stay married than that she deal with her inability to make decisions. An-mei wants her daughter to address the personality deficiencies that are the cause of her circumstances. Believing that Rose needs to assert her identity by acting on her own behalf, An-mei admonishes: "You must think for yourself, what you must do. If someone tells you, then you are not trying" (130). An-mei's advice is embedded in the broader context of her Chinese worldview. When Rose complains that she has no hope, and thus no reason to keep trying to save her marriage, An-mei responds: "This is not hope. Not reason. This is your fate. This is your life, what you must do" (130). An-mei believes life is determined by fate, by immutable celestial forces. But like Lindo Jong, she sees fate as having a participatory element. Earthly matters admit the influence of human agency. Consequently, her admonition to Rose is focused on what Rose must "do."

As a child Rose observes that both her parents believe in their *neng-kan*, the ability to do anything they put their minds to. This belief has not only brought them to America but has "enabled them to have seven children and buy a house in the Sunset district with very little money" (121). Rose notes that by taking into account all the dangers described in *The Twenty-Six Malignant Gates*, An-mei has "absolute faith she could prevent every one of them" (124).

However, An-mei's optimism about her ability to manipulate fate is challenged when her youngest child, Bing, drowns. An-mei does everything she can to recover her son, but she realizes she cannot "use faith to change fate" (130). Tragedy teaches her that forethought is not the same thing as control. Still, she wedges a white Bible—one in which Bing's name is only lightly pencilled in under "Deaths"— beneath a short table leg as a symbolic act, "a way for her to correct the imbalances of life" (116). Although An-mei accepts that her power over fate is limited, she continues to believe that she can positively influence her circumstances. The idea of balance she is enacting is a fundamental element of *yin-yang* philosophy, according to which two complementary forces "govern the universe and make up all aspects of life and matter" (Rossbach 21). As Johndennis Govert notes, "to remove an obstruction to your happiness, regain a state of health, or create a more harmonious household, *yin* and *yang* must be in balance" (7). An-mei may use a Bible to balance the kitchen table, but she rejects the Christian beliefs it represents. Rose notes that her mother loses "her faith in God" after Bing's death (116). The belief system that governs An-mei's actions is Chinese, an amalgam of luck, house gods, ancestors, and all the elements in balance, "the right amount of wind and water" (122).

In contrast to her mother, Rose lacks a means by which she can delineate or systematize her notions of causality and responsibility. Moreover, she eschews any real sense that people can have control over their circumstances. As a teenager Rose is appalled to discover she is powerless to prevent little Bing from falling into the ocean as she watches. Later Rose thinks "that maybe it was fate all along, that faith was just an illusion that somehow you're in control. I found out the most I could have was hope, and with that I was not denying any possibility, good or bad" (121). When her husband Ted wants a divorce, Rose compares the shock she receives to having the wind knocked out of her: "And after you pick yourself up, you realize you can't trust anybody to save you—not your husband, not your mother, not God. So what can you do to stop yourself from tilting and falling all over again?" (121). Added to her sense of helplessness is the suspicion that whenever she is forced into making a decision, she is walking through a minefield: "I never believed there was ever any one right answer, yet there were many wrong ones" (120). Rose's lack of any sort of a belief system fosters a crippling passivity characterized by a fear that whatever she chooses will turn out badly. Her inability to make even the smallest decisions becomes the equivalent, in Ted's mind at least, of her having no identity.

Ironically, once Rose realizes that Ted has taken away all her choices, she begins to fight back. She seizes on the metaphor An-mei has used to explain the lack of Wood in her personality: "If you bend to listen to other people, you will grow crooked and weak. You will fall to the ground with the first strong wind. And then you will be like a weed, growing wild in any direction, running along the ground until someone pulls you out and throws you away" (191). Inspired by the weeds in her own neglected garden that cannot be dislodged from the masonry without "pulling the whole building down" (195), Rose demands that Ted let her keep their house. She explains, "You can't just pull me out of your life and throw me away" (196). For the first time in her life she stands up for what she wants without soliciting the advice of others. After her assertion of selfhood, Rose dreams that her "beaming" mother has planted weeds that are "running wild in every direction" in her planter boxes (196). This image, which suggests that An-mei has finally accepted Rose's nature instead of trying to change her, is consistent with the desires the Joy Luck daughters share regarding their mothers. Each one struggles to feel loved for who she is. In part the younger women's insecurity stems from having a different set of cultural values than their mothers. The older women try to encourage their daughters but do not always know how to cope with the cultural gap that separates them. As Lindo states: "I wanted my children to have the best combination: American circumstances and Chinese character. How could I know these two things do not mix?" (254). But Rose's dream-image submerges the fact that Rose has finally acted on her mother's admonition to speak up for herself. An-mei has guessed that Ted is engaged in "monkey business" with another woman, and it is at the moment when Rose realizes her mother is right that she begins to move intuitively toward standing up for her own needs and desires. As it turns out, An-mei is correct in wanting Rose to listen to her mother rather than to her bored and sleepy-eyed psychiatrist in order to be "strong and straight." Ultimately, An-mei's belief that one's fate involves making choices instead of being paralyzed as a victim is validated by Rose's assertion of her identity.

A third element of traditional belief in *The Joy Luck Club* is *feng shui*, or geomancy. The most opaque yet potentially the most important aspect of Chinese cosmology to Tan's exploration of identity, *feng shui* plays a pivotal role in Lena St. Clair's story "The Voice from the Wall," which chronicles her mother Ying-ying's gradual psychological breakdown and withdrawal from life. Ten-year-old Lena, having no knowledge of her mother's past, becomes convinced that her mother is crazy as she listens to Ying-ying rave after the death of her infant son. Even before Ying-ying loses her baby, however, her behavior appears to be erratic and compulsive. When the family moves to a new apartment, Ying-ying arranges and rearranges the furniture in an effort to put things in balance. Although Lena senses her mother is disturbed, she dismisses Ying-ying's explanations as "Chinese nonsense" (108). What Lena does not understand is that her mother is practicing the ancient Chinese art of *feng shui* (pronounced "fung shway"). Translated literally as "wind" and "water," *feng shui* is alluded to only once in the book as An-mei Hsu's balance of "the right amount of wind and water" (122). Although the term "*feng shui*" is never used overtly in conjunction with Ying-ying St. Clair, its tenets are fundamental to her worldview.

Stephen Skinner defines *feng shui* as "the art of living in harmony with the land, and deriving the greatest benefit, peace and prosperity from being in the right place at the right time" (4). The precepts of *feng shui* were systematized by two different schools in China over a thousand years ago. The Form School, or intuitive approach, was developed by Yang Yün-Sung (c. 840-888 A.D.) and flourished in Kiangsi and Anhui provinces. Practitioners focus on the visible form of the landscape, especially the shapes of mountains and the direction of watercourses. The Compass School, or analytical approach, was developed by Wang Chih in the Sung dynasty (960 A.D.) and spread throughout Fukien and Chekiang provinces as well as Hong Kong and Taiwan (Skinner 26). The analytic approach is concerned with directional orientation in conjunction with Chinese astrology. As Walters notes, Compass School scholars have traditionally "placed greater emphasis on the importance of precise mathematical calculations, and compiled elaborate formulae and schematic diagrams" (10). Geomancers using this approach employ an elaborate compass called the *lo p'an*, astrological charts and horoscopes, numerological data, and special rulers.

According to Susan Hornik, the beliefs encompassed by *feng shui* date back 3,000 years to the first practice of selecting auspicious sites for burial tombs in order to "bring good fortune to heirs" (73). As Skinner explains, "Ancestors are linked with the site of their tombs. As they also have a direct effect on the lives of their descendants, it follows logically that if their tombs are located favourably on the site of a strong concentration of earth energy or *ch'i*, not only will they be happy but they will also derive the power to aid their descendants, from the accumulated *ch'i* of the site" (11). By the Han dynasty (206 B.C.), the use of *feng shui* was extended to the selection of dwellings for the living (Hornik 73). The basic idea is to attract and channel *ch'i*, or beneficial energy, and "accumulate it without allowing it to go stagnant" (Skinner 21). Since *ch'i* encourages growth and prosperity, a wise person will consider how to manipulate it to best effect through *feng shui*, the study of placement with respect to both natural and man-made environments. As a form of geomancy *feng shui* is "the exact complement of astrology, which is divination by signs in the Heavens" (Walters 12), but it is based on a different presupposition. Whereas the course of the stars and planets is fixed, the earthly environment can be altered by human intervention through *feng shui*. The practice of *feng shui* offers yet another variation of the belief that people have the power to affect their destiny.

Thus Ying-ying St. Clair's seemingly idiosyncratic actions and their nonsensical explanations in "The Voice from the Wall" are grounded in a coherent system of beliefs and practices concerned with balancing the environment. Since Ying-ying feels her surroundings are out of balance, she does everything she can to correct them. For instance, she moves "a large round mirror from the wall facing the front door to a wall by the sofa" (108). *Ch'i* is believed to enter a dwelling through the front door, but a mirror hung opposite the entrance may deflect it back outside again. Mirrors require careful placement so as to encourage the flow of *ch'i* around a room. Furniture, too, must be positioned according to guidelines that allow beneficial currents of *ch'i* to circulate without stagnating. Through properly placed furniture "every opportunity can be taken to correct whatever defects may exist, and to enhance whatever positive qualities there are" (Walters 46). Hence, Ying-ying rearranges the sofa, chairs, and end tables, seeking the best possible grouping. Even a "Chinese scroll of goldfish" is moved. When large-scale changes are impossible, *feng shui* practitioners frequently turn to symbolic solutions. Strategically placed aquariums containing goldfish are often prescribed for structural problems that cannot be altered, in part because aquariums symbolically bring all Five Elements together into balance (Collins 21). In Ying-ying's case, a picture is substituted for live goldfish, which represent life and growth.

Ying-ying's attempt to balance the living room follows a *feng shui* tradition: "If beneficial *ch'i* are lacking from the heart of the house, the family will soon drift apart" (Walters 42). But Ying-ying is also compensating for negative environmental and structural features that she cannot modify. The apartment in the new neighborhood is built on a steep hill, a poor site, she explains, because "a bad wind from the top blows all your strength back down the hill. So you can never get ahead. You are always rolling backward" (109). In ancient China the ideal location for a building was in the shelter of hills that would protect it from bitter northerly winds. However, a house at the very base of a sloping road would be vulnerable to torrential rains, mudslides, and crashes caused by runaway carts. Ying-ying's concern with psychic rather than physical danger is consistent with modern applications of *feng shui*, but her notion of an ill wind sweeping downhill is based on traditional lore. In addition to the unfortunate location of the apartment building, its lobby is musty, a sign that it does not favor the circulation of *ch'i*. The door to the St. Clairs' apartment is narrow, "like a neck that has been strangled" (109), further restricting the entrance of beneficial energy. Moreover, as Ying-ying tells Lena, the kitchen faces the toilet room, "so all your worth is flushed away." According to the Bagua map derived from the *I Ching*, the ancient Chinese book of divination, every building and every room has eight positions that correspond to various aspects of life: wealth and prosperity; fame and reputation; love and marriage; creativity and children; helpful people and travel; career; knowledge and self-cultivation; and health and family (Collins 61-62). Heidi Swillinger explains the problem of a dwelling where the bathroom is located in the wealth area: "Because the bathroom is a place where water enters and leaves, and because water is a symbol of wealth, residents in such a home might find that money tends to symbolically go down the drain or be flushed away."[5] Even if the St. Clairs' bathroom is not actually in the wealth area, *feng shui* guidelines dictate that it should not be placed next to the kitchen in order to avoid a clash between two of the symbolic Elements, Fire and Water.

In light of the bad *feng shui* of the apartment, Ying-ying's unhappiness with it is logical. Once she finishes altering the living room, she rearranges Lena's bedroom. The immediate effect of the new configuration is that "the nighttime life" of Lena's imagination changes (109). With her bed against the wall, she begins to listen to the private world of the family next door and to use what she hears as a basis for comparison with her own family. It is not clear whether Lena's bed has been moved to the "children" area of the room, which would enhance her *ch'i*, but certainly the new position is more in keeping with the principles of good *feng shui*, which indicate a bed should be placed against a wall, not a window (Walters 53). From this standpoint, Ying-ying's inauspicious positioning of the crib against the window appears to be inconsistent with her other efforts. Lena notes, "My mother began to bump into things, into table edges as if she forgot her stomach contained a baby, as if she were headed for trouble instead" (109). Since according to *feng shui* theory protruding corners are threatening (Collins 47), Ying-ying's peculiar neglect toward sharp table edges along with her placement of the crib suggest that her efforts at generating good *feng shui* are suspended with regard to her unborn baby.

When the baby dies at birth, apparently from a severe case of hydrocephalus and spina bifida, Ying-ying blames herself: "My fault, my fault. I knew this before it happened. I did nothing to prevent it" (111). To Western ears her self-accusation sounds odd, for birth defects such as spina bifida are congenital, and nothing Ying-ying could have done would have prevented the inevitable. However, her Eastern worldview dictates that fate can be manipulated in order to bring about good effects and to ward off bad ones. Ying-ying believes that her violation of good *feng shui* principles constitutes negligence, causing the baby to die. She is accusing herself not merely of passivity but of deliberate complicity with a malignant fate.

The burden of guilt Ying-ying carries over an abortion from her first marriage is the root of her disturbed mental state during her pregnancy. Her bumping into table edges may even be a form of self-punishment. In any case, whether she has subconsciously tried to harm the fetus or has merely failed to fend off disaster through the use of *feng shui*, in blaming herself for the baby's death Ying-ying is clearly wrestling with her responsibility for the death of her first son. In her mind the two events are connected: "I knew he [the baby] could see everything inside me. How I had given no thought to killing my other son! How I had given no thought to having this baby" (112). Instead of finding any resolution after the baby dies, Ying-ying becomes increasingly withdrawn. She cries unaccountably in the middle of cooking dinner and frequently retreats to her bed to "rest."

The presence of *feng shui* in the story suggests that however displaced, demoralized, and severely depressed Ying-ying may be, she is not "crazy," as Lena fears. Ying-ying's compulsion to rearrange furniture does not presage a psychotic break with reality but rather signals that, transplanted to a foreign country where she must function according to new rules and expectations, Ying-ying relies on familiar practices such as *feng shui* and astrology to interpret and order the world around her, especially when that world is in crisis. Lena, of course, is locked into a ten-year-old's perspective and an American frame of reference. She shares Jing-mei Woo's problem of being able to understand her mother's Chinese words but not their meanings. Whereas Clifford St. Clair's usual practice of "putting words" in his wife's mouth stems from his knowing "only a few canned Chinese expressions" (106), Lena's faulty translation of her mother's distracted speech after the baby dies reflects a lack of sufficient personal and cultural knowledge to make sense of Ying-ying's references to guilt.

Ying-ying's story, "Waiting Between the Trees," traces the origins of her decline to a much earlier time. At sixteen Ying-ying is married to a man who impregnates her, then abandons her for an opera singer. Out of grief and anger, she induces an abortion. However, after this defiant act she loses her strength, becoming "like the ladies of the lake" her mother had warned her about, floating like "a dead leaf on the water" (248-49). Unfortunately, Ying-ying's Tiger characteristic of "waiting patiently for things to come" (248) turns from easy acceptance of whatever is offered into listlessness and acquiescence over a period of fourteen years: "I became pale, ill, and more thin. I let myself become a wounded animal" (251). She confesses, "I willingly gave up my *chi*, the spirit that caused me so much pain" (251). Giving up her vital energy is tantamount to giving up her identity. By the time Clifford St. Clair takes her to America, she has already become "an unseen spirit," with no trace of her former passion and energy. Nevertheless, she retains her ability to see things before they happen. Her prescience stems from her trust in portents, which constitutes another facet of her belief system. When she is young, a flower that falls from its stalk tells her she will marry her first husband. Later on, Clifford St. Clair's appearance in her life is a sign that her "black side" will soon go away. Her husband's death signals that she can marry St. Clair.

Years later, Ying-ying can still see portents of the future. She knows Lena's is "a house that will break into pieces" (243). Ying-ying also continues to think in terms of *feng shui*. She complains that the guest room in Lena's house has sloping walls, a fact which implies the presence of sharp angles that can harbor *sha*, malignant energy signifying death and decay. With walls that close in like a coffin, the room is no place to put a baby, Ying-ying observes. But it is not until Ying-ying sees her daughter's unhappy marriage that she accepts responsibility for the fact that Lena has no *ch'i* and determines to regain her own fierce spirit in order to pass it on to her daughter. Ying-ying knows she must face the pain of her past and communicate it to her daughter so as to supply Lena with the personal and cultural knowledge of her mother's life that she has always lacked. By recounting her life's pain, Ying-ying will in essence reconstruct her lost identity. To set things in motion, she decides to topple the spindly-legged marble table in the guest room so that Lena will come to see what is wrong. In this instance Ying-ying manipulates her environment in a literal as well as a symbolic sense, drawing on her traditional Chinese worldview once more in order to effect the best outcome for her daughter's life.

Unlike her mother, Lena has no consistent belief system of her own. She inherits Ying-ying's ability to see bad things before they happen but does not possess the power to anticipate good things, which suggests that Lena has merely internalized "the unspoken terrors" that plague Ying-ying (103). According to Philip Langdon, "second- or third-generation Chinese-Americans are much less likely to embrace *feng shui* than are those who were born in Asia" (148). Not only is Lena a second-generation Chinese-American, she is half Caucasian, which makes her Chinese heritage even more remote. Nonetheless, Lena is profoundly affected by Ying-ying's way of perceiving the world. As a child Lena is obsessed with knowing the worst possible thing that can happen, but unlike her mother, she has no sense of being able to manipulate fate. Thus, she is terrified when she cannot stop what she supposes to be the nightly "killing" of the girl next door, which she hears through her bedroom wall. Only after Lena realizes that she has been wrong about the neighbor family does she find ways to change the "bad things" in her mind.

Lena's muddled notions of causality and responsibility persist into adulthood. In "Rice Husband," she still views herself as guilty for the death of Arnold Reisman, a former neighbor boy, because she "let one thing result from another" (152). She believes there is a relation between her not having cleaned her plate at meals when she was young and Arnold's development of a rare and fatal complication of measles. She wants to dismiss the link as ridiculous, but she is plagued by doubt because she has no philosophical or religious scheme by which to interpret events and establish parameters for her personal responsibility: "The thought that I could have caused Arnold's death is not so ridiculous. Perhaps he was destined to be my husband. Because I think to myself, even today, how can the world in all its chaos come up with so many coincidences, so many similarities and exact opposites?" (154). Whereas Ying-ying's belief system affords her a sense of certainty about how the world operates, Lena's lack of such a system leaves her in confusion.

It is Lena's uncertainty about causality together with her failure to take purposive action that leads Ying-ying to believe her daughter has no *ch'i*. Lena tells herself, "When I want something to happen—or not happen—I begin to look at all events and all things as relevant, an opportunity to take or avoid" (152). But Ying-ying challenges her, asking why, if Lena knew the marble table was going to fall down, she did not stop it. By analogy she is asking Lena why she does not resolve to save her marriage. Lena muses, "And it's such a simple question" (165). It is unclear whether Lena has already decided not to rescue the marriage or whether she is simply confused about her capacity to act on her own behalf. But the fact that Lena cannot answer her mother's question quietly privileges Ying-ying's perspective on the situation, much as Anmei's viewpoint of Rose's predicament is validated in "Without Wood."

Marina Heung has pointed out that among works which focus on mother-daughter relations, *The Joy Luck Club* is "remarkable for foregrounding the voices of mothers as well as of daughters" (599). However, Tan goes further than "foregrounding" the mothers; she subtly endorses their worldview at strategic points in the text. Whereas Rose, Lena, and Jing-mei are paralyzed and unable to move forward in their relationships and careers and Waverly is haunted by a lingering fear of her mother's disapproval, Suyuan, Lindo, An-mei, and even Ying-ying demonstrate a resilient belief in their power to act despite having suffered the ravages of war and the painful loss of parents, spouses, and children. Out of the vast range of Chinese religious, philosophical, and folkloric beliefs, many of which stress self-effacement and passivity, Tan focuses on practices that allow her characters to make adjustments to their destinies and thereby preserve and perpetuate their identities. Suyuan Woo is most striking in this regard. She goes outside of conventional Chinese beliefs to make up her own means of dealing with fate. Suyuan invents "Joy Luck," whereby she and her friends in Kweilin "choose [their] own happiness" at their weekly mah jong parties instead of passively waiting for their own deaths (25). Joy Luck for them consists of forgetting past wrongs, avoiding bad thoughts, feasting, laughing, playing games, telling stories, and most importantly, hoping to be lucky. The ritualistic set of attitudes and actions that Suyuan and her friends observe keep them from succumbing to despair. When the war is over, Suyuan holds on to the main tenet of her belief system—that "hope was our only joy"—by refusing to assume a passive role in the aftermath of tragedy. She never gives up hope that by persistence she may be able to locate the infant daughters she left in China. When Suyuan says to Jing-mei, "You don't even know little percent of me!" (27), she is referring to the complex interplay among the events of her life, her native culture and language, and her exercise of her mind and will. These things constitute an identity that Jing-mei has only an elusive and fragmentary knowledge of.

The references in *The Joy Luck Club* to traditional beliefs and practices such as astrology, *wu-hsing*, and *feng shui* emphasize the distance between the Chinese mothers and their American-born daughters. Tan hints through the stories of Lindo and Waverly Jong that a degree of reconciliation and understanding is attainable between mothers and daughters, and she indicates through Jing-mei Woo's journey that cultural gaps can be narrowed. In fact, Jing-mei Woo starts "becoming Chinese" as soon as she crosses the border into China (267). But overall, Tan's portrayal of first-generation immigrants attempting to transmit their native culture to their offspring is full of situations where "meanings" are untranslatable. The breakdown in communication between mothers and daughters is poignantly encapsulated in "American Translation," the vignette that introduces the third group of stories in the book. A mother tells her daughter not to put a mirror at the foot of her bed: "'All your marriage happiness will bounce back and turn the opposite way'" (147). Walters notes that mirrors are "regarded as symbols of a long and happy marriage" but also that "care has to be taken that they are not so placed that they are likely to alarm the soul of a sleeper when it rises for nocturnal wanderings" (55). According to *feng shui* principles, a mirror "acts as a constant energy reflector and will be sending [a] stream of intensified power into the space over and around [the] bed, day and night. It will be a perpetual cause of disturbance" during sleep (Lam 105). The daughter in the vignette is "irritated that her mother s[ees] bad omens in everything. She had heard these warnings all her life." Lacking an understanding of the cosmological system to which her mother's omens belong, the daughter simply views them as evidence that her mother has a negative outlook on life.

When the woman offers a second mirror to hang above the headboard of the bed in order to remedy the problem, she is seeking to properly channel the flow of *ch'i* around the room. The mother comments, "this mirror see that mirror—*haule!*—multiply your peach-blossom luck." The daughter, however, does not understand her mother's allusion to peach-blossom luck, which "refers to those who are particularly attractive to the opposite sex" (Rossbach 48). By way of explanation, the mother, "mischief in her eyes," has her daughter look in the mirror to see her future grandchild. She is acting in accordance to the ancient Chinese belief that the "mysterious power of reflection" of mirrors, which reveal "a parallel world beyond the surface," is magical (Walters 55). The daughter, unfortunately, can only grasp literal meanings: "The daughter looked—and *haule!* There it was: her own reflection looking back at her." The mother is incapable of translating her worldview into "perfect American English," so the daughter's comprehension remains flawed, partial, incomplete. Whether or not she apprehends, from her literal reflection, that she herself is the symbol of her mother's own peach-blossom luck is ambiguous. In the same way, the uneasy relations between the older and younger women in *The Joy Luck Club* suggest that the daughters understand only dimly, if at all, that they are the long-cherished expression of their mothers' Joy Luck.

Notes

1. For a discussion of existential unrepeatability and the role of memory in *The Joy Luck Club*, see Ben Xu, "Memory and the Ethnic Self: Reading Amy Tan's *The Joy Luck Club*," *MELUS* 19.1 (1994): 3-18. An interesting treatment of language, storytelling, and maternal subjectivity in Tan's novel can be found in Marina Heung, "Daughter-Text/Mother-Text: Matrilineage in Amy Tan's *Joy Luck Club*," *Feminist Studies* 19.3 (1993): 597-616.

2. Jing-mei Woo thinks her mother's "telltale Chinese behaviors" are expressly intended to embarrass her, including Suyuan's predilection for yellow, pink, and bright orange (143, 267). When Jing-mei arrives in China, she notices "little children wearing pink and yellow, red and peach," the only spots of bright color amidst drab grays and olive greens (271). Tan seems to suggest through this detail that Suyuan's color preferences reflect not only her personal taste but Chinese patterns and traditions. According to Sarah Rossbach, yellow stands for power, pink represents "love and pure feelings," and orange suggests "happiness and power" (46-47). In this light, Lindo Jong's criticism of Suyuan's red sweater in "Best Quality" is ironic since it is Lindo who provides evidence that red is regarded by the Chinese as an auspicious color connoting "happi-

ness, warmth or fire, strength, and fame" (Rossbach 45). In "The Red Candle" Lindo mentions not only her mother's jade necklace and her mother-in-law's pillars, tables, and chairs but also her own wedding banners, palanquin, dress, scarf, special eggs, and marriage candle as being red.

3. Jing-mei Woo, born in the same year as Waverly (37), is a Metal Rabbit, and like Waverly, she exhibits a "Rabbit-like" sensitivity to criticism, especially when it comes from her mother.

4. The Chinese system of astrology has Buddhist origins, while the theory of the Five Elements derives from Taoist thought. Holmes Welch observes that "there was little distinction—and the most intimate connections—between early Buddhism and Taoism" (119).

5. Similar reasoning obtains in "Rice Husband" when Ying-ying tells Lena that a bank will have all its money drained away after a plumbing and bathroom fixtures store opens across the street from it (149). Lena comments that "one month later, an officer of the bank was arrested for embezzlement."

Works Cited

Collins, Terah Kathryn. *The Western Guide to Feng Shui*. Carlsbad, CA: Hay House, 1996.

Govert, Johndennis. *Feng Shui: Art and Harmony of Place*. Phoenix: Daikakuji, 1993.

Heung, Marina. "Daughter-Text/Mother-Text: Matrilineage in Amy Tan's *Joy Luck Club*." *Feminist Studies* 19.3 (1993): 597-616.

Hornik, Susan. "How to Get that Extra Edge on Health and Wealth." *Smithsonian* Aug. 1993: 70-75.

Jackson, Dallas. "Chinese Astrology." *Los Angeles Times* 20 Feb. 1991, Orange County ed.: E2. *News*. Online. Lexis-Nexis. 15 Mar. 1997.

Lam, Kam Chuen. *Feng Shui Handbook*. New York: Henry Holt, 1996.

Langdon, Philip. "Lucky Houses." *Atlantic* Nov. 1991: 146+.

Maspero, Henri. *Taoism and Chinese Religion*. Trans. Frank A. Kierman, Jr. Amherst: U of Massachusetts P, 1981.

Rossbach, Sarah. *Living Color: Master Lin Yun's Guide to Feng Shui and the Art of Color*. New York: Kodansha, 1994.

Scott, Ann. "Chinese New Year: The Year of the Tiger." *United Press International* 5 Feb. 1986, International sec. *News*. Online. Lexis-Nexis. 15 Mar. 1997.

Skinner, Stephen. *The Living Earth Manual of Feng-Shui*. London: Routledge, 1982.

Swillinger, Heidi. "Feng Shui: A Blueprint for Balance." *San Francisco Chronicle* 8 Sept. 1993: Z1. *News*. Online. Lexis-Nexis. 15 Mar. 1997.

Tan, Amy. *The Joy Luck Club*. New York: G.P. Putnam, 1989.

Walters, Derek. *Feng Shui: The Chinese Art of Designing a Harmonious Environment*. New York: Simon & Schuster, 1988.

Welch, Holmes. *Taoism: The Parting of the Way*. Revised ed. Boston: Beacon, 1966.

Xu, Ben. "Memory and the Ethnic Self: Reading Amy Tan's *The Joy Luck Club*." *MELUS* 19.1 (1994): 3-18.

Youngblood, Ruth. "Baby-Poor Singapore Looks to Dragon for Help." *Los Angeles Times* 29 Nov. 1987, sec. 1: 41. *News*. Online. Lexis-Nexis. 15 Mar. 1997.

"That Was China, That Was Their Fate":
Ethnicity and Agency in *The Joy Luck Club*_____

Patricia P. Chu

"In Your Bones": The Mother-Daughter Romance

My discussions of Eaton and Mukherjee have emphasized the cultural work they do in attempting to find a way to portray Asian women that addresses various ideological agendas. The prime agenda is to interpellate the Asian woman immigrant as a subject whose interior life is not only accessible and sympathetic to American readers but whose story in some way redefines Americanness. By using the codes of sentimental and domestic fiction, both authors seek to complicate their readers' ideas of American subjectivity by presenting Asian women immigrants as already possessing, or readily understanding, deeply American ideals of love, self-determination, and individual happiness; such narratives seek, ultimately, to establish the newcomers not only as less alien but as quintessential American subjects. Amy Tan's best-selling first novel *The Joy Luck Club* (1989) contributes to this project by introducing life-defining episodes from the lives of four Chinese immigrant mothers and their American-born daughters. Although Tan's novel is one of numerous matrilineal Asian American texts published in the last ten years, its extraordinary popular success suggests that Tan has been particularly successful in positioning herself and her work in relation to readers who are not Asian American.[1] Indeed, students of various ethnicities in my contemporary American literature courses have described the book's portrayals of mother-daughter relations as universal stories with which they themselves identify.

Whereas Eaton used the short-story form and Mukherjee a highly compressed, episodic format to convey insights into the multiple experiences of various immigrant characters, Tan's innovation is the use of the four-layer mahjong club to structure the development of four mother-daughter pairs. One critic has suggested that the introduction of multiple narratives about two generations of Chinese American women is inherently challenging to stereotypical readings that treat Chinese women as fungible because they share a defining Chinese "essence," and Melani McAlister argues, along the same lines, that the novel's complex representation of Chinese American subjectivities requires careful attention to the full range of temperaments, class variations, and differences in personal history, particularly among the four mothers.[2]

In *The Joy Luck Club*, Tan's contribution to the problem of narrating Asian American subject formation lies in her elaboration of an established form, the mother-daughter plot, in which the immigrant mother's desire for America becomes focused on her American-born daughter. In this plot, the American offspring fulfills multiple functions that I have previously linked with white romantic partners in narratives about immigrants for whom marriage and child rearing are seen as remote and unlikely. For instance, Tan's daughters both personify America and mediate their mothers' assimilation into American society. Though the mothers' desire for their daughters' love and understanding is not sexualized, it tends to displace the mothers' heterosexual relationships in importance and to be charged with the burden of compensating for multiple losses, including romantic disappointments and a range of losses attributable to emigration, war, and natural disaster.[3] Because of the intensity attributed to mother-daughter relations in such stories and the structural similarities these dyads bear to romantic partnerships in earlier assimilation narratives, I consider such mother-daughter plots another form of the narrative I've described as the immigrant romance. From the daughters' perspectives, the functions of the immigrant mother are similarly complex. Tan's novel is typical, but usefully explicit, in spelling out these functions in *Joy Luck*. The mothers both personify China and Chineseness in their daughters' minds and mediate as the daughters seek to construct narratives of Chinese female subjectivity that will be enabling to them in their task of Chinese American self-formation.

At the same time, *Joy Luck* challenges this sense of intergenerational differences by suggesting that the mothers and daughters are united by blood and gender. The "in your bones" trope of kinship as an organic, ineffable link is reinforced by the allusions to the common issues the book attributes to the characters' gender socialization. The majority of the stories deal with the protagonists' feelings of helplessness in the face of oppressive domestic relationships; this internalized helplessness is then addressed primarily as a psychological hurdle that must be overcome through individual efforts of will.

By looking at the ways Tan first constructs her generational dialogues as intercultural ones and then seeks to envision rapprochement between the two poles for each mother-daughter dyad, we see that ultimately the imagined similarity turns on the problem of women's agency and that the portrayal of women's agency as essentially the *same* in both the United States and China rests in this novel on a kind of historical amnesia about twentieth-century Chinese political and social history. Such amnesia, I suggest, is neither unique to Tan nor a sign of individual deficiency on her part, but it is suggestive of the ways in which American culture selectively takes in and constructs Chinese culture. Because I read the novel's ending as gesturing beyond intercultural understanding within America toward a horizon of international cooperation between China and the United States, the terms on which the novel suggests such an understanding might be built are suggestive of larger cultural assumptions governing perceptions of Asians and Asian Americans.

* * *

Let's begin, then, by speaking briefly about the relationship between the "mother-daughter romance," as I shall call it, and the utopian myth of the immigrant's Americanization that underlies it, noting that Tan's version shares with the generic myth certain values central to American thinking: the belief in America as a land of opportunity, the bonds between parents and children, and the power of the individual to control his or her own future through acts of will (agency).[4] In the immigration myth, immigrants abandon an old world, which, like the home of a mythic hero, has become incomplete, disordered, or intolerable, to brave the journey to America, which is figured as a promised land of greater economic and social opportunity as well as greater freedom and justice.[5] Although the immigrant may encounter substantial difficulties in America, he or she typically overcomes these difficulties by remaining true to the initial dream of American society's fairness and openness, working hard, and looking forward to the greater success and assimilation of his or her American-born children. This narrative typically emphasizes the power of the immigrant's agency and the ultimate attainability of the American dream and denies that obstacles such as racism or economic exploitation are systemic or insurmountable. This utopian view of American immigration is the foundation of Tan's text.[6]

Built directly upon this foundation is the mother-daughter narrative, which affirms the desire of each generation for the respect and understanding of the other, and the importance of maternal legacies of wisdom and character transmitted from mother to daughter. This plot, in which each mother guides her daughter to claim greater agency in her own life, tallies nicely with the immigration plot. Together, the two plots comply with a fictional condition deeply embedded in American popular culture, the premise that heroic individuals can triumph over all obstacles.

* * *

The novel opens with a short episode—a prelude to the first four stories—that epitomizes the whole book's skillful blending of the mother-daughter romance and the immigration myth. In the mother-daughter romance, mothers seek their daughters' understanding and offer in turn a legacy of gendered, ethnically marked identity and empowerment. On one level, the text insists that this legacy is transmitted instinctively and genetically—"through the bones," as one character will say—but the text as a whole makes *narrative* the prime medium for transmission of the maternal legacy. The primary function of the prelude, then, is to signal that the stories to follow will fulfill the crucial functions of cultural transmission and translation. This opening story also embodies three components of the maternal narratives that are shortly offered at greater length: first, a narrative in which girls and women are educated to accept social powerlessness as their due, first in long-ago China and then in contemporary America; second, a counter-narrative of female empowerment through individual efforts of will; and third, a narrative of successful immigration and assimilation, processes that provide avenues of escape from the closed system of Chinese society. As we shall see, these elements all return us to the problem of conceptualizing Chinese women's agency.

In the story, an old woman remembers a swan she once bought in Shanghai, which, according to the vendor, had transcended its original identity as a duck by stretching its neck in the hope of becoming a goose. Instead, it became something better: a swan "too beautiful to eat." As the woman carries the swan to America—both travelers stretching their necks in aspiration—she fantasizes:

> "In America I will have a daughter just like me. . . . Over there nobody will look down on her, because I will make her speak only perfect American English. And over there she will always be too full to swallow any sorrow! She will know my meaning, because I will give her this swan—a creature that became more than what was hoped for."
>
> But when she arrived in the new country, the immigration officials pulled the swan away from her, leaving the woman fluttering her arms and with only one swan feather for a memory. And then she had to fill out so many forms she forgot why she had come and what she had left behind.
>
> Now the woman was old. And she had a daughter who grew up speaking only English and swallowing more Coca-Cola than sorrow. For a long time now the woman had wanted to give her daughter the single swan feather

and tell her, "This feather may look worthless, but it comes from afar and carries with it all my good intentions." And she waited year after year, for the day she could tell her daughter this in perfect American English. (unpaginated)

This Chinese American "ugly duckling" tale captures a number of ideas central both to this text and to other narratives of immigration: the old world as a place of limited possibility; the immigrant as the one duck who will not accept her appointed place in that society; America as the site of the immigrant's dream of transformation, the land of unbounded possibility; the blurring of the immigrant's vision and sense of self when confronted with the realities of an alien and inhospitable land; the transference of hope (the swan feather) to the immigrant's offspring; the dream of vicarious assimilation through those offspring, who will be both like and unlike their parents (fully comprehending the parent yet fully assimilated); and, finally, the fear of alienation from and rejection by the offspring. The daughter's affinity for Coca-Cola and unfamiliarity with sorrow serve as shorthand for issues to be elaborated in the novel: the danger that the material comfort, even luxury, symbolized by the drinking of bubbly, unnourishing Coca-Cola will also lead to malnourished character development, a callousness and lack of imagination bred by the very prosperity, and shelter from suffering, that the mother has risked so much to offer. The story ends with the immigrant mother poised between hope that her daughter may still be brought to understand the world of meaning symbolized by the swan's feather and fear that the moment for transmitting that legacy may never arise.

The opening chapter, which follows this passage, emphasizes this interweaving of the mother-daughter and assimilation plots. June Jing-mei Woo, whose mother, Suyuan, has just died, is invited by her mother's friends ("aunties") and her father to take her parent's place at the weekly meeting of the mahjong club her mother founded, the Joy Luck Club. Like bridge, mahjong is a four-handed "card" game (played with engraved tiles rather than cards). June knows she is to play her mother's hand at this meeting, but this turns out to be true on more levels than one. After the game, her father and "aunties" reveal that June's half sisters, lost in China in their infancy, have at long last been located. Alas, it has happened too late for them to meet their mother, Suyuan. Thus, June is to go to China to greet them in her mother's place, break the news of her death, and bear witness to her life. When June doubts that she knows her mother well enough to perform this task, her aunties erupt in dismay:

> "Not know your own mother?" cries Auntie An-mei with disbelief. "How can you say? Your mother is in your bones!" . . .
>
> "Tell them stories she told you, lessons she taught, what you know about her mind that has become your mind," says Auntie Ying. "You mother very smart lady." . . .
>
> "Her kindness."
>
> "Her smartness."
>
> "Her dutiful nature to family."
>
> "Her hopes, things that matter to her."
>
> "The excellent dishes she cooked." . . .
>
> And then it occurs to me. They are frightened. In me, they see their own daughters, just as ignorant, just as unmindful of all the truths and hopes they have brought to America. They see daughters who grow impatient when their mothers talk in Chinese, who think they are stupid when they explain things in fractured English. . . . They see daughters who will bear grandchildren born without any connecting hope passed from generation to generation. (40-41)

Thus, June, a drifting copywriter who has not yet found her true subject, is officially assigned the task of remembering and representing her mother (both speaking for and portraying her). By implication, she is chosen to be the chronicler for her mother's generation. Clearly, June is Amy Tan's fictional surrogate, for she inherits not only the immigrant offspring's classic call to remembrance but the writer's call to authorship. Male writers, like James Joyce's Stephen Dedalus, are often portrayed as eagerly seizing the hammer and anvil of authorship ("to forge in the smithy of my soul the uncreated conscience of my race" [*Portrait of the Artist*, 276]); by contrast, women writers, especially ethnic women writers, often need the legitimation of outside authorization for their writing.[7] Here Amy Tan offers her alter ego, June, official family cover for taking up the perhaps unwomanly or unfilial task of writing for publication: it is a duty to her mother, family, and community. The link between June and the author is further suggested by this novel's dedication, which addresses the book to Tan's mother and grandmother and offers it as a kind of memory in response to remembered conversations. In short, the charge of *The Joy Luck Club* initiates a roundelay of interlaced first-person stories in which June, as the author's surrogate, imagines the voices and stories of the mothers and daughters. Only Suyuan, being dead, does not voice her own first-person narrative; instead, June takes her two turns in the narrative as well as the mahjong game.

The Two-Worlds Problem

Both the immigration and mother-daughter plots turn upon the tension between sameness and difference: the immigrant passes from an old world defined as a dystopia of exhausted possibilities and tragic narrative outcomes to the utopian new world, where opportunity and happy endings beckon. This scheme is evident in the immigrant attitudes summed up respectively by An-mei Hsu, an immigrant, and June Woo, speaking for her mother Suyuan:

[An-mei:] My mother, she suffered. She lost her face and tried to hide it. She found only greater misery and finally could not hide that. There is nothing more to understand. That was China. That was what people did back then. They had no choice. They could not speak up. They could not run away. That was their fate. (241)

[June:] My mother believed you could be anything you wanted to be in America. You could open a restaurant. You could work for the government and get good retirement. You could buy a house with almost no money down. You could become rich. You could become instantly famous. . . .

America was where all my mother's hopes lay. She had come here in 1949 after losing everything in China: her mother and father, her family home, her first husband, and two daughters, twin baby girls. But she never looked back with regret. (132)

The thread that links these two disparate worlds is of course the story of the immigrant herself, whose consciousness mediates between the two cultures, and potentially unites them, as he or she moves from one place to the next. The coexistence of loss, transience, and change, on the one hand, and the will to establish continuity and progress, on the other, is the essence of the immigration plot; the image of the old woman's swan feather gains its resonance from this tension.

In the mother-daughter plot, the tension between sameness and difference resides in the mother-daughter dyad itself, as each party struggles to overcome perceptions of the other's differentness and to locate the qualities they have in common. Such a plot is ideally suited to examining how ethnicity is constructed as a source of intergenerational difference as well as commonality ("Your mother is in your bones!" [40]). The text constructs its implied reader as occupying the American pole of Chinese-American binarism, so that we readers share the American daughters' search for the essences of their respective Chinese mothers. That search brilliantly folds together the two plots defining both ethnicity and femininity while providing a basis for assessing Tan's success in negotiating with existing preconceptions about Chinese womanhood. In this regard, the text expresses two opposed impulses: the impulse to expose and distance itself from American stereotypes of Chinese as un-American, nonrational, or backward and the tendency to reinforce these stereotypes by accentuating the alienness of Chinese thinking and character.

When the novel invokes the old world/new world opposition we saw in the quotations just discussed, its positioning of China as an inferior term that helps to define American modernity and progressiveness is reminiscent of the East/West split that raised such sharp critical questions in Bharati Mukherjee's *Jasmine*. As we have seen, critics attuned to the complexity of South Asian social and political history were affronted by that novel's tendency to portray India primarily as the negative term in a first world/third world comparison that ultimately celebrates the United States as the more modern, civilized society where women are more assertive and better treated, and even terrorists' motives can be cogently explained (as justified economic frustration, in the American gunman's case, and as opposed to knee-jerk religious fanaticism in the Sikh nationalists' case). In scrutinizing Tan's negotiation of the problem of first-world bias in her representations of pre-Communist China, let us draw upon Johannes Fabian's concept of "allochronism," or temporal distancing, in anthropological writing.[8] According to Rey Chow's succinct summary of this concept, anthropologists tend to position themselves and their subjects as "coeval," inhabiting the same temporal world, while in the field, with the implication that the writers and their subjects are equally modern and equal in other ways as well. When the scholars depart and write up their notes, however, this sense of "shared time is replaced by a more linear, progressive use of time that enables the distinctions between 'primitive' and 'developed' cultures" in which the subjects of study, placed in a static, "primitive" time, are thereby distanced from the progressive, linear temporality of the writers. In Chinese area studies, Chow argues, this "casting of the other in another time" has contributed to a reverence for classical China and an attitude of "realpolitik contempt" toward modern China, with a corresponding lack of interest in the full psychological complexity of modern Chinese as post-colonial, diasporic subjects.[9] I want to suggest that what Chow describes as Western disinterest in the complex subjectivities of modern Chinese people—that is, resistance to modernity in the Chinese—

resembles the historical American resistance to the ideas of Americanness and assimilability in Asian Americans because both are rooted in a conceptualization of Asia as "other." This othering, and the tendency to fall back on familiar, static stereotypes (such as those of classical China or the inscrutable Chinese), may take place partly because it is easier to conceptualize a subject one is writing about as static, rather than dynamic, and of course it is easier to draw upon existing concepts than to create new ones.

The Joy Luck Club is in many ways an effort to disturb and challenge orientalist conventions for representing Chinese women, yet Tan's decision to emphasize retrospective maternal narratives of pre-Communist China, addressed to daughters who stand in for a late-1980s American readership, necessarily raises the specter of allochronism, and the risk of representing the Chinese mothers as belonging to a fundamentally different, and other, narrative universe from their daughters.

* * *

It's in the daughters' stories, set in contemporary America, that Tan is most overtly concerned with debunking orientalist stereotypes about Chinese women, and as a result her portrayal of the mothers' nature is divided. In these scenes, we find the American-born daughters struggling with the tendency to view their mothers in ways that combine immaturity (in the form of uncertainty about their own independence) with orientalism. That is, they see their mothers as powerful, controlling beings whose psychology is unfathomable both because as daughters they still retain an exaggerated image of their mothers' powers from childhood and adolescence and because, rightly or wrongly, the daughters chalk up seemingly unfathomable differences to the fact that their mothers are Chinese. The novel is winning and persuasive when it suggests that images of the mothers as superhuman others are largely projections of the daughters' own fears and fantasies, as in the story where Waverly Jong learns to see her mother not as a malignant adversary scheming to break up Waverly's new romance but simply as an old woman waiting for her daughter's acceptance (184). In addition to these moments, which humanize the mothers by highlighting their vulnerability, Tan undercuts Western stereotypes in the mothers' narratives. For instance, Lindo and An-mei identify fortune cookie epigrams as "American" nonsense (262), and Ying-ying St. Clair (the daughter of a wealthy family) explains that she was unimpressed by the trinkets offered by her American suitor as gifts but pretended to make a fuss over them so as not to disrupt his illusions of cultural superiority (250).

However, the text also provides scenes that serve to validate orientalist stereotypes of Chinese alterity by portraying the mothers as guardians of ancient Chinese wisdom or powers—powers their life stories cannot adequately explain. This sort of problem occurs, for instance, when Ying-ying St. Clair, on a visit to her unhappily married daughter, Lena, proposes to help by drawing upon her own "tiger spirit"—a manifestation of her and Lena's Chinese birth sign—to release Lena's (252). Given that the four stories devoted to Ying-ying and Lena have portrayed Ying-ying as a psychically fragile person (permanently traumatized by an abusive first husband, an abortion, a well-intentioned but uncomprehending American husband, and a miscarriage), that she has always been rather remote from Lena, and that she has been passive in her two marriages, the text's insistence on her underlying "tiger spirit" feels like an attempt to substitute a romantic, generic ideal of Chinese folk wisdom for a conclusion more consistent with her previous, individualized psychological profile. By awkwardly forcing this romanticized element into an ostensibly realistic chapter about Lena's failing romantic relationship, the text ends up implying that the mother is culturally and psychically alien—of a different universe—after all. At such moments, the text ceases to critique the orientalism of particular characters and becomes orientalist itself.[10]

Lindo's Agency

This text, then, continues the Asian American exploration of the problem of defining Asian American difference within a broader claim of commonality with other Americans. On what terms, the text seems to ask, can we recognize these mothers as American in their core values yet still retaining values that are Chinese? Most importantly, which values, common to subjects in both cultures, transcend the "East is not West" fallacy?

Tan's answer to this problem draws upon feminist thinking to invoke the struggle for personal agency—control of the decisions that define one's life—as common to girls and young women in both China and America. In the end, I think Tan's difficulty is that she bases her understanding of female agency on her experiences as a middle-class American in a postfeminist era without being fully aware of how privileged this position is. In the stories of two yuppie daughters (Lena and Rose), the key to regaining self-respect, claiming better treatment from males, and beginning a new life is simple self-assertiveness. Thus, Rose Hsu Jordan, whose passive dependence on her husband has extinguished his interest in her, learns that she can force him to make a generous divorce settlement, and even scare him, merely by deciding to become self-assertive again. "The power of my words was that strong," she concludes (196). Rose's passivity, explained as both an individual psychic deficiency and a symptom of feminine conditioning, vanishes so quickly that one wonders why she didn't clear it up sooner. Although somewhat simplistic, such solutions are appropriate for these characters because, for women of their class and era, other elements necessary for their "liberation" from debilitating marriages are available to them: education, the possibility of supporting themselves, family support, legal rights, and a well-established public ideology of women's equality. The novel doesn't really need to acknowledge this environment as the product of the American women's movement because this social context is familiar to American readers. On the other hand, because the novel lacks historical self-consciousness about the enabling conditions for female self-assertion in America, it naively universalizes its lessons about self-empowerment, disregarding the more serious obstacles to autonomy faced by Chinese women, as we shall see by examining the circumstances for self-empowerment described in Lindo Jong's story, "The Red Candle." Whereas a sense of self-worth may be a necessary condition for women's survival or liberation in China, it isn't a sufficient guarantee of either unless other conditions also prevail. Thus, the novel's understanding of female agency, and its efforts to compare Chinese and American female oppression, are dependent on simplistic analogies between two groups of women whose differing social conditions aren't fully clarified by the book's optimistic treatment.

* * *

Before assessing what is marginalized by Tan's narrative method, it's only fair to acknowledge what is achieved: clear plots in which heroic young women, undergoing trials by ordeal, arrive at epiphanies of character that carry them through their ordeals and, implicitly or explicitly, to America. Lindo Jong's story, "The Red Candle," is the most compact and winsome version of this type of story. It goes like this: she is betrothed at age two to marry into a rich family, the Huangs. When she is twelve, her peasant family is ruined by river floods. They have to move far away but leave her to be brought up by the Huangs. Before leaving, her mother insists that Lindo uphold the family honor by devoting her life to fulfilling the family's marriage contract. Lindo's natal family then disappears completely from her life. Although the Huangs treat her more like a servant than a family member, Lindo remains and does her best to please them, both because of her mother's wishes and because there is no alternative. After her marriage at sixteen, she's relieved to find that her husband, who's slightly younger, avoids touching her. This means she can sleep in peace but can't produce the required male heir despite the threats and confinement imposed by

Huang Taitai, her mother-in-law. Having recognized that a servant girl whom she likes is concealing an illegitimate pregnancy, Lindo uses bogus supernatural tokens to persuade Huang Taitai that the family will be cursed by her continued presence and blessed if they trade her in for the servant, whose pregnancy the Huangs have not yet noticed. The Huangs accordingly bribe Lindo to accept a quiet divorce and leave town; they marry their son to the pregnant servant and thereby (it's implied) get their heir (so to speak). Lindo escapes with honor and a nest egg, to Beijing and thence to America, rescues the servant from ruin, and saves the Huangs from patrilineal extinction in the process.

The features of Lindo's story that recur, with variations, in those of her friends are these: a young girl or young woman is forced to face extreme adversity or injustice, either alone or with the support of a powerless mother. Aside from her mother, the heroine has no friends or allies either within or beyond the family circle. The heroine's initial condition of hopeless victimization is represented as emblematic of the condition of all women in China, which is basically seen as a static feudal society. Each heroine, however, discovers within herself a reservoir of self-esteem, resourcefulness, and dissatisfaction with her prescribed low status, and each finds a way to escape her entrapment and come to America.

These positive qualities, which appear in each mother's story at some point, are most clearly defined in the case of Lindo. The text portrays her in-laws, both son and mother, as a self-absorbed pair who see her as a combination of servant, breeding stock, and chattel (indeed, many traditional Chinese proverbs compare the taking of a wife to the purchase of livestock). But Lindo survives and ultimately escapes the marriage because of outstanding personal qualities, which are depicted as intrinsic to her and are, in terms of the social milieu depicted, inexplicable. These qualities, the greatest of which is courage, define Lindo; they are also, I would argue, definitive within this text of the immigrant sensibility—that which marks the Chinese mothers as unfit for their old world milieu and destined to become Americans. In the Chinese scenes, almost everyone else accepts the status quo and criticizes those who don't. Only the young protagonists have a version of "Hamlet's dis-ease": they recognize that the world is out of joint. But whereas Hamlet, as a prince, feels "born to set it right," these young women are placed in a fictional Chinese world where both individual justice and systemic social change seem impossible. They cannot set things right; they can only seek survival, then freedom, for themselves. Therefore, they must come to America.

The sign of this Americanizing discontent is usually a scene in which the young woman rallies her spirits and determines to take charge of her future. In Lindo's story, the possibility of controlling her own fate comes to her as an epiphany of psychological autonomy, which takes place, appropriately enough, before a mirror. In Lindo's life, the Fen River represents the inevitability of fate; it's a Fen River flood that ruins her peasant family, forcing them to leave town and abandon her to the Huangs' tender mercies. Four years later, as she considers casting herself into the river to avoid her wedding—a gesture combining defiance with defeat—she's distracted and heartened by the power of the wind, which exerts terrific force on both the river and the humans in her view. Her formative scene of self-recognition follows: "I wiped my eyes and looked in the mirror. I was surprised at what I saw. I had on a beautiful red dress, but what I saw was even more valuable. I was strong. I was pure. I had genuine thoughts inside that no one could see, that no one could ever take away from me. I was like the wind" (58). Here Lindo grants herself the subjectivity no one else has offered her. In the story, she has been conditioned all her life to deny her desires, imagination, and will, a schooling the novel identifies with Chinese female experience. Now she alone recognizes and values her own interiority, the intelligence that both parents and in-laws have systematically sought to stifle lest it foster discontent and rebellion. Strikingly, intelligence is linked by Lindo with a new perception of her sexuality as something strong and good that she herself commands. Because Lindo's intelligence and the mental freedom it adds to her life are unrecognized by those around her, it is an invaluable weapon in her struggle for survival and freedom. This invisible source of strength, as well as the real freedom she seeks, is henceforth linked with the wind, which has the power to manipulate the river of fate and the power to carry her to America.

Similar scenes of courage and decisiveness, definitive immigrant traits, appear in all the mothers' stories. Suyuan Woo, waiting out the Sino-Japanese War in Guilin, takes charge of her life by forming the original Joy Luck Club, a mahjong club, to keep her hope alive at a time when the Chinese are being slaughtered by the Japanese. This carefully nourished hope in turn enables her to flee to safety and to preserve the lives of her two infant daughters. Nine-year-old An-mei Hsu takes her future into her hands when she accepts her mother's invitation to leave her uncle's house ("full of dark riddles and suffering that I could not understand," like China in this book) and follow her mother into an unknown life elsewhere (218). And even Ying-ying, whose spirit has been broken by her abusive first husband in China, holds the attention of Clifford St. Clair, her American suitor, for four years until her first husband's death frees her to marry St. Clair, her ticket to America. These moments of decision define the young women both as subjects capable of articulating themselves in narrative and as agents who seek to control their lives and set them apart from the nonimmigrant Chinese who appear in the book.

An-mei Hsu's stories, "Scar" and "Magpies," describe a similar reversal of fortune in another traditional Confucian household. An-mei's mother, the young widow of a scholar, has been tricked into accepting a position as the fourth wife (actually, the third concubine) of a wealthy merchant named Wu Tsing. When An-mei's mother was freshly widowed, she had met Wu Tsing's second wife at a Buddhist shrine. Second Wife, who wanted to find a docile concubine to keep her husband at home, invited the young widow to spend the night as their guest, sent her husband to rape her, and spread rumors that the guest had seduced the host. As a result, the young woman was cast out by members of her family, who believed the rumors rather than seeking and crediting the account of their daughter. (The family of An-mei's father is not mentioned.) With nowhere else to go, An-mei's mother has grimly accepted her new position in order to survive. By bringing An-mei with her, she expresses love for her daughter—according to Tan—yet also seems to guarantee that An-mei's prospects will be bleaker than her own. (I wonder what mother would really have done this, for by bringing An-mei from her family's household into Wu Tsing's, she transforms An-mei, for practical purposes, from the orphan of a scholar being raised by her kin into the daughter of a slave.) For, although An-mei's mother is young, wellborn, and attractive, her status—already at the bottom of society—is low even among Wu's concubines. She is too virtuous and refined to combat the manipulative tactics of Second Wife, who works constantly to ensure her own preeminence at everyone else's expense.

In the story's denouement, An-mei's mother commits suicide and dies two days before the first day of the lunar new year. Although the ghost of the departed traditionally returns to settle accounts on the third day after death, this return is particularly threatening, it seems, when it falls on the first day of the new year because of the Chinese understanding that on this day "all debts must be paid, or disaster and misfortune will follow" (240). In mortal terror of this supernatural threat, the prodigal husband Wu Tsing dons the Chinese equivalent of sackcloth and ashes, vows to honor his fourth wife as his first and only wife and the mother of his only son, and declares that he will treat An-mei as his own legal daughter. As a result, An-mei recalls this as the day she gained both a voice and the agency it symbolizes: "And on that day, I learned to shout" (240).

This story relies upon the same narrative trick used in "Red Candle" with deeply problematic results. Having stacked the odds against her victim, reinforcing the impression of young women's total isolation in traditional Chinese society, the text fails to provide a plausible source of assistance or escape for her heroines. Therefore, a "happy" ending involving some restitution, however incomplete, can only be effected by the extreme means of threatening to invoke the wrath of supernatural forces. In An-mei's case, we are asked to believe that, after years of dominating Wu Tsing and his household, Second Wife will give way permanently to the nine-year-old An-mei out of deference to her mother's ghost, although An-mei has never been taught to fight by her excessively self-effacing mother. An-mei's mother, who isn't even named in the story, has always accepted injustice with resignation and never fought directly for anything, even her mother's respect, before committing suicide. It's said that in Chinese society a young woman's suicide was often investigated, and publicly perceived, as a sign of family abuse, and so suicide was the ultimate form of protest available to young women (Wolf, *Women* 122). But An-mei's story doesn't broach this level of social reality. By insisting on the importance of the timing, it implies that the fear of ghosts alone—not the fear of public censure or the awakening of Wu's nonexistent conscience—will permanently set right the household, which for so long has been distorted by Wu's abuse and abrogation of his moral authority and Second Wife's exploitation of his flaws. Moreover, An-mei's idea of justice is (understandably, but severely) limited by her acceptance of the household's gendered power relations: she looks forward to putting Second Wife in her place but never considers Wu Tsing to have been the true author of her mother's tragedy. Nor does it occur to her to question the demeaning ranking and competition set up among the various wives and their children. Of course, she is in no position as a child to question the social order so fundamentally, but the story is, after all, recounted by the adult An-mei many decades later in an effort to incite her daughter Rose to stand up to her adulterous husband.

Later, when the adult An-mei recounts her mother's suicide as a triumphant endgame that protected the child An-mei's interests (240), she places her mother in a tragic world much like that of many European operas in which young women's greatest triumphs are as victims, their agency confined to dramatic acts of self-destruction. For An-mei, her mother's tragic world is remote, mythical, and quintessentially Chinese. An-mei, having lived forty years in America, has escaped this world but is a respectful witness to it. In a passage already quoted, she concludes that, although things are different in modern China, in the China of her youth her mother's story was typical: "My mother, she suffered. . . . That was China. That was what people did back then. They had no choice. They could not speak up. They could not run away. That was their fate" (241).

What Lindo Knows

The "just say yes" fable of self-determination, which can readily be recognized by American readers as simplistic but not entirely removed from reality for the middle-class American daughters, is more problematic in a story like Lindo's because Tan cannot assume an equivalent understanding of the Chinese social context in her American readership, nor does she provide quite enough context in this story or elsewhere in the novel. As a result, Tan's novel tends to give the impression that Lindo Jong, An-mei Hsu, and to a lesser extent Ying-ying St. Clair passed readily from a very traditional Confucian society into the American middle class with little mention of such mediating forces as the questioning of traditional family structures by Chinese reformers, feminist movements within China, the influence of Western education and ideas on Chinese elites, and the struggles of Chinese on many levels—including the level of domestic social structures—to modernize their country.[11] Such forces, which are reduced to the level of rumor in a story like "The Red Candle," would help prepare Chinese women and men of the educated classes for immigration to America and a relatively easy transition into the professional classes here, in contrast to others, who, coming to the United States without English or readily negotiable professional credentials, connections, or capital, would probably enter the ranks of the working poor.[12] In Tan's novel, the characterization of the fourth mother, Suyuan Woo, is most free of the problem of improbable discontinuities in class identity. Since she was trained as a nurse and married to two professional men (a Kuomintang officer and then a journalist, June's father) in China, it's easier to imagine Suyuan picking up English and sending her children to college. What is present in the American stories, but absent from most of the Chinese ones, is the middle term identified by Rey Chow, the Chinese woman as a modern subject, and what that subject represents, the vision of early-twentieth-century China as a country in which modern and traditional elements coexist, a country that, like the United States, is constantly changing.

One way in which Tan occludes this period is by making the Chinese mothers a generation older than they logistically need to be: because the American daughters are the children of *second* marriages, the mothers' childhood memories describe a China one generation earlier, and hence less touched by modernization, than the story's two-generation format requires.[13] Other issues raised by Lindo's story are the exaggerated contrast between her mind and those of the other characters in her story and the issue of social support for her rebellion.

Lindo, for instance, undergoes a highly conventional education yet independently develops values and intellectual resources that might reasonably be expected of a more educated, cosmopolitan person. From age two onward, she is told that she is going to be the property of the Huangs and that the family honor demands that she fulfill this marriage contract by sacrificing her body and will. She is subjected to a number of fortune-telling sessions, taught domestic skills, asked to believe that her worth depends on her usefulness to the Huangs, and lectured inexplicitly on her reproductive duties. What does Lindo teach herself? Despite her youth and isolation, she knows not only about sex but about sexual behavior, she knows her own worth and the worthlessness of the Huangs' words and she knows how to assess and manipulate evidence independently (such as the matchmaker's lying about the candles, her husband's disinclination to touch her, the signs of the servant girl's pregnancy, and the "signs" she invents to convince the

Huangs to release her from the marriage). Moreover, she transcends her conventional moral education when she is kind and affectionate toward her bratty husband (despite their inimical positions in an exploitative family structure, she recognizes his humanity), and compassionate toward the hapless servant despite the girl's "promiscuity" and their difference in status. If we relied on this novel, Lindo's reliance on empirical observation rather than conventional class or moral prejudices would seem to set her apart from almost everyone else in China—or at least from everyone else in "The Red Candle." In addition, her practice of judging people by their conduct rather than their class status might be considered in the light of arguments that the very idea of an "inner self" distinguishable from one's outer social status is arguably a Western one. Lindo's empowering emphasis on her mental life—her "interiority"—is certainly not without Chinese literary precedent, but it also aligns her with Western fictional heroines whose mental purity transcends the limits or mortifications of their flesh.[14] Finally, she seems to be the one disbeliever in a community where everyone else takes the authority and supernatural power of dead ancestors literally. If the Chinese people around her are really so homogeneous in their thinking, how does Lindo, an isolated girl confined to these two households, arrive at a mind set so different, so seemingly Western?

When we next see young Lindo, she's in Beijing, copying English words and planning to enter the United States as a college student (of theology, no less). Arriving in America, she amuses herself with jokes about the signs in Chinatown, gets a job in a fortune cookie factory, and uses night school English classes to woo her future husband. Given the Huangs' feudal approach to female education, when did she learn to read Chinese and manage money? How did she learn of America, much less decide to come here? Once here, how does she jump from a cookie assembly line into the middle class? Glossed over are the obstacles to legal entry, and physical and social mobility, faced by most working-class immigrants. Instead, Lindo's lighthearted initiation into America seems more like that of an exchange student with a work-study job.

Such questions, however, beg a more fundamental one: how could Lindo have survived in China after she left the Huangs? Her own mother had preemptively refused to shelter her, and everyone in the village would have known she was the Huangs' daughter-in-law. Even had she found a way to reach the city, who would have sheltered, fed, or hired an unknown young woman from the provinces with no references? The absence of social support for runaway or castaway women is to become a central concern, and a central explanation for wife abuse, in Tan's next novel (*The Kitchen God's Wife*); in *Joy Luck* that absence implicitly explains the high tolerance for domestic abuse of Lindo, An-mei, and Ying-ying. It doesn't, however, explain how Lindo survived the sudden independence for which she had never been prepared.

In Lindo's case, Tan simply attributes an educated, arguably American, consciousness to her character. This serves the optimism of the immigration plot well, because it overstates the possibility of upward mobility in the United States. It serves the task of portraying actual immigrants' experiences less well, however, for it understates the working-class immigrant's struggle to survive (particularly when language barriers and race-based obstacles come into play) as well as the foreign student's loneliness, cultural isolation, and financial anxiety. Admittedly, the class disparity between the narrator's mind and her ostensible background is greatest in Lindo's narratives, and the resulting overstatement of the character's freedom and agency, while historically implausible, is part of the book's charm. Given the difficulty of Tan's cross-cultural project, it seems better that she has chosen to overstate rather than understate Lindo's intelligence and agency. It is merely regrettable that "The Red Candle" depends on portraying other Chinese characters as self-absorbed, maliciously exploitative, and unthinking in their adherence to the letter, but not the spirit, of their traditional religious beliefs.

By contrast, Tan's characterizations of An-mei and Ying-ying make more developmental sense but risk understating their intelligence and agency. Given the traditional upbringing each describes, it's plausible that these two internalize and unwittingly pass on the ethos of self-denial that this text characterizes as a female Chinese legacy. An-mei, for instance, approves of her mother's extreme acts of self-sacrifice (48, 240), and Ying-ying, even while criticizing and manipulating Clifford St. Clair's orientalist view of her as a helpless female in need of rescue, also colludes with that view by concealing her real past from him. In the United States, she permits him to mistranslate her name, birth date, personal history, and thoughts to fit his condescending view of her (104, 106, 109, 250-51), thereby driving her to mental illness and reducing her, in her daughter's eyes and her own words, to a ghost.

At the same time, since An-mei and Ying-ying come from more privileged families, it's disappointing that Tan seems to conceive them as both uneducated and indifferent to public events. Ying-ying, for instance, comes from a wealthy scholar's family, grew up not far from a major port (Wuxi, close to Shanghai), marries an Irish American, and lives in the United States for about forty years before ostensibly offering her life story to her daughter in "Waiting Between the Trees." Yet, when she recalls the tumultuous era of her birth and infancy (1914-18), a period when the fall of the last Chinese dynasty was about to herald thirty years of continuous warfare, she describes 1914 as "the year a very bad spirit entered the world," a spirit that, according to her, "stayed in the world for four years" and caused people to starve and die (248). Ying-ying explains her survival, in similar terms, as an astrological accident: born in the Year of the Tiger, she happens to be endowed with the superior tiger spirit she's now passing on to Lena. I've already discussed the representational and psychological problems with this "just say grr" empowerment scene; I want now to question the speech's assumptions about Ying-ying's historical consciousness. What "very bad spirit" is Ying-ying recalling? If she's thinking only of local disasters, why say "the world" to her American daughter? It's true that in the West, World War I may have ended in 1918, but China's struggles to resist Japanese imperialism, which begin in 1914, became worse in

1919, when the Western powers' failure to honor Chinese interests in the Versailles peace treaty provoked student demonstrations and fueled the nationalist May Fourth Movement (Chow Tse-tung, *May Fourth*, 84-116). On the "world" level, China's troubles neither began in 1914 nor ended in 1919. It's true that Ying-ying would have been only an infant at the time. But she's supposed to be the child of a scholar as well as someone who cagily survived a traumatic wartime marriage and found a way to immigrate. Having introduced these details, which seem meant to give Ying-ying both psychological specificity and complexity—she is both a sometime victim and an adaptive survivor—the novel then trivializes them by having the character think and speak as a generic peddler of stereotypical folk wisdom. And, since this is an *internal* monologue presumably conducted in Chinese rather than English, why should it be represented in ersatz pidgin English?

A Chinese Account: Pa Chin's *Family*

The line between wishing for Chinese characters to be portrayed in a manner that presumes a modern consciousness—avoiding the temporal distancing of Chinese women as passive, accepting victims in a primitive, static culture—and asking that all Chinese be portrayed as having enlightened, arguably Westernized minds free of traditional beliefs construed by Westerners as "superstitions"—is admittedly a fine one. I have argued that several portions of Tan's novel are problematic. First, it portrays a majority of Chinese as unquestioning and rather literal in their acceptance of traditional social hierarchies and traditional beliefs in evil omens, ghosts, astrological signs, and the like, which when presented as divorced from the fuller social context seem to function as markers of alterity, producing, as Sau-ling Wong has remarked, a pleasing "Oriental effect" of congruence between the text and the reader's orientalist expectations ("Sisterhood," 187). In my reading, such moments, combined with gullibility and mean-spiritedness (in "The Red Candle") or faux pidgin English and psychological and historical incoherence (in "Waiting Between the Trees"), contribute to an underestimation of the heterogeneity and sophistication of Chinese minds. In addition, the Chinese narrators fail to convey a sense that their stories take place in a country where conventional wisdoms are questioned and discussed, not only by elites but eventually by people in all walks of life. Finally, these lapses contribute to distortions in the novel's conception of the necessary and sufficient conditions for young women to escape unhappy marriages and control their futures in China. To give the book its due, some chapters gracefully avoid these gaffes and work toward conveying a sense of the characters' modernity. I find the stories about Suyuan Woo, for instance, moving and persuasive.

To flesh out this discussion about agency and Chinese consciousness, a useful comparison might be made with a domestic novel by an influential Chinese writer born in 1904, a text that addresses one of Tan's central themes, young people attempting to rebel against the tyranny of their elders. *Family*, an autobiographical novel composed by the radical Chinese writer Pa Chin in 1931, is said to be his masterpiece.[15] According to Olga Lang's introduction, it was an immediate hit with Chinese readers, who responded to its attacks on the old Chinese family system, which "deprived the young of their freedom of action and their right to love and marry according to their own choice" (Introduction, viii). After the Communist revolution of 1949, Pa Chin's work was perceived as having helped "to create among the intellectuals an emotional climate which induced them to accept the Communist revolution," and so it continued to be read, for another seventeen years, until the Cultural Revolution (xxi-xxii). Set in a provincial capital city, Chengtu, in 1931, and incorporating the novelist's experiences during the 1920s, the novel depicts the struggles of three brothers (Chueh-hsin, Chueh-min, and Chueh-hui) to claim autonomy within a wealthy clan ruled by their elderly grandfather (or *Yeh-yeh*), the Venerable Master Kao. The brothers, their cousins, and their friends attend cosmopolitan schools, read Western literature, and are caught up with the new social ideas of the May Fourth Movement. Chueh-hui, the youngest son, often seems to speak for the author, an anarchist, in his youthful intolerance for hypocrisy and oppression. His character is established early in the novel in a typical diary entry:

> That book *Yeh-yeh* gave me—"On Filial Piety and the Shunning of Lewd-ness"—was still on the table. I picked it up and skimmed through a few pages. The whole thing is nothing but lessons on how to behave like a slave. It's full of phrases like "the minister who is unwilling to die at his sovereign's command is not loyal; the son who is unwilling to die at his father's command is not filial," and "of all crimes, lewdness is the worst; of all virtues, filial piety is the best." The more I read, the angrier I became, until I got so mad I ripped the book to pieces. With one less copy of that book in the world, a few less people will be harmed by it. (85-86)

By pitting the younger generation against the elder and focusing particularly on the effects of arranged marriage and forced concubinage, the novel makes the simple point that Chinese attitudes toward traditional beliefs varied even within generations and classes. In contrast to the empowering suicide in "Magpies," for instance, Pa Chin describes the suicide of an adolescent slave girl, Ming-feng, who loves Chueh-hui but is chosen by the Venerable Master (the one who so disapproves of lewdness) to be sold as a concubine to another rich elderly man. Although her mistress disapproves, she refuses to help, claiming that she can't go against the patriarch's word. Her sweetheart, Chueh-hui, has secretly promised to help and even marry her, but he is not told of the plan and when she tries to tell him is too busy with his exams and his radical paper even to find out what is troubling her. Pa Chin writes: "Her hopes were completely shattered. They even wanted to take away the love she depended upon to live, to present her verdant spring to a crabbed old man. Life as a concubine in a family like the Fengs' could bring only one reward: tears, blows, abuse, the same as before. The only difference would be that now, in addition, she would have to give her body to be despoiled by a peculiar old man whom she had never met. . . . After eight years of hard work and faithful service that was her only reward" (204). When Ming-feng drowns herself in the family's lake, her action has no effect on old Master Kao. He simply sends another maid in her place and purchases a third to do Ming-feng's chores for the Kaos. There is no scandal, no investigation, no fear or thought of her ghost; the death is hushed up within the family compound, and only the few who care remember her. At the same time, Pa Chin describes a greater range of responses to the problem than we hear of in Tan's stories. In the days before the "wedding," Ming-feng often overhears others disparaging the transaction, such as the angry woman in the kitchen who cries, "A young girl like that becoming the 'little wife' of an old man who's half dead! I wouldn't do it for all the money in the world!" (210). (Only in the kitchen does anyone refer to the money old Master Kao will receive for Ming-feng.) Ironically, all this disapproving gossip deeply humiliates Ming-feng but never reaches Master Kao's venerable ears.

The phenomenon of covert, passive dissent among decent people who confuse compliance with virtue is bitterly dissected in this novel. In the novel's climax, which sheds further light on traditional Chinese beliefs, a pregnant woman is sacrificed to protect the supposed interests of the Venerable Master shortly after his death. It seems the women of the elder and middle generations have become obsessed with the belief that, if Jui-chieh, the wife of the oldest brother, Chueh-hsin, should give birth while Master Kao's corpse is still in the house, she would emit a "blood-glow" that "would attack the corpse and cause it to spurt large quantities of blood" (296). This can only be prevented by sending the pregnant woman to give birth beyond the city gates on the far side of a bridge. Pa Chin describes "the curse of the blood-glow," a superstition that overtly places the interests of the dead over those of the living, as something most people in the household discount but are too timid to criticize openly. Lest we think that only the educated, Westernized youth question the myth, the author includes a scene in which Chueh-hsin's middle-aged servant begs the third brother to avert the move: "I don't think she ought to go, Third Young Master. Even if she must, it ought to be to some place decent. Only rich people have all these rules and customs. Why doesn't First Young Master speak up? We servants don't understand much, but we think her life is more important than all these rules" (299). Despite the urgent (but prudently covert) pleas of this servant and of his brothers, Chueh-hsin fails to defend his wife for fear of being called "unfilial." The rest of the household follows his cues, and the expectant mother dies in agony in an isolated house outside the city. Later, Jui-chieh's mother clearly holds the Kaos responsible for her death.

By contrast, Tan has An-mei Hsu describe a cannibalistic gesture of her mother's with apparent approval. After An-mei's family has cast her mother out, forcing the young widow to become a concubine, the mother returns to nurse her mother, Popo, on her deathbed, where she uses flesh and blood from her own arm to brew a medicinal broth for the dying woman. An-mei cites this not only as a metaphor for filial piety but as a gesture that she personally witnessed, recognized as an ancient Chinese custom, and admired; she came to "love her mother" by witnessing this scene:

> My mother took her flesh and put it in the soup. She cooked magic in the ancient tradition to try to cure her mother this one last time. She opened Popo's mouth, already too tight from trying to keep her spirit in. She fed her this soup, but that night Popo flew away with her illness.
>
> Even though I was young, I could see the pain of the flesh and the worth of the pain. (48)

King-kok Cheung wonders whether this is an actual Chinese custom, and so do I.[16] While we might ask the same question about Pa Chin's "curse of the blood-glow," my point is that the two writers position ordinary Chinese very differently in relation to the questionable practices evoked. Moreover, Tan positions herself here as an inside authority instructing her readers about Chinese culture, just as An-mei is suppos-edly instructing Rose; given such positioning, the text does not signal that the custom described may be an invention or a metaphor. By con-trast, Pa Chin implicitly addresses an audience of fellow Chinese who are presumably equipped to assess the literal or poetic truth of his "curse" within Confucian family life.

Unlike Tan, Pa Chin portrays traditional beliefs as held selectively in accordance with existing social hierarchies. The interests of old, rich, powerful men are invoked even after death, while the ultimate protest of a pure-hearted slave girl goes unheeded. Why does the su-perstition of the blood-glow require the removal of the living rather than the dead? Could it be that this is a way for the middle generation to parade their filial piety at a time when they are struggling over the es-tate? Or is this action one more battle in the Third and Fourth House-holds' undeclared domestic warfare with the First Household, now led by Chueh-hsin? Clearly, the death of the patriarch makes this a good time for the other households to test and destroy the influence of Chueh-hsin, the eldest son of his generation, which this move accom-plishes. Since the story of Jui-chueh's death is the culminating incident in the novel, the ghoulish curse is also clearly selected by the author to epitomize the older generation's abuse of the young. No doubt Pa Chin was influenced by reformers such as the eminent writer Lu Hsun, who chose cannibalism as a metaphor for the oppressiveness of the Chinese feudal system in his notorious satire, "The Diary of a Madman."[17] In contrast to such moments in Tan's novel, where acts or beliefs that would be considered foolish, bizarre, or unbelievable in a Westerner are justified as Chinese customs, traditional beliefs in *Family* are inter-woven with other interests—as Christian beliefs might be in an Amer-ican story—and are observed according to individual interests and temperaments. The curse of the blood-glow, for instance, is readily dis-counted not only by the "Westernized" masters and the younger gener-ation but by their servants and Jui-chieh's mother, who are ruled by their feelings for Jui-chieh. Thus, Pa Chin's novel, like Tan's, depicts prerevolutionary China as a site of questionable traditional practices, hypocrisy, and cruelty, but it does not ask readers to misapply cultural relativism by justifying these things as acceptable to Chinese.

Family also conveys the difficulty of resisting custom, even for the wealthy, educated heirs of the clan. In one chapter, the brothers' favorite female cousin, Chin, an admirer of Ibsen, contributes a feminist editorial advocating short hair for women, but she lacks the nerve to cut her own hair. Her timidity isn't without cause; when she broaches the subject to her mother, the latter casually threatens to take her out of school and marry her off early to a rich stranger. In this period, elite female education was still valued primarily for its influence on women as future wives and mothers, an attitude conveyed by Mrs. Kao's resistance to Chin's attempt at critical thinking (Croll, *Feminism*, 153-84). Coached by a freethinking schoolmate, Chin is able to see her mother's threat in collective terms:

> Before long there suddenly appeared a lengthy highway stretching to infinity, upon which were lain spreading corpses of young women. It became clear to her that this road was built thousands of years ago; the earth on the road was saturated with the blood and tears of those women. They were all tied and handcuffed and driven to this road, and made to kneel there, to soak the earth with their blood and tears, to satiate the sex desire of wild animals with their bodies. . . .
>
> Then, last but not least [came the question]: "Are you willing to give up the one you love, and hand yourself over to be the instrument of sexual satisfaction to some stranger?" . . . Justice was so dim, remote and uncertain. Her hope was completely dashed. (202)

Chin resolves privately to "take a new road," but she is so inexperienced in testing authority that she cannot even tell if her mother's remarks are serious, or communicate her vision to her.

Fortunately, Chin's principles are not put to the ultimate test faced by Ming-feng because her male cousins finally are motivated by earlier family tragedies to resist this sort of coercion. When her sweetheart, the second son, Chueh-min, is threatened with an arranged match, he runs away and stays away until Venerable Master Kao (still alive at this point in the novel) agrees to suspend the engagement, altering the family climate so that Chin is left free to continue her studies and to marry Chueh-min later. However, this resistance is only possible with the support of the brothers' radical schoolmates, who hide him for several weeks; Chin, whose consciousness has been raised by her classmate's discussion of these issues and by witnessing other unhappy lovers; and Chueh-hui, still enraged by the recent death of Ming-feng. Fortunately, the grandfather capitulates and reconciles with Chueh-min before either disowning him or dying.

The novel suggests that, oppressed as young men are by the system, they are still less isolated than their female peers. Throughout the novel, it is the young men who are invested with the possibility of saving themselves and others, and the young women who wail, suffer, and die for their mistakes. It is so much harder for the women to rebel that the brothers are held doubly responsible—for themselves and their loved ones. Chin, the most privileged and feminist of the cousins, hesitates to write a feminist article until she is coaxed by Chueh-hui, the journalist; she dares not even cut her hair or argue with her mother. However, during Chieh-min's exile from the Kao household, she is sustained not only by friends but by access to the modern ideas she has imbibed at school and in her cousins' company. Ming-feng, by contrast, lacks both an ideology of freedom—she longs for it but does not understand herself to be entitled to it, as Chin does—and a network of supporters.

While this highly autobiographical novel is clearly more concerned with male agency, the women's weaker resolve and more limited scope for action seem to reflect not only the author's individual perceptions, and his synthesis of Chinese and Western literary conventions for portraying female agency, but also an underlying recognition of women's greater oppression. Ironically, the only heroine who exercises real agency in *Family* is Ming-feng, whose suicide refuses and indicts the Venerable Master and steels Chueh-hui's resolve to rebel. When the family system becomes too intolerable for Ming-feng, she can only rebel and escape through suicide, whereas Chin has the support of her classmates and cousins and Chueh-hui finds ways both to rebel at home and eventually to flee to Shanghai, there to pursue his studies, activism, and literary work.[18]

By examining a Chinese novel that treats the same period Tan claims for her Chinese characters' girlhood and youth, we can gain additional perspective on the stories Tan chooses to tell: we see that the oppressive family system Tan describes in her novel was being questioned on a national level by Chinese reformers (the brothers in Chengtu read Beijing-based publications and correspond with like-minded students in Shanghai); that traditional beliefs in ghosts, ancestors, astrology, and the like were held literally by some (arguably, by older and less-educated people), disbelieved by others, and applied selectively by others; and that acts of rebellion and resistance—the claiming of individual agency—required not only individual will (Ming-feng has that) but a network of supporters. Such a network needed to be sustained both by a coherent alternate ideology, strong enough to counter the moralistic condemnation of Confucian thinking, and by material resources. By this novel's standards, the view of Chinese female agency in Lindo's story, "The Red Candle," and An-mei's "Magpies" must be considered incomplete and simplistic. At the same time, Pa Chin's sinocentric perspective sets off more clearly Tan's shaping of her Chinese stories to fit the demands of her (Asian) American genre, the mother-daughter romance. Set in a Chinese society that is distant and picturesque, yet contained by the novelist's simplifying representational choices, the mothers' stories serve to complement and set off the daughters' more familiar, arguably more banal problems as middle-class American women. The women's claiming of agency as a central theme in a majority of the stories serves agreeably to unite the stories of the two generations.

The Mother-Daughter Romance

I have suggested that in Tan's intricate mother-daughter version of the immigrant romance the repeated rapprochements of mothers and daughters who discover they are not so very different is one way of addressing, in a sentimental plot, contradictions inherent in American attitudes toward immigration—specifically the contradiction between the country's ideology of inclusion and its systematic mechanisms for excluding unwelcome newcomers. In this context, the novel's doubled presentation of the mothers as both alien and familiar is central to its ideological force as a set of utopian immigration stories: the mothers must be sufficiently alien to provide "diversity" but sufficiently American to enter mainstream society without radically disturbing or transforming its flow. The text works by giving substance to the American daughters'/readers' combined attraction to, and anxieties about, the mothers' alienness and then relieving those anxieties with assurances of underlying sameness. A good example of this is "Best Quality," in which June worries that her mother, Suyuan, may have done away with her tenants' cat, a fear reminiscent of anti-Chinese literature emphasizing exotic/repulsive practices from footbinding and opium smoking to the consumption of cats and dogs. As June moves toward recognition that her late mother remains close to her because she is, figuratively and literally, in her bones (197-209), the cat reappears, further dispelling June's vague fears about her mother's differentness. In this regard, the text's representation of a group of middle-class women as exemplary immigrants and citizens serves a reconciling function; the class of these mothers and daughters renders them readily assimilable into middle-class American life, while their gender somewhat distances them from the negative images of Asian males that have been generated by nineteenth-century observations of working-class male sojourners, on one hand, and Asian soldiers and leaders in modern wars in Asia and the Pacific Rim on the other.

The final chapter, in which June takes her late mother's place in a reconciliation with her long-lost half sisters in China, carries the logic of symbolic reconciliation one step further, offering an image of understanding between (ethnic) Americans (June and her father) and Chinese (their relatives) in an era of increased American interest in future ties with China. In this chapter, June's successful first contacts with her Chinese relatives capture larger American attitudes toward China. The basis for June's happy encounters, and metaphorically for cross-cultural understanding, is, in brief, that the Americans come to value ethnic diversity (both outside and within themselves) while the Chinese become familiar, seemingly "the same" at heart, through their acceptance of global capitalism. Thus, the sixty-year estrangement of June's father, Canning Woo, from his aunt is eased by the amenities of their Westernized luxury hotel, Polaroids, hamburgers, and apple pie. Even Coca-Cola, the symbol of American callousness in the novel's opening, is recoded as a sign of China's reassuring Westernization when it appears in the Woos' hotel room bar with other familiar name brands. Belying the remote, impoverished China of the mother's tales, Mr. Woo's elderly aunt tells him that her sons are cleaning up and conspicuously consuming without fear in China's newly liberalized economy: "My sons have been quite successful, selling our vegetables in the free market. We had enough these last few years to build a big house, three stories, all of new brick, big enough for our whole family and then some. . . . You Americans aren't the only ones who know how to get rich!" (296). Even at this moment of seeing China as a modernizing country, the return of the two-worlds problem can be heard in the elderly lady's dialogue: Chinese success is described in comparison with American norms. Described through a tourist's eye, June's perceptions of contemporary China generally share this presumption of a framing American perspective. Conveniently occluded from this perspective are questions about the Chinese government's policy of embracing capitalism but not democracy; ironically, Tan's book was published in 1989, the year the massacre at Tiananmen Square dramatized the limits of official tolerance for democratic movements in the People's Republic of China.

Finally, how does this novel construct Chinese American ethnicity? In the concluding image, the Polaroid portrait of June with her half sisters, the Chinese sisters prove to be uncanny replicas of the absent mother, both alien and familiar. The alien in manageable form, they appear with June to enact Suyuan's long-cherished wish of assimilating her Chinese past and her American future: "The gray-green surface changes to the bright colors of our three images, sharpening and deepening all at once. And although we don't speak, I know we all see it: Together we look like our mother. Her same eyes, her same mouth, open in surprise to see, at last, her long-cherished wish" (288). From the mother's perspective, the Polaroid represents the happy denouement of the immigration myth set forth at the novel's beginning. Through June and her father, the mother has told her story. The American daughter has understood, will become a successful American version of her mother, and will carry forward her tradition, her wishes, her lineage. And, in terms of the immigrant romance, the American daughter who listens and honors her mother both stands in for the American reader and mediates the mother's self-presentation to that reader.

From June's perspective, the "return" to China represents a return to origins. She begins the novel by taking her late mother's place at the mahjong table, described as "the East, where things begin" (41). In "Best Quality," she comes to a temporary resolution in her mourning by recognizing her mother's presence within herself (209), but this is not quite enough. By ending the book with "A Pair of Tickets," depicting the "reunion" with the lost sisters in China, Tan suggests that the Chinese American's work of remembering the mother/motherland is incomplete without this return and that there is something still unknown about the mother that can only be found in China—something that is represented by the unknown sisters. June's nervousness about the meeting with her half sisters seems driven by fear that, because they came first and grew up in China, they will judge her as a substitute for her mother and will find her deficient in ethnic consciousness and moral character—traits that the novel as a whole conflates with Chinese life experience. By appearing at this moment in June's story—a few months after her mother's death—the sisters threaten to assume in June's mind the role of the demanding, judgmental mother of June's childhood, the mother described in "Two Kinds" (132-44). The mothers and half sisters stand for both China and Chineseness, then, and for a psychologically significant other June is seeking to internalize in building a whole adult self. The sense is that part of that self is an inherited core of Chineseness, or of the Chinese feminine (the missing siblings cannot, in Tan's novel, be *brothers*), but that completion of her adult self requires the integration of that aspect within a subjectivity that will be strengthened by acknowledging its presence—this is the work of the Chinese American daughter. The recognition of affinity captured by the Polaroid, then, functions as a sign that June has passed the test of the mother-like sisters' inspection and that the work of mourning/reconstruction represented figuratively by the novels' many maternal narratives has been successful. The American daughter has constructed her Chinese aspects appropriately, lending complexity to her American self without rendering it fundamentally different; the threat of radical difference is embodied by the mothers and their stories—enough to be enjoyed—but is contained in a narrative frame emphasizing the daughter's psychological work and the sentimental story of the finding of the long-lost sisters. Thus, the phrase "your mother is in your bones," which might once have meant that Chinese Americans could not be considered American, now means they share with other Americans an enriching access to a matrilineal heritage of protofeminist individualism and enterprise.

Notes

1. Matrilineal Asian North American narratives of note include Cynthia Kado-hata's *The Floating World*, Julie Shikeguni's *A Bridge between Us*, Sky Lee's *The Disappearing Moon Cafe*, and the texts cited in note 3. For an analysis of Tan's popular success, see Sau-ling Cynthia Wong, "Sugar Sisterhood': Situating the Amy Tan Phenomenon," in *The Ethnic Canon: Histories, Institutions, and Interventions*, ed. David Palumbo-Liu (Minneapolis: U of Minnesota P, 1995), 175-210.

2. Melani McAlister, "(Mis)Reading *The Joy Luck Club*," *Asian America: Journal of Culture and the Arts 1* (winter 1992): 102-18.

3. My reading of Tan's treatment of this theme may be taken as a sequel to my study of daughterly self-formation in Maxine Hong Kingston's *The Woman Warrior*, which was in turn enriched by the mother-daughter studies cited therein. The mother-daughter plot may be read as a feminist alternative to the male immigration plots of romantic desire for white women and the abjection of Asian women. It may be placed in dialogue with oedipal male narratives such as Frank Chin's and David Mura's, in which American-born sons re-create themselves by separating and differentiating themselves from fathers perceived as deficient. It may also serve as a paradigm for reading Asian American men's narratives such as Gus Lee's *Honor and Duty*.

Some of the most prominent and effective Asian American fictional examples include Kim Ronyoung's *Clay Walls*, Fae Myenne Ng's *Bone*, and Velina Hasu Houston's *Tea*. Biographical works structured by this plot include Denise Chong's *The Concubine's Daughter*, Lydia Minatoya's *Talking to High Monks in the Snow*, and, of course, Eaton's "Leaves."

4. *Myth* here denotes an archetypical plot that shapes numerous individual narratives defining the American sense of self and nation, both fictional and nonfictional. Although I have argued that Asians have often been portrayed and perceived as fundamentally un-American, Tan clearly invites cross-racial identification by modeling her immigrant Chinese women after this myth of the immigrant as quintessential American self.

5. The idealism with which Chinese in particular have traditionally regarded America is embedded in their names for it: Beautiful Country and Gold Mountain.

6. A classic immigrant success story that largely incorporates this plot is Abraham Cahan's *The Rise of David Levinsky* (1917; New York: Penguin, 1993). Levinsky does not marry but considers this a deviation from the usual pattern of transferring one's aspirations to one's children. An orphan whose assimilation is linked with his commercial success as a cloak manufacturer, Levinsky claims agency primarily through his capacity for entrepreneurial initiative and risk taking. Levinsky's rise through his own "luck and pluck" in turn resonates with the formula for personal success popularized in Horatio Alger's stories for boys. See for instance, Horatio Alger Jr., *Ragged Dick and Struggling Upward*, ed. Carl Bode (1868, 1890; New York: Penguin, 1985). For various reasons, such opportunities tend not to be the focus of female immigration narratives.

In addition to these male paradigms, my account of the immigration myth draws upon my reading of Asian American immigration narratives and upon William

Boelhower's multiethnic studies of immigration narratives. See his "Ethnic Trilogies" and "Brave New World."

7. Here James Joyce's fictional alter ego, Stephen Dedalus, announces his intention to create a new literary voice, which will be both modern and distinctly Irish. Dedalus differs from Tan's June in his willingness to authorize *himself* in order to renounce traditional obligations, but he shares with her the objective of creating a literature for his community, his "race." Dedalus's greater ambition, to create a literature that will define his community as a people, goes beyond June's immediate aim, but it significantly resembles the collective Asian American project of literary self-authoring.

8. Johannes Fabian, *Time and the Other: How Anthropology Makes Its Object* (New York: Columbia UP, 1983), cited in Rey Chow, *Women and Chinese Modernity: the Politics of Reading between West and East* (Minneapolis: U of Minnesota P, 1991). Most of the Chinese episodes in Tan's novel occur between 1914 and 1946, the beginning of World War I and the end of World War II from the Western point of view. However, since the interwar period was one of continuous civil war and unrest for China, I use the term *pre-Communist* to refer to the period between the fall of the Manchu dynasty (1911) and the establishment of the People's Republic of China (1949), a time when China lacked a strong central government.

9. Rey Chow, *Women and Chinese Modernity*, 30-31. See also Sau-ling Cynthia Wong's discussion of temporal distancing in Amy Tan's work ("Sugar Sisterhood," 185-86). While I concur with her analysis, my work is more concerned with how this allochronism enables readers to overlook the problems raised by the novel's representations of female agency, how it contributes to the erasure of modern Chinese subjectivities from the text, and how it contributes to the construction of the mother-daughter romance as an immigration narrative.

10. Melani McAlister reads this as a moment when Ying-ying asserts that she must change her relationship with Lena ("(Mis)Reading," 112). Her deft reading avoids crediting all Chinese mothers with ancient folk wisdom; it does, however, accept a highly optimistic view of Ying-ying's agency, the view that she could reverse the effects of a lifetime of passivity and poor communication by speaking frankly with her daughter on this single occasion.

11. Historian Jonathan Spence argues in *The Search for Modern China* (New York: Norton, 1990) that with the abdication of the last Ching emperor in 1912 the following decades of social and political upheaval were also characterized by an ongoing search for new ideas about how to govern China, with Western liberal democracies and the Russian socialist system emerging as the most significant foreign models. Significant histories of feminist movements in China, which may counter the notion of classical China as socially unchanged for the first five decades of this century, are offered by Elisabeth Croll, *Feminism and Socialism in China* (London: Routledge, 1978); Kazuko Ono, *Chinese Women in a Century of Revolution, 1850-1950*, trans. Kathryn Bernhardt et al., ed. Joshua A. Fogel (1978; Stanford: Stanford UP, 1989); and Kay Ann Johnson, *Women, the Family, and Peasant Revolution in China* (Chicago: UP of Chicago, 1983). Such histories, combined with the novel about to be discussed, confirm Tan's sense that Chinese women had few means of resisting the sex-gender system characterized by arranged marriages, but they also provide a more complex and

varied sense of how the Chinese inhabited this system and how it could continue despite being a source of misery for so many.

12. On the experiences of Chinese women immigrants in America, see Judy Yung, *Unbound Feet: A Social History of Chinese Women in San Francisco* (Berkeley: U of California P, 1995).

13. For instance, Ying-ying St. Clair is born in 1914. In the "Moon Lady," which takes place in 1918, she depicts her father, "a dedicated scholar of ancient history and literature," emending ancient poetry with his gentleman guests while her mother, oblivious to the literary discussion, discusses herbal cures for sore feet (an oblique reference to foot binding?) with other women (70-71). This tranquil scene, replete with traditionally gendered topics of instruction, contributes to the episode's allochronism. At the time, the country was embroiled in civil war, it lacked a stable central government, and it was confronting the outrage of Japan's twenty-one demands (Chow Tse-tung, 9-10). Tan's story does not evoke a peaceful interlude in a period of turmoil, an upper-class family wilfully denying events that might affect them or others, or the memories of a child registering but unable to interpret the troubles of her adult relatives; rather, it evokes an idealized classical China free of political or social tensions. If we take the American episodes to be "contemporary" in 1989, the year of publication, we should imagine the mothers as women in their seventies; Canning Woo is seventy-two in the novel's "present" (268).

14. Concepts of the self vary within cultures, but a useful starting point might be Alan Roland's discussion of the Western philosophical roots of psychoanalytic concepts of self, as contrasted with May Tung's account of Chinese concepts of the self. See Alan Roland, "How Universal Is the Psychoanalytic Self?" (3-21, esp. 3-13), and May Tung, "Insight-Oriented Therapy and the Chinese Patient" (175-86), both in Alan Roland, *Cultural Pluralism and Psychoanalysis: The Asian and North American Experience* (New York: Routledge, 1996).

15. Pa Chin, *Family*, trans. Sidney Shapiro (1931, 1972; Prospect Heights, Ill.: Waveland, 1989).

16. King-kok Cheung, "Re-viewing Asian American Literacy Studies," in *An Interethnic Companion to Asian American Literature*, ed. King-kok Cheung (Boston: Cambridge UP, 1997), 30, n. 16.

17. In his 1918 satire "The Diary of a Madman," Lu's mad diarist writes: "I take a look at history; it is not a record of time but on each page are confusedly written the characters 'benevolence, righteousness, and morals'" and "Desperately unsleeping, I carefully look it over again and again for half the night, and at last find between the lines that it is full of the same word 'cannibalism!'" He goes on: "Having unconsciously practiced cannibalism for four thousand years, I am awakening now and feel ashamed to face a genuine human being!" See Lu Hsun, "The Diary of a Madman," *New Youth* 4, no. 5 (May 15, 1918): 414-24 (trans. and qtd. in Chow Tse-tung, 308).

18. The novel's ending replicates the author's permanent departure from Chengtu in 1923. His studies and literary work led him to Shanghai, Nanjing, and Paris, but he returned to Shanghai in 1928. He chose to remain in China for the rest of his life, and his novel reflects a commitment to the need for and possibility of change within China that is, understandably, absent from Tan's.

Works Cited

Chow Tse-tung. *The May Fourth Movement: Intellectual Revolution in Modern China*. Cambridge: Harvard UP, 1960.

Croll, Elisabeth. *Feminism and Socialism in China*. London: Routledge, 1978.

Joyce, James. *A Portrait of the Artist as a Young Man*. 1916. New York: Viking-Penguin, 1976.

Mukherjee, Bharati. *Jasmine*. New York: Fawcett Crest-Random House, 1989.

Wolf, Margery. "Women and Suicide in China." In *Women in Chinese Society*, ed. Margery Wolf and Roxanne Witke. Stanford: Stanford UP, 1975. 111-41.

Wong, Sau-Ling Cynthia. "'Sugar Sisterhood': Situating the Amy Tan Phenomenon." In *The Ethnic Canon: Histories, Institutions, and Interventions*, ed. David Palumbo-Liu. Minneapolis: U of Minnesota P, 1995. 175-210.

Narrative Beginnings in Amy Tan's
The Joy Luck Club:
A Feminist Study_____

Catherine Romagnolo

> Like virginity, literary introductions are often seen as an awkward embarrassment, an obstacle to be overcome as quickly as possible in order to facilitate vital experiences. On the other hand, "the first time" is a supremely privileged moment, to be lingered over, contemplated, and cherished. Which is the more telling conception we can only begin to imagine.
>
> —Steven Kellman, "Grand Openings and Plain"

> Even feminist narratology . . . has tended to focus on women writers or female narrators without asking how the variables "sex," "gender," and "sexuality" might operate in narrative more generally.
>
> —Susan S. Lanser, "Queering Narratology"

Few extensive studies of narrative beginnings exist, and not one takes a feminist perspective. Offering almost exclusively formalist readings, existing analyses neglect the ideological implications of beginnings, especially as they relate to gender, race, and cultural identity.[1] Even as scholars overlook ideological valence in narrative beginnings, their own readings often indicate, perhaps unexpectedly, that social and cultural concerns adhere to any conception of beginnings. For example, Steven Kellman, one of the first to study narrative beginnings in an extended analysis, evokes ways that cultural bias is embedded in these studies. The sexualized metaphor he uses to illustrate the trouble inherent in starting a literary text testifies to this bias. The problem with his description arises when one considers the historical importance placed on female purity and virginity in numerous cultures. Not only is the conception of virginity as an "awkward embarrassment" a specifically heteronormatively masculinist perspective, but it also posits the proverbial pen-as-penis, page/text-as-female-body metaphor with whose ideological valences we are all familiar. Furthermore, the analogy obscures cultural differences that shape the relationship of a given individual to gendered sexuality. Similarly, A. D. Nuttall, while recognizing that his text on narrative beginnings is a "spectacle of alternating (male) authority and (male) sequence [that] will certainly be unpleasing to some people,"[2] never interrogates this exclusively white male focus (vii). These studies serve as examples of the way gender concerns, however invisible, are often already linked to beginnings. They invite us to examine seriously the identificatory variables that have been elided and to take up the challenge identified by Susan S. Lanser to explore how social categories operate in narrative (250).

The Joy Luck Club by Amy Tan is an ideal vehicle with which to begin such a project.[3] It is suggestive of a new way to look at narrative beginnings, one that emphasizes a destabilization of conceptions of history that exclude women, particularly those of non-European descent. This way of reading narrative beginnings encourages an interrogation of the relevance of both European American and Asian American cultural and national origins for Asian American female subjects, as well as promoting a resistance to the notion of an alternatively authentic origin. If we attend to the ideological significance of beginnings in Tan's novel, a critique of the very concept of origins—especially in its relation to "American," "Chinese," and "Chinese American" identity— becomes apparent. Moreover, doing so illuminates the discursive constructedness of authenticity, origins, and identity, thereby problematizing reductive cultural representations of female, American, and Asian American subjectivity. Building on recent scholarship about Asian American literature and subjectivity, which has suggested that *The Joy Luck Club* has been misread,[4] this essay attempts to extend, if not disrupt, the readings of many scholars from different disciplines who impose certain kinds of master narratives onto this novel.[5] While these readings are not so much "wrong" as they are incomplete, an examination of this text's narrative beginnings can at once help us to theorize narrative with an attentiveness to difference and to recognize this help as integral to the cultural work Tan's novel performs.

Narrative beginnings, as suggested by the example of *The Joy Luck Club*, assume a symbolic primacy in relation to social identity. Because, as Tan's text demonstrates, they represent one way to conceptualize origins and contest the representational inadequacies of patriarchal, nationalist rhetoric, narrative beginnings often take on figurative status as metaphorical origins and embody the significance of origins in nationalist discourse. Origins and their relation to national identity and questions of authenticity are discussed by a wide variety of cultural and literary critics working in such diverse fields as post-colonial studies, U.S. minority discourse, and feminist theory. Such scholarship has interrogated the recovery of authentic cultural, literary, and historical origins, a nationalist recovery initially embarked upon in an effort to reveal the falsity of stereotypical conceptions of identity and to propose an "authentic" representation in their place. Although a thorough overview is beyond the scope of this essay, this scholarship broadly asserts that the importance placed upon authenticity can lead to discrimination and exclusion. Norma Alarcón et al., for example, explicate the problems associated with nationalism and the "denial of sexual or racial difference" within the nation-state (1). Etienne Balibar theorizes the ironic connection between racism and nationalism, even within what he calls "nationalism of the dominated" (45). And Dana Takagi, in the context of Asian American studies, contends that a fixation upon reclaiming authentic origins can occlude the experiences of marginalized members of a community: "At times, our need to 'reclaim history' has been bluntly translated into a possessiveness about the Asian American experience or perspectives as if such experiences or perspectives were not diffuse, shifting, and often contradictory" (33). In conjunction with such critiques of origins as grounds for social identity, many similarly oriented critics maintain the importance of narrative and narrative form to explicating gender, nation formation, national identity, and individual subjectivity. For example, Lisa Lowe argues that formal attributes of Asian American narratives express "an aesthetic of 'disidentification' and 'infidelity'" (32). Through formal and thematic "contradictions," she explains, this aesthetic critiques exclusionary conceptions of American and Asian American cultural identity. Contributing to such critical debates, my study of Amy Tan's novel demonstrates the importance of focusing on *narrative beginnings*, specifically, as sites at which these questions about origins, authenticity, and narrative converge.

Using Tan's text as a point of entry, I propose a more fully elaborated way of defining narrative beginnings in order to facilitate understanding of their ideological function and textual significance. Theorists such as Gerald Prince, Nuttall, and James Phelan have defined narrative beginnings in various ways. Prince, for example, defines them as "the incident[s] initiating the process of change in a plot or action . . . not necessarily follow[ing] but . . . necessarily followed by other incidents" (10). Nuttall, on the other hand, chooses to narrow his discussion to the actual opening lines and/or pages of a narrative text, claiming that these openings are "naturally rooted, are echoes, more or less remote, of an original creative act" (viii). Phelan, taking another approach, breaks his understanding of opening lines and/or pages into four separate categories: "exposition . . . initiation . . . introduction . . . entrance" (97). These definitions, while useful, fall short of distinguishing the different ways that beginnings may be conceptualized in narrative fiction. In effect, they have been unable to yield a discussion of the many ideological functions a beginning may serve within a narrative. The example of *The Joy Luck Club*, however, can serve as a source of critical insight from which we might generate a broader framework for the consideration of narrative beginnings. Working with Tan's novel, then, I schematize a critical paradigm for the study of four categories of narrative beginnings:

Structural Narrative Openings—The beginning pages or lines of a narrative, as well as the opening pages/lines of chapters or section breaks. This beginning is the most easily identified and most frequently studied.

Chronological Narrative Beginnings—The chronologically earliest diegetic moments in a narrative. Often there exist several simultaneously occurring textual moments that compete, in a sense, for the status of chronological beginning.

Causal Beginnings—The diegetic moment or moments that represent the catalyst for the main action within a narrative. They initiate or set into motion the conflict of the narrative.

Thematic Origins—The topic of origins or beginnings when it is interrogated or explored by the characters, narrator, or by the author her/himself. This beginning occurs on the story or content level of a narrative.

By working through this particularized framework that Tan's novel helps us to formulate, I propose that we can advance our understanding of both this text in particular and the broader narratological as well as cultural matters it thematizes.

Structural Narrative Openings: Repetition and Revision

The Joy Luck Club begins with what has been described by Asian American writer and cultural critic Frank Chin as a "fake" myth of origin:

> Then the woman and the swan sailed across an ocean many thousands of li wide, stretching their necks toward America. On her journey she cooed to the swan: "In America I will have a daughter just like me. But over there nobody will say her worth is measured by the loudness of her husband's belch. Over there nobody will look down on her, because I will make her speak only perfect American English. And over there she will always be too

full to swallow any sorrow! She will know my meaning, because I will give her this swan—a creature that became more than what was hoped for." (3)

This "fake Chinese fairy tale" is so described both because, according to Chin, it overstates the misogyny of Chinese society, and because it represents a misappropriation, a "faking," of Chinese culture (2). The implication of this misappropriation, Chin argues, is that Chinese Americans—particularly women—like Tan and her characters are so assimilated that they have lost touch with their "Chinese" cultural origins. Consequently, they have produced new feminized "versions of these traditional stories," which in trying to pass themselves off as authentic only represent a further "contribution to the stereotype," a stereotype which facilitates the emasculation of Asian American men (3).

We may take this myth to exemplify the structural opening, that is, the beginning lines/pages of Tan's novel. While other theories of narrative beginnings might identify this section of the text as the beginning, its purpose is not as self-evident as might be suggested. It is neither a "fake fairy tale" nor an "echo of an original creative act" (Nuttall viii). In fact, while the structural opening of *The Joy Luck Club* may initially appear to be trying (and failing, according to Chin) to establish and mythologize an authentic and originary moment of immigration from China to U.S.A. for the "Joy Luck aunties," it, in fact, disrupts the very notion of authenticity, especially in regard to origins. Although the first half of the myth seems to imply an unproblematic transition between Chinese and American cultures, by its ending, the contradiction between an idealized version of assimilation to "American" subjectivity and the fragmentation of identity that historically marks immigrant experiences becomes clear: "But when she arrived in the new country, the immigration officials pulled her swan away from her, leaving the woman fluttering her arms and with only one swan feather for a memory. And then she had to fill out so many forms she forgot why she had come and what she had left behind." Instead of either idealizing an essential Asian origin or mythologizing a melting-pot ideology of U.S.

immigration, Tan's structural narrative opening marks the way "America" strips the woman of her past, her idealized hopes for the future in the United States, and excludes her from an "American" national identity: the woman is still waiting "for the day she could tell her daughter this [narrative] in perfect American English" (3). By opening with a fabricated myth of origin, Tan's novel foregrounds the ideological implications of a search for beginnings and exemplifies the importance of narrative beginnings to an understanding of this text.

As Chin's response attests, Tan invokes a mythic sensibility in these opening lines, yet undermines the authority of nationalist myths of origin that attempt to uncover an uncorrupted past ethnic identity in which the members of the nation can "rediscover their authentic purpose" (Hutchinson 123). Through an ironic use of mythic form, language, and tone, Tan utilizes repetition for subversion. Repetition in this sense is a performance, which has "innovation," to use Trinh Minh-Ha's term, as its goal. Trinh explains:

> Recirculating a limited number of propositions and rehashing stereotypes to criticize stereotyping can . . . constitute a powerful practice. . . . Repetition as a practice and a strategy differs from incognizant repetition in that it bears with it the seeds of transformation. . . . When repetition reflects on itself as repetition, it constitutes this doubling back movement through which language . . . looks at itself exerting power and, therefore, creates for itself possibilities to repeatedly thwart its own power, inflating it only to deflate it better. (190)

Tan's opening myth utilizes mythic characters such as "The old woman" juxtaposed with historically rooted figures like immigration officials. It invokes mythic situations seemingly ungrounded in time such as a journey across an ocean "many thousands of li wide" contrasted by modern cultural icons like Coca-Cola. Her myth, then, reflects upon itself as national mythology, revised. In its self-reflexivity and difference, this formal and generic repetition serves to deflate the power of the so-called original. That is, by mimicking supposedly authentic nationalist mythologies, the self-consciously illegitimate status of Tan's myth exposes the inability of any nationalist project to recover a genuinely original, pure cultural history. Like Homi Bhabha's concept of mimicry, Tan's myth "problematizes the signs of racial and cultural priority, so that the 'national' is no longer naturalizable" (87). Because culture is always hybrid, any project that asserts purity must necessarily be "fake." This "fakeness" should not, however, be read as inauthenticity, but as a deconstruction of the very concept of authenticity.

The self-conscious repetition and revision of Tan's myth simultaneously destabilizes the notion of an authentic cultural origin (which gives rise to essentialist conceptions of gendered and racialized identities) and dislodges stereotypical representations of Chinese culture. For although the language of this structural opening might evoke a mythological aura, in its content, Tan's opening myth reflects the hybridity of immigrant subjectivity. That is, it signifies the historical "relationships of unequal power and domination" (Lowe 67) that accompany Chinese immigration to the United States. Moreover, it combines and interrogates stereotypically "Chinese" cultural symbols like the swan and "American" cultural emblems like Coca-Cola: "Now the woman was old. And she had a daughter who grew up speaking only English and swallowing more Coca-Cola than sorrow." In such cases, Tan utilizes overdetermined cultural symbols, which most readers would recognize as the trite, even clichéd, images that have come to signify the respective cultures. And yet, because of the way in which they are deployed, the repetition of these stereotypes cannot take hold as authentic representations; their authority is subverted. The symbol of the swan, stereotypically representative of Chinese women as graceful, silent, and docile, is hybridized and re-appropriated within Tan's narrative. It comes to symbolize both the woman's past ("the old woman remembered a swan she had bought many years ago in Shanghai for a foolish sum") and her idealized hopes for the future as an

American ("I will give her this swan—a creature that became more than what was hoped for"). In combining these contradictory impulses or desires (nativism and assimilation), the symbol becomes unstable, unfixed, never to be resolved within Tan's revisionist myth. Furthermore, as this symbol (the swan) is torn away from the old woman when she reaches the United States, we apprehend both the historical violence of immigration as well as the illusory nature of nativist and assimilationist mythology: "She forgot why she had come and what she had left behind" (3).

Tan also invokes a stereotypical emblem of Americanness in the materialistic and modern cultural icon, Coca-Cola. Yet, like the symbol of the swan, this sign is already unstable and dislocated from its supposed referent. For, while Coca-Cola has come to represent "Americanness," in fact, in this period of late-capitalism the corporation of Coca-Cola is found throughout the world. The transnational character of this icon registers the economic and cultural imperialism entailed in the success of Americanization on a global scale, while contradicting its status as American for it both is and is not American. This instability continuously interrogates what it means to be "American." That is, the Coca-Cola icon does not have as its referent some real originary "America," but alludes to a popular representation of Americanness as tied especially to diversity ("I'd like to buy the world a Coke"). This image is not only a cultural myth unto itself; it also points back to other media representations of America, which refer back yet again to the popular representation of America in "melting pot" ideology, a construction which has historically contributed to the elision of a United States that is, in reality, fraught with racial contradictions. Thus, through the chain of signifiers set in motion by the Coca-Cola icon, Tan's myth not only subverts the authority of cultural symbols but also confirms cultural identity to be discursively constructed. Finally, through the placement of these icons in an opening narrative which undermines its own status as a myth of origin, *The Joy Luck Club* structurally reaffirms the inadequacy of such "authentic" cultural symbols to represent the "original essence" of their cultures. The final effect of this myth, then, is not a reconciliation of contradictions—assimilation and nativism—but a dialogic representation of an immigrant experience that struggles with both of these impulses.

By positioning an obviously spurious myth at the structural opening of *The Joy Luck Club*, Tan gives her own text a false originary moment and thus further critiques the notion of origins. The duplicity of this opening structurally and symbolically undermines the text's status as an "immigration novel" that could somehow refer to and represent the "authentic" female immigrant experience. That is, by placing a false myth of origin—which refers only to other illusory origins—in the inaugural pages of her text, Tan implies metaphorically that the novel can never be said to recover any sort of authentic, definitive experience. In searching for the originary moment of Tan's writing, contrary to the "original creative act" that Nuttall finds in his dynasty of white-male authors, one finds an obvious "fake," a performative, symbolic repetition of an originary moment, which itself is discursively constructed (viii). Through this self-conscious performance, the novel argues that any claims of ethnic and/or national authenticity are suspect; they can only be said to allude intertextually to other discursive constructions.

Tan's structural opening is additionally significant in that it acts as a synecdoche for the thematic concerns of the novel. Through its preoccupation with a search for authenticity, origin, and/or the defining moment of one's identity, the story helps us to recognize links between structure and thematic origins. This thematic interest in beginnings is placed in dialogue with the text's structural openings, reinforcing its cultural critique. For example, Suyuan Woo, who has already died as the novel opens, has spent her entire life in an unsuccessful quest to recover the fateful moment when she left her babies on the roadside in Kweilin while fleeing from the invasion of Japanese soldiers. Symbolically, she tells her daughter Jing-mei (June): "The East is where things begin, . . . the direction from which the sun rises, where the wind comes from" (22). An-mei Hsu is also preoccupied with a quest. Her narrative tells the story of an attempt to recover the source of her psychic pain as well as a search for a mother who was absent for much of her childhood. She speaks of this past as a wound: "That is the way it is with a wound. The wound begins to close in on itself, to protect what is hurting so much. And once it is closed, you no longer see what is underneath, what started the pain" (40). And Ying-ying St. Clair, who is similarly in search of a lost self, remembers the sense of loss that accompanied her youth: "The farther we glided, the bigger the world became. And I now felt I was lost forever" (79).[6]

Despite the almost compulsive search for origin and identity displayed by the stories within this novel, each quest in its own way repudiates the existence of its goal. For example, although Suyuan claims that the East is where all begins, we learn that this "East" is not static; in fact, it moves and changes just as her Kweilin story changes each time she tells it. Although June takes her mother's place on the East side of the mah jong table, the East shifts places: "Auntie Ying throws the dice and I'm told that Auntie Lin has become the East wind. I've become the North wind, the last hand to play. Auntie Ying is the South and Auntie An-mei is the West" (23). Similarly, An-mei learns that underneath the multiple layers of memory that compose one's sense of self, there is no authentic core: "you must peel off your skin, and that of your mother, and her mother before her. Until there is nothing. No scar, no skin, no flesh" (41). And Ying-ying finds that although as she ages she feels closer and "closer to the beginning" of her life, that beginning, that origin is fluid—not fixed, but variable. She suggests this fluidity in speaking of the traumatic day in her childhood when she falls from a boat and is separated from her family. This moment in her life comes to represent, for her, the origin of her loss of self and the beginning, in a sense, of her adult life: "And I remember everything that happened that day because it has happened many times in my life. The same innocence, trust, and restlessness; the wonder, fear, and loneliness. How I lost myself" (83). Further undermining any sense of fixed

---

origins, Ying-ying's beginning also represents an end, a loss; for her, coming to a recognition of one's self entails a loss of a sense of wholeness.[7] The quests embarked upon by these women, therefore, repudiate the ability to recover any type of static identity which might solidify exclusionary conceptions of gendered and racialized subjectivity; at the same time, however, they stress the importance of the histories of these characters to their ongoing sense of agency, highlighting an idea of history as not completely knowable, but nevertheless significant to the discursive construction of identity.

Alternative Structural Openings: Authenticity and Truth

Although Tan's introductory tale possesses great significance, it merely represents the first of the structural narrative openings in her novel. In fact, *The Joy Luck Club* is constructed in such a manner that it has at least four section openings and sixteen chapter openings (four sections each with four chapters). Moreover, each of the characters has at least two narratives (which, with the exception of Suyuan, each narrates herself) and each of these narratives has at least one opening of its own, not necessarily coinciding with the opening pages of a section or a chapter; thus, the number of conceivable structural narrative openings is quite large. Although these separate stories are tied to one another through content and theme, each on its own arguably qualifies as a narrative with individual structure including an opening and a closing, however open that closing may be. (It seems to me that a reader could start this text at any one of these openings and still comprehend the narrative.) This proliferation of structural openings, in combination with the text's use of thematic origins, undermines the concept of an originary moment in obvious ways. That is, because each opening represents a new structural beginning, it signifies a challenge, contradicting any claim the first opening might make as the originary moment of the text. Thus, this repetition of openings symbolically represents the way in which a search for origins/authentic beginnings uncovers multiple possibilities, none clearly the most privileged, each possible origin continually displacing/deferring the privilege onto other possibilities.

Furthermore, it becomes clear in a close reading of these alternative openings that many are, in and of themselves, revisionist originary myths working to destabilize essentialist notions of authenticity and truth. The opening to the second section of the novel, "The Twenty-six Malignant Gates," for example, expresses a seemingly ambiguous message about cultural mythology and truth. For, while it exposes the book *The Twenty-Six Malignant Gates* as simply a fairy tale intended to keep young children obedient, this tale proves itself to be quite powerful. The mother in the opening narrative uses the myth in *The Twenty-Six Malignant Gates* to bolster her authority and support what she views to be best for her child—staying close to home: "'Do not ride your bicycle around the corner.' . . . 'I cannot see you and you will fall down and cry and I will not hear you.' 'How do you know I'll fall?' whined the girl. 'It's in a book, *The Twenty-Six Malignant Gates*, all the bad things that can happen to you outside the protection of this house.'" If we read this opening as a comment on the use of mythology in nationalist projects, Tan's revisionist myth can be seen as illustrative of the way in which the invocation of an "authentic" mythology/past may be used to manipulate subjects of a nation into loyalty to the "mother" country:

> "Let me see the book."
>
> "It is written in Chinese. You cannot understand it. That is why you must listen to me."
>
> "What are they, then?" The girl demanded. "Tell me the twenty-six bad things."
>
> But the mother sat knitting in silence.
>
> "What twenty-six!" shouted the girl.
>
> The mother still did not answer her.
>
> "You can't tell me because you don't know! You don't know anything!" (87)

Similar to the recovery or enforcement of a national language and the naturalization of ethnic and national identity, the mother's use of the "mother-tongue" (Chinese) in her invocation of this myth implies that the daughter's ethnic purity is questionable while simultaneously reinforcing the legitimacy of the myth. Both uses, then, are attempts to prevent the daughter from questioning the authority of the myth and to assert the daughter's inferiority to the mother's authenticity. The daughter, in recognizing and rejecting this authority and authenticity, exposes the actual status and purpose of the myth and in the process suggests a goal of nationalist mythology.

Yet, while the first half of this narrative seems to subvert claims of originality and truth, the ending of the narrative appears, at first, to reinforce the power of the very myth the opening exposes. Although the daughter uncovers the constructed nature of *The Twenty-Six Malignant Gates*, the prophecy her mother claims to extract from this myth comes to fruition: "And the girl ran outside, jumped on her bicycle, and in her hurry to get away, she fell before she even reached the corner" (87). Clearly, we are not to suppose that the myth actually predicted this child's injury; instead, we understand this ending to represent the ability of the myth to enter the child's imagination and prompt her to attribute her fall to the story's premonitory power. Thus, the narrative argues that the power of national mythology lies in the subject's imagination, not in some intrinsic truth.

Chronological and Causal Beginnings: History and Time

While the numerous structural openings of this novel are, like the structural openings of all novels, clearly located in fixed textual positions, the chronological beginning of Tan's narrative is not. The earliest diegetic moment is, perhaps, easy to identify in a single linear narrative; but a text like *The Joy Luck Club* is difficult to view as a single entity at all. It seems more appropriate to refer to the text's *narratives*.

And yet, even when we recognize their plurality, the actual earliest moments, or chronological beginnings, of all of these narratives are elusive. This fact is represented structurally in the complex chronological arrangement of Tan's text, as well as thematically in each of the stories. The numerous flashbacks and concurrent narratives that characterize the chronological organization of *The Joy Luck Club* challenge the idea of history as linear and objectively knowable. Each section of the text is narrated from a different perspective, many of the incidents occurring simultaneously. For example, through flashbacks, we learn about Lindo Jong's first arranged marriage, which coincides with Suyuan Woo's experience in Kweilin. Both stories take place during the Japanese invasion of China, and yet the two experiences are markedly different. For Lindo, the war remains a backdrop to her personal experiences, while, for Suyuan, the war represents a catalyst for a personal tragedy from which she will never fully recover. We cannot choose one woman's experience as more representative than the other's, nor can we choose one view of the war's impact over another. In understanding these simultaneously occurring events and experiences as equally important, we as readers will find it impossible to choose one as the definitive chronological beginning of the novel. This non-linear structure, accordingly, undermines the teleology often associated with traditional narrative sequence, which, as feminist theorists like Margaret Homans, Nancy K. Miller, and Rachel Blau DuPlessis have asserted, is linked to restrictive conceptions of femininity.[8] The novel combines what is traditionally seen as the "personal" history of women with the typically male-centered "public" history of war, destabilizing the hierarchical relationship between these seemingly opposing narratives. It undermines a nationalist conception of history as progress, as a "shared real or imagined past . . . [that] defines the present in the trajectory toward a common future" (Moallem and Boal 251).[9] This conception of history is reinforced by nationalist narrative, which as Mary N. Layoun argues, strives "to give the impression of coherence" (251). And, as Alarcón, Kaplan, and Moallem explain, this coherence is enmeshed in patriarchy, engendering exclusion of women from participation in the nation-state, which according to these critiques, is the "central site of 'hegemonic masculinity'" (Alarcón et al. 1). Tan's structure counters this narrative by depicting the many disjointed trajectories that history takes through the stories of these individual women. Unlike national historical myths, which tend to imply progress toward either successful immigration/assimilation or a return to authentic cultural origins, the directions that history takes in the stories of Tan's women cannot be perceived in terms of progress. Instead, the movements from China to the United States and back to China are lateral, significant because of the material effects they have upon the women of Tan's story. Thus, the text implies a more complex understanding of the relationship among cultural origins, history, and the development of individual female and cultural identities.

Just as a chronological beginning to the novel itself is impossible to locate, so too are the causal beginnings of the individual characters' narratives. Causal beginnings, like chronological beginnings, are especially elusive in modern and postmodern narratives. These narrative moments are not connected to any fixed textual location or to any particular place in time. Borrowing from Prince's definition of a "narrative beginning"(Prince 10), they are instead defined as the moment or moments in a story that represent the catalyst for the main action. This beginning is clearly the most subjective in that each reader may have his/her own interpretation of what qualifies as the catalyst. And yet, despite its subjective nature, it can be key in identifying important cultural work being performed by a text. As *The Joy Luck Club* progresses, we read a narrative about each mother-daughter relationship first from the daughter's perspective and then from the mother's. Inhibiting the reader's ability to locate a causal beginning to the struggles within each mother/daughter narrative, the text structurally and causally links each daughter's present problems directly to her own childhood in the United States as well as to her mother's past in China. For example, in "American Translation" we hear from Lena's point of view about her unhappy marriage to Harold. And later in "Queen Mother of the Western Skies" we read about the same situation from her mother Ying-ying's viewpoint. Ying-ying attributes her daughter's instability in the present directly to her own past weakness: "Now I must tell my daughter everything. That she is the daughter of a ghost. She has no *chi*. This is my greatest shame. How can I leave this world without leaving her my spirit?" (286). Lena, however, finds a different origin to her present marital strife, seeing it as something she deserves for mistakes made as a child: "I still feel that somehow, for the most part, we deserve what we get. . . . I got Harold" (168). The mothers return to their Chinese roots to understand their daughters' present strife, while the daughters locate the origin of their pain in their American childhoods. Neither causal beginning is placed in a more structurally prominent position; nor is one legitimized by content over the other. The novel leaves the reader vacillating between two causes, two origins of the daughters' identities; it thereby disrupts a sense of sequentiality, portraying identity as "simultaneously" constructed, a state of being described by Ketu H. Katrak as a "simultaneous present of being both here and there . . . challeng[ing] the linearity of time and specificity of space by juxtaposing . . . here and now . . . with histories and past geographies" (202). The text, therefore, acknowledges an integral continuity between the past in China and the present in the United States.

Thematic Origins: Subjectivity and Deferral

The representation of thematic origins is, perhaps, best illustrated through the repetition of Suyuan Woo's "Kweilin" story, a self-created myth of origin, which she and other characters begin to tell over and over again. Like Tan's novel itself, the deferred telling of Suyuan's full story can be read as manifesting a compulsion to recover the defining moment of one's identity at the same time her tale refutes the possibility of such a recovery. June searches for knowledge of her own beginnings through her mother's story, in much the same way that Suyuan attempts to recover her whole self by repetitively beginning her originary story. June describes her mother's obsession with the telling of this story:

> Joy Luck was an idea my mother remembered from the days of her first marriage in Kweilin, before the Japanese came. That's why I think of the Joy Luck as her Kweilin story. It was the story she would always tell me when she was bored, when there was nothing to do. . . . This is when my mother would take out a box of old ski sweaters sent to us by unseen relatives from Vancouver. She would snip the bottom of a sweater and pull out a kinky thread of yarn, anchoring it to a piece of cardboard. And as she began to roll with one sweeping rhythm, she would start her story. Over the years she told me the same story, except for the ending, which grew darker, casting long shadows into her life, and eventually into mine. (7)

Significantly, like the yarn of the sweaters Suyuan unravels, she dismantles the complex weave of her story each time she begins to tell it, re-forming it, like the balls of yarn she tightly winds, into a new and reusable shape constructed from the substance of the previous form. Suyuan's story and the way that she relates it thematically represent the text's conception of the past and its connection to individual identity; for the organized pattern of the sweater may also be read to symbolize both History and authentic subjectivity. Like Suyuan, Tan's novel attempts to snip the threads that hold these tightly knitted structures together, unraveling them as it constructs new ideas of history and identity which are at once subjective, personal, and polymorphous.

Just as the story evolves when Suyuan tells it to June, it is also significantly altered by the several characters who advance the narrative after Suyuan's death, each storyteller attempting to decipher the "truth" of this originary story. And yet, the novel asserts no version of this narrative as definitive, just as it posits no authoritative representation of history; each remains in dialogue with the other, none on its own signifying an essential truth. The concepts of storytelling and history, then, are directly connected to one another, as we see when closely examining the final telling of the Kweilin story. When June travels to China to meet her sisters, her father again begins to tell her mother's story, this time attempting to close it. In its final version, however, the historical event of the invasion of Kweilin by Japanese soldiers seems to permeate the "personal" story of Suyuan's lost babies. This conflation of the personal and historical dismantles the dichotomy of personal/private vs. historical/public and interrogates notions of truth and the power of representation:

> "Japanese in Kweilin? says Aiyi [June's Aunt]. "That was never the case. Couldn't be. The Japanese never came to Kweilin."
>
> "Yes, that is what the newspapers reported. I know this because I was working for the news bureau at the time. The Kuomintang often told us what we could say and could not say. But we knew the Japanese had come into Kwangsi Province. We had sources who told us how they had captured the Wuchang-Canton railway. How they were coming overland, making very fast progress, marching toward the provincial capital." (321)

The contradictions between personal experiences and documented history exemplified by this passage clearly exhibit the text's play with notions of history and objectivity, for they make apparent the fact that the representation of historical events is as manipulable and subject to questions of power as storytelling. Thus, by complicating notions of historical objectivity and truth, Tan examines the way in which political power affects the representation of historical events as well as an understanding of individual subjectivity.

The completion of Suyuan's story is continually deferred in an attempt to recover an irretrievable past which represents her unknowable beginning. The deferral of this narrative, however, may also be seen to signify an anxiety over representation, which, as we have seen, is a theme continually worked through in Tan's novel. The inability of the other *Joy Luck Club* characters to tell Suyuan's story in its entirety, therefore, symbolizes the impossibility of depicting an authentic subject through language. This same anxiety is expressed when June's aunties tell her that she must visit her sisters and tell them of her mother: "What will I say? What can I tell them about my mother? I don't know anything. She was my mother" (31). June's apprehension, expressive of the novel's concern with the representation of subjectivity, is never quelled and the question of how to represent an authentic subject is not definitively answered. Instead, the metaphoric search for an authentic and stable identity represented by the search for origins in the Kweilin story is, like the story itself, destined to remain infinitely fragmented and ultimately irretrievable, for it refers only to other discursive representations whose "truth" can never be discerned.

Although we as readers learn more about Suyuan each time the Kweilin story is begun, we never receive the complete story, only fragments that we must try to piece together to compose the whole narrative. The text, nonetheless, renders this act of construction impossible, for it mixes fact, myth, and incomplete memories seemingly indiscriminately among the narrative pieces. Accordingly, neither the reader nor June can distinguish between them: "I never thought my mother's Kweilin story was anything but a Chinese fairy tale" (12). Although we might suspect much about the origins of the Joy Luck Club to be fable, neither the text nor Suyuan distinguishes this element of the narrative as more or less truthful than the other fragments. Moreover, June's interpretation of the new versions of the story (told by her aunties and her father) are inextricably colored by her previous knowledge. Instead of referring to a "real" event for her, the story as told by her mother's friends only refers back to stories her mother had told her. She remembers the refrain from one of those stories ("You are not those babies") and can only think of her sisters the way they were represented in her mother's narratives, as babies:

The babies in Kweilin. I think. I was not those babies. The babies in a sling on her shoulder. Her other daughters. And now I feel as if I were in Kweilin amidst the bombing and I can see these babies lying on the side of the road, their red thumbs popped out of their mouths, screaming to be reclaimed. Somebody took them away. They're safe. And now my mother's left me forever, gone back to China to get these babies. (29)

Even Suyuan's knowledge of her own story is intertextual, for it refers back to prior versions of the story as well as to other narratives, all of which are inseparably combined with the language of fairy tale and myth:

Oh, what good stories! Stories spilling out all over the place! We almost laughed to death. . . . We feasted, we laughed, we played games, lost and won, we told the best stories. And each week, we could hope to be lucky. That hope was our only joy. And that's how we came to call our little parties Joy Luck. (11-12)

The language used here, like that of the first opening myth, ironically mimics the language of fairy tale, causing the line between fact and fiction to be irreparably blurred for both June and the reader. We cannot always separate what is performance from what is factual; thus we are forced to interrogate our own notions of truth, as well as the nature of history and identity.

It only appears to be ironic that I wish to conclude my discussion of narrative beginnings in *The Joy Luck Club* with a look at the ending of the novel, for it seems clear that these beginnings have resonance throughout the entirety of the novel, its close being no exception. It has been argued that Tan's text ends on a note of reconciliation, forcing to quiescence all of the contradictions and interrogations raised throughout; however, if we choose to examine the ending(s) in light of the novel's many beginnings, such a reading is, perhaps, dislodged. That is, by focusing on the way the beginnings of this text foreground a search for origins, we see that the endings to the many narratives actually leave the conclusion of this quest quite open.

Because the endings of Suyuan's and June's stories are the most easily perceived as conciliatory, it is on their conclusions that I will focus most closely. Suyuan's search as well as the telling of her story, as I have intimated, is displaced onto June throughout the text. And although it might be argued that this quest achieves resolution through June's trip to China, the fact that Suyuan dies before returning herself to China means that she can never be said to have actually achieved her goal; symbolically, she never recovers her origins. Instead, the displacement of this achievement onto June leaves it indefinitely deferred, the goal eternally displaced. Similarly, June's search for her mother/origin is displaced onto her sisters. When she finally reaches China she sees her mother in the faces of her two sisters ("Together we look like our mother. Her same eyes, her same mouth, open in surprise to see, at last, her long-cherished wish"); however, the text acknowledges that the daughters "look like," or signify their mother, but they are not actually her (332). June, therefore, can only recover the sign of her mother/origin, never her actual mother. Additionally, although the daughters, as representatives of their mother, see her "long-cherished wish" come to fruition, Suyuan herself does not.

Finally, in much the same way the denouement of June and Suyuan's story is displaced and deferred, so are the resolutions of the other mother-daughter stories. For, none of these narratives actually end in resolution. Like the other stories, Waverly and Lindo's narrative ends with unresolved questions: "What did I lose? What did I get back in return? I will ask my daughter what she thinks" (305). Certainly, adhered to these questions is a hope for future answers, but no real sense of closure. Instead, the perception of closure comes exclusively through June and Suyuan's story, which, as we have seen, simultaneously offers and rescinds this sense of resolution for the reader. Thus, by giving a sense of closure without "real" resolution, Tan's novel subverts the notion that the contradictions set up by both the content and form of her novel can be reconciled. For as Trinh has argued: "Closures need not close off; they can be doors opening onto other closures and functioning as ongoing passages to an elsewhere (-within-here). . . . The closure here . . . is a way of letting the work go rather than of sealing it off" (15).

Narrative beginnings in *The Joy Luck Club* invoke questions about origins, cultural identity, individual subjectivity, gendered identity, and history; they, therefore, enable a critical interrogation and reconfiguration of these ideas. Destabilizing a nationalist conception of cultural, national, and historical subjectivity, which relies heavily upon the recovery of origins, Tan's text suggests an alternative narrative based upon a feminist, contingent, contradictory, and heterogeneous conception of history. The understanding that narrative beginnings are integrally connected to questions of narrativity and social identity undermines notions of authentic subjectivity accomplished through the recovery of an originary historical moment. This study, through an illustrative reading of *The Joy Luck Club*, stresses the necessity of focusing instead on a broader, more fluid sense of the historical and material conditions giving rise to gendered and racialized subjectivities. This way of considering narrative beginnings is vital to ensuring that we attend to difference on all levels and in all formal elements of narrative, a focus which helps to make visible the roles these cultural factors play in our critical reading and writing practices.

From *Studies in the Novel* 35, 1 (Spring 2003): 89-107. Copyright © 2003 by the University of North Texas. Reprinted by permission.

Notes
I would like to acknowledge the help and support of the following mentors, friends, and colleagues: Kandice Chuh, Brian Richardson, Emily Orlando, and Scott A. Melby.
1. Although Edward Said's *Beginnings* is an example of an extensive philosophical examination of the concept of beginnings, Said does not include in this study a consideration of the formal functions of beginnings within narratives; nor does he consider the implications of social identity in relation to formal beginnings.

2. Nuttall's use of parentheses in this statement is particularly telling in that it seems to reveal a certain reluctance to admit that his all-male study may not be universally representative.

3. This study of narrative beginnings in *The Joy Luck Club* is part of a larger project on beginnings in women's literature. The framework for the larger project has been derived through my examination of Tan's text.

4. See Lisa Lowe, Melani McAlister, and Malini Johar Schueller for discussions of the misreading of Tan's novel. Lowe, for example, points to the tendency of *The Joy Luck Club* to be appropriated as a text that "privatizes social conflicts and contradictions" by figuring "broader social shifts of Chinese immigrant formation" as a "generational conflict" and "'feminized' relations between mothers and daughters" (78). She has asserted that *The Joy Luck Club* actually critiques the way this trope of mother-daughter relationships has become a symbol for Asian American culture and has rendered cultural and class differences in conceptions of gender invisible (80). Malini Johar Schueller uses Lisa Lowe's theories of ethnic and racial subjectivity to discuss how Tan's text works to "affirm a politics of resistance and difference," and to emphasize the "discursive nature of gender and ethnic identity" (74). Also see Patricia Hamilton and Yuan Yuan, who both offer alternative, perhaps less universalizing, readings of the "generational conflict."

While, as my examples show, many scholars have recently sought to look beyond the generational conflict that so clearly underestimates this text's complexity, most have not recognized the important role narrative form plays in *The Joy Luck Club*. I will be stressing this role.

5. For example, some feminist scholars, such as Bonnie Braendlin and Gloria Shen, read Tan's text as a universal exploration of mother-daughter relationships. Similarly, such scholars of American literature as Walter Shear tend to identify *The Joy Luck Club* as an example of the "successful-immigrant" narrative. And still further, many scholars of Asian American literature such as Sau-ling Cynthia Wong read Tan's text as a narrative which encourages orientalist views of the Chinese American community.

6. Although there is not space to discuss each example, all of Tan's characters are involved in a search for an origin of some type. Each daughter, for example, searches in some way for her own origins as she seeks to know her mother. Furthermore, as Schueller has noted, this search for mothers may be interpreted as a metaphoric search for the motherland.

7. Each character's search for a definitive moment of identity formation is similarly undermined. For instance, although each daughter comes closer to a complete knowledge of her mother, she can never fully achieve her goal, for much of the mother's past is unknowable. Moreover, the mothers represent only a small portion of the daughters' discursively constructed identities, which are variously formed by the stories their mothers tell, their education in U.S. schools, and their exposure to the media's representations of their cultural heritage.

8. Although many feminist scholars of narrative assert that sequential narrative form is inherently conservative and restrictive, this essay takes the position that narrative form in and of itself is without inherent ideological value; the ideological valences are instead attributable to the "social uses that can be made of [narrative form]," to use

Margaret Homans's words (7). See Brian Richardson in his recent essay "Linearity and Its Discontents: Rethinking Narrative Form and Ideological Valence," where he discusses this issue extensively, arguing against those who would assert inherent political value in literary form.

9. For scholarship on narratives of nationalism, see *Between Woman and Nation*, eds. Kaplan et al.

Works Cited

Alarcón, Norma, et al. "Introduction: Between Woman and Nation." *Between Woman and Nation: Nationalisms, Transnational Feminisms, and the State*. Eds. Caren Kaplan, Norma Alarcón, and Minoo Moallem. Durham: Duke UP, 1999.

Balibar, Etienne, and Immanuel Wallerstein. *Race, Nation, Class: Ambiguous Identities*. New York: Verson, 1991.

Bhabha, Homi K. *The Location of Culture*. New York: Routledge, 1994.

Braendlin, Bonnie. "Mother/Daughter Dialog(ic)s In Around and About Amy Tan's *The Joy Luck Club*." *Synthesis: An Interdisciplinary Journal* 1.2 (Fall 1995): 41-53.

Chin, Frank. "Come All Ye Asian American Writers of the Real and the Fake." *An Anthology of Chinese American and Japanese American Literature*. Eds. Jeffery Paul Chan et al. New York: Penguin, 1991.

DuPlessis, Rachel Blau. *Writing Beyond the Ending: Narrative Strategies of Twentieth-Century Women Writers*. Bloomington: Indiana UP, 1985.

Hamilton, Patricia L. "*Feng Shui*, Astrology, and the Five Elements: Traditional Chinese Belief in Amy Tan's *The Joy Luck Club*." *MELUS* 24.2 (Summer 1999): 125-45.

Homans, Margaret. "Feminist Fictions and Feminist Theories of Narrative." *Narrative* 2 (1994): 3-16.

Hutchinson, John. "Cultural Nationalism and Moral Regeneration." *Nationalism*. Eds. John Hutchinson and Anthony B. Smith. New York: Oxford UP, 1994. 122-31.

Katrak, Ketu H. "South Asian American Literature." *An Interethnic Companion to Asian American Literature*. Ed. King-kok Cheung. Cambridge: Cambridge UP, 1997. 192-218.

Kellman, Steven G. "Grand Openings and Plain: The Poetics of First Lines." *Sub-Stance* 17 (1977): 139-47.

Lanser, Susan S. "Queering Narratology." *Ambiguous Discourse: Feminist Narratology and British Women Writers*. Chapel Hill: U of North Carolina P, 1996. 250-61.

Layoun, Mary N. "A Guest at the Wedding." *Between Woman and Nation*. Eds. Caren Kaplan et al. Durham: Duke UP, 1999. 92-107.

Lowe, Lisa. *Immigrant Acts*. Durham: Duke UP, 1996.

McAlister, Melani. "(Mis)Reading *The Joy Luck Club*." *Asian America: Journal of Culture and the Arts* 1 (1992): 102-18.

Miller, Nancy K. "Emphasis Added: Plots and Plausibilities in Women's Fiction." *PMLA* 96 (1981): 36-48.

Moallem, Minoo, and Iain A. Boal. "Multicultural Nationalism and the Poetics of Inauguration." *Between Woman and Nation*. Eds. Caren Kaplan et al. Durham: Duke UP, 1999. 243-63.

Nuttall, A. D. *Openings: Narrative Beginnings from the Epic to the Novel*. Oxford: Clarendon Press, 1992.

Phelan, James. "Beginnings and Endings: Theories and Typologies of How Novels Open and Close." *Encyclopedia of the Novel*. Ed. Paul Schellinger. Chicago: Fitzroy Dearborn, 1998. 96-99.

Prince, Gerald. *A Dictionary of Narratology*. Lincoln: U of Nebraska P, 1987.

Richardson, Brian. "Linearity and its Discontents: Rethinking Narrative Form and Ideological Valence." *College English*. 2000.

Said, Edward W. *Beginnings*. New York: Basic Books Inc., Publishers, 1975.

Schueller, Malini Johar. "Theorizing Ethnicity and Subjectivity: Maxine Hong Kingston's *Tripmaster Monkey* and Amy Tan's *The Joy Luck Club*." *Genders* 15 (Winter 1992): 72-85.

Shear, Walter. "Generational Differences and the Diaspora in *The Joy Luck Club*." *Critique* 34.3 (Spring 1993): 193-99.

Shen, Gloria. "Born of a Stranger: Mother-Daughter Relationships and Storytelling in Amy Tan's *The Joy Luck Club*." *International Women's Writing: New Landscapes of Identity*. Ed. Anne E. Brown and Marjanne E. Goozé. Westport: Greenwood P, 1995. 233-44.

Takagi, Dana Y. "Maiden Voyage: Excursion into Sexuality and Identity Politics in Asian America." *Asian American Sexualities: Dimensions of the Gay and Lesbian Experience*. Ed. Russell Leong. New York: Routledge, 1996. 21-37.

Tan, Amy. *The Joy Luck Club*. New York: Ivy Books, 1989.

Trinh T. Minh-Ha. *When the Moon Waxes Red: Representation, Gender, and Cultural Politics*. New York: Routledge, 1991.

Wong, Sau-ling Cynthia. "'Sugar Sisterhood': Situating the Amy Tan Phenomenon." *The Ethnic Canon: Histories, Institutions, and Interventions*. Ed. David Palumbo-Liu. Minneapolis: U of Minnesota P, 1995. 175-210.

Yuan, Yuan. "The Semiotics of China Narratives in the Con/Texts of Kingston and Tan." *Critique* 40.3 (Spring 1999): 292-303.

The Joy Luck Club After Twenty Years:
An Interview with Amy Tan_____
Robert C. Evans

In an interview conducted not long before the twentieth anniversary of the first appearance of *The Joy Luck Club* (publication date March 22, 1989), Amy Tan reflected on a number of factors that helped shape the book, on the ways it has been read, on the film that resulted from the work, and on a variety of other topics. Speaking by phone and coping good-naturedly both with feedback from the interviewer's primitive tape recorder and with requests for attention from one of her small dogs, Tan talked at length about the importance of "voice" in fiction. Her own voice—calm, friendly, thoughtful, generous, and good-humored—will be familiar to anyone who has ever encountered her previous interviews.

* * *

RCE: It's been almost exactly twenty years since the publication of **The Joy Luck Club** ***established you as a well-known writer. Have your attitudes or approaches to writing changed very much in the course of those two decades? Do you approach your writing differently today than you did then?***

AT: My approach has changed, mostly because I know so much more about publishing and being published, so one part of it is the degree of self-consciousness that I did not have when I was writing my first book. And it was also different because I didn't know that the first book was going to even be published or read or sold or anything, and it was more of a writing exercise, so I had a great deal more freedom in doing things without (again) that self-consciousness that I was making mistakes. The actual stories were things I could just spell out without worrying that people would interpret it in a certain way, assume things were completely autobiographical or partly, or that they would make fun of the way that I created the story. The way that I write now also is a little bit more haphazard because of my schedule, and then also because I am such a glutton for research that I have a disorganized amount of research. I don't have, for example, that material that has been sitting there for all those many years before I wrote my first book, so what I have now seems to be more amorphous, and these questions that I have seem to be more undefined, in a way, or less urgent, and I have to find the one that is the most urgent and work on it. It's not as though I have no ideas; I have too many of them, and I have to be honest with myself and say which is the one that is the most important to me and which are the ones I have to discard because maybe I am thinking about writing [about] them to impress somebody.

I'm hoping that my craftsmanship is getting better, that I'm understanding my craft better, and that is apart from what anybody says about my work. I've learned that I have to disregard with more effort what people say about my work, because it does influence how I think about my work. When I go into my room, I need that sense that I'm not being watched and, again, recapturing what happened in 1987 when I started writing the first book. That's a *very* long-winded [laughs] way of saying yes, my approach has changed, but what comes with that are the principles I started with, which are to know my reasons for writing, to remember always, each day that I write, that it is the process of writing that is the most important and not the end result or what anyone has to say about it, and that I always discover something within that, and to revise and revise and revise and not be afraid to try things and then throw them away.

RCE: Over the years, and especially when you were at work on **The Joy Luck Club,** *who provided the most valuable and helpful feedback about your writing, and what, precisely, made that feedback valuable?*

AT: The person who was the most valuable in terms of craft and what a story was and what voice is is the person who is now my editor, Molly Giles. She was the one I met in Squaw Valley, which was the first writers' conference I went to, and I chose her as the writer who would give me one-to-one advice on the manuscript that I had submitted. You could have chosen an agent or editor and I chose a writer because I had read her work and really liked her work, admired her work. So, over the years, she's given me feedback on all my stories—very honest reader type of feedback as well as that of an editor, and because she's somebody who knows me from the beginning and what I'm capable of doing, she has absolute confidence in me. The other person, obviously, that's very influential in my storytelling and my reasons for writing is my mother. She was a natural storyteller, and she was somebody who spoke about things absolutely honestly, and she would have been able to detect anything that seemed disingenuous, and she read my first stories and really got the sense of what they were about. I don't know which one you would consider to be more of an influence; one is reason, one is craft.

RCE: When you read fiction yourself, what do you look for or hope to find? What, in your opinion, makes a work of fiction satisfying or worth reading? What makes a work of fiction disappointing to you?

AT: I know almost from the first page if it's a story that I want to read, and it has a lot to do with language. It has to do with voice, and within "voice," of course, is language, but I'm not talking about fancy words or sentence construction, but it's the nature of what this voice observes in the world, and so there is a history, a sense of observation, that is in there, and it's always evident within the first page, and sometimes I feel it in the first sentence or paragraph. I want to feel the story is *felt*, meaning there is that storytelling quality that is an honest story. When I get to the point where I think it's pyrotechnics then I lose interest, even though I might *admire* the writing very much. I'm not really keen on writing that is very distanced emotionally, and that's not to say that that's not good writing–*that* comes down to a preference. And so I hear people talk about writers they really admire and it's one of those "not for me" kind of judgments. I like intelligence within writing so that within the sentences there is also (it could be) a sense of history, or a kind of observational association, and it doesn't have to be that you went and got your Ph.D. in history that makes me appreciate that. It has to do with natural knowledge of the world and the history that informs one personally. An example of that at the highest level is García Márquez, where just very naturally, as the story unfolds, you just get a sense of a whole world at a particular time.

RCE: You once described what you do as "the artful arrangement of words." Can you elaborate a little bit on that statement? What, in particular, did you mean by "artful"?
AT: Well, it says "artful" and it should be almost "art*less*," meaning not apparent. The artfulness is the craft of it and taking language and being very much aware of the choice of words, of how they sound, the combinations and the rhythms, and so it is always an art, I think, the craftsmanship of sentences, the sensuality in the imagery within the words. That was something I was always aware of when I began writing, and it was an interest of mine when I was a linguistics major and when I read things myself and was fascinated by Middle English and prosody. I would read my work aloud; I was told that I should do that when I started writing fiction, and as I read things aloud I developed that sense of rhythm and what was conveyed in the actual language chosen that matched what was being said, what the sentiment was or the imagery. So I think that is part of the "artful

arrangement of words," but that should not stick out and say, "Look what I did; isn't that clever how I put these words together here?" It should be artless. It's almost awful to be aware of this now as somebody who's been writing for longer, seeing it in other people's work and then rereading my work later and seeing things that are very jarring to me and not honest—"not honest" meaning the motives were mostly, you know, maybe to be a little too clever.

RCE: You also once referred, in an interview, to what you called "the grunt work of writing." Can you explain that phrase a little bit more? What exactly does such "grunt work" involve?

AT: [Pauses to think] Oh, boy . . . the "grunt work" is . . . you know, it's funny, "grunt" makes it sound like it's awful. I really like research, and I really like revision, but sometimes the grunt work is also going through a mass of stuff and being confused and not being able to see the thread that clearly. And so, going through all of that over and over again—it's mind-boggling to me, and it's effort, real effort, and that's what I mean by "grunt work." The part that I think is grunt work also that probably people don't think about is to get one's office in order, and by that I mean arrange all the books that are needed in a particular place and then all the journals that are part of the research in a certain way, and write down, copy, going through the journals, copy on computer (actually typing in) what I had written in the journals so it gets back into my mind again all the freshness of the ideas that I had over the last two, three years, or ten years, or whatever it is. So that's part of it; I guess you would call that "grunt work."

RCE: How much do you revise your work, and when you are revising, what kinds of changes do you tend to make? Do you save the various drafts of your work?

AT: I know people think I'm exaggerating when I say it's sometimes a hundred times that I revise, but the reason why I say "a hundred times" is that every day, when I open up my files to start working on them, I usually begin at the beginning, and I read through for continuity leading up to that point in the story that I have now started anew. And as I go through those early pages there are inevitably things that I change. I didn't save all my early drafts when I first started writing, but I do have some early ones. And now they're automatically saved; I work on a Mac, and there's something called "iDisk" and everything—I guess!—every single draft is saved if it has any change to it. I've never gone back to see if that's really true, but that's my understanding. And then I do print out things because I get a different sense of what I've written when I print it out and read it that way. I would say that I revise a *lot*. I also do a big revision where I just remove whole chunks of things or even abandon a whole, you know, two hundred pages of something I've started.

RCE: Do critics or commentators ever help you see meanings or dimensions in your work that you hadn't suspected before?
AT: Umm, you know I read a lot of early reviews and I would say that it was more confusing than anything. It was disconcerting; even if they were good reviews, I felt that they had interpreted the work differently from what it meant to me or what my intentions were. That didn't mean that they had bad interpretations, because as a former English literature major, I feel that there's value in work and whatever the reader brings to that and how they interpret it. And of course the bad reviews just paralyzed me, and as a consequence I stopped reading reviews. What I take, then, as my feedback is my editor, and I realized that I could only listen to one editor. The more people who would be involved with reading things, the more opinions I would get, and the more I would be uncertain as to what I was doing. [Sound of small dog barking with plaintive annoyance] I'm sorry; I've a little dog here complaining about my being on the phone. So I have not really—I'm sure there are some reviews somewhere that I've read about different things, but I've deliberately not

read things, and I actually tell people "do not tell me what the reviews say." But I've had a few people say some things to me; often they're things like, "I completely disagree with that person's trashing your book" [laughs]. I remember reading some things where people had made a remark about a fault in a book having to do with structure or something, and I did think it was instructive. I don't consider myself a perfect writer, beyond criticism. With many things I believe that I have to also know what my own voice is, and that there are some people who are going to say something about a book—any book—and that it will be a reflection of the things that they want to read or write.

RCE: *Much of the academic criticism dealing with* The Joy Luck Club *tends to focus on themes or ideas rather than on its style or craftsmanship. When you're writing, how concerned are you with matters of style and expression, as opposed to themes?*
AT: In some way, it's inseparable, but definitely the style is what I call "voice," and that is, in the beginning, everything. I can't begin something unless I know the voice, whether it's a certain intimacy or knowledge that that person has, the way they talk about things, the rhythm. . . . I'm perfectly capable of writing sentences that are much more complex sentences, but I choose sometimes a style, I guess, or a voice that would have a different cadence, and probably in the early work would have the cadence of how my mother spoke. And, in some ways, I think that the cadence is also mirrored in statements in the Bible, which was an influence, at least rhythmically, because my father was a pastor. So, yes, I have to begin with all of that. But the imagery that's part of the voice is the way that the voice would say something, and the saying of something creates imagery. I'm very much aware of the voice qualities of imagery, but it's not as though I start with an image and say, "Okay, here's the image I want and then how do I work into that?" I often find the images more spontaneously; when I'm writing in my journal, I'm *really* free and

I'm writing by hand and these are things that just come out without editing, and I see then in the voice that I've been writing these things in the moment, in the heat of the moment of what I've observed, that oftentimes these images spontaneously come up. And again, that has to do with just the observations and what the voice is. When I write down notes, too, and when I'm having these ideas—say something has happened that day—I do try to write it in a particular kind of voice, and that's all part of it.

RCE: Do you recall which authors may have had the most influence on your art at the time you were working on **The Joy Luck Club?** *In general, which other writers of fiction do you value most, and why? Are there any contemporary writers that you particularly admire?*

AT: Well, one of the writers very early on—probably the first published writer who ever read my work and was very helpful and encouraging—was Amy Hempel, and I admired (and still admire) her work very much. I happened to meet her personally at a friend's house; she was mutual friends with people in San Francisco, and she was my example, or my early mentoring example, of writing that, whatever it said, she called it "what's the news?"—that it's something new, that you don't say things that everybody knows about. And I guess it's that getting rid of cliché or getting rid of a way of looking at things in the same way. I think what happens is, and I'm aware of this, that when I look at a thing in the same way, I'm not looking at it, really, I'm just covering it with the same blanket that's always been there, so you have to get rid of that and find what is there that is freshly discovered or freshly felt. And the other is the rhythm of her sentences: there was nothing wasted there, it was like density, and so when I did my early work I was very much aware of those two qualities in Amy Hempel's work.

The other person was Louise Erdrich. I was reading her work *Love Medicine*, and the voices in that, which were different; I became very aware of these different qualities of voice and a sense of internal voices. And it was also because she had written, in *Love Medicine*, about a community—that these voices came from a community of people; they were linked through that, that the stories did not have to be structured in a traditional novelistic sense. The funny thing is that my first book does begin with a crisis of emotion, and it ends with addressing that notion of having lost a mother, and so I had more of a traditional shape in one very general way. But the idea of different voices, and looking for different qualities in those voices, was very much influenced by *Love Medicine*.

*RCE: Issues of ethnicity are very prominent in commentary on your work, especially in commentary on **The Joy Luck Club**. I was wondering how important ethnicity was to you when you were writing the book and how crucial a theme you think it is in the book itself. Why and how do you think the book is capable of appealing to readers who are not Asian or readers who are not female?*

AT: You know, when I first started writing I thought it was going to be a drawback, and in fact in the early stories I wrote I tried to strip it of any kind of ethnicity and make it generically American. And—who was it?—I think it was Amy Hempel or somebody else who said something about authenticity of voice. That's when I realized that I just have to write in a way that really does relate to something in my life. Now, a lot of that was what I *didn't* know—part of it that I'd never thought about: the things that were said to me and the history that underlay a lot of that. As I was writing, I was beginning to learn more about that—doing interviews with my mother—and that, naturally, required me to do some reading of history, and then I became addicted to wanting to have this dual knowledge of personal history and a larger history and a mythic history (I guess that's three things!). . . .

What I didn't expect was that more people than I would have expected were interested in those details, but interested in them to the point that for them that was the story. The story became an instruction manual for certain people on differences in culture or in some very funny things, like whether you should bring a bottle of wine to a Chinese family's dinner. There were people who looked upon some details as representational of a whole culture, and that was disturbing to me.

RCE: *I'm wondering what reactions you had to the film of* The Joy Luck Club *and how active a role you played in work on that film.*

AT: Well, I had a very active role, and I didn't want an active role when people first approached me about it. I've had this problem with trying to stay focused on writing, and these opportunities come up and somehow my resolve gets aborted. I became involved with this movie and ended up cowriting the screenplay with the real screenwriter, Ron Bass. He outlined the whole story and we talked through it and then I would take the first stab at writing what would look like a screenplay, and then he would comment extensively on all of that, so I was learning how to write a screenplay at the same time I was writing it for an actual movie that was being produced. And then I was a producer, so I had a lot of decision-making power, I guess. I chose not to use it for everything, and I didn't want to be involved in all of it.

I felt that the movie was very true emotionally to the book, but from the beginning I knew that we would create something that was not a mirror image of the book. And that's how I feel about everything that has come out of this book, when people do things—like a play, or we just did this opera—I feel it needs to be re-created, that there's a certain part of it that was the impetus for the story, and there are certain elements that are integral, but to follow the same structure of the story itself is a mistake, because it was created for a particular form. So the movie is necessarily different in some ways and it felt, to me, very true to the original story.

RCE: Can you talk a little bit about your experiences as an English major? Did they have any influence on your later career as a writer?

AT: You know, I loved to read from the time I was able to first read—well, even before that, I loved to *hear* stories. I don't think I had an active sense that I was reading so that one day I could be a writer. If there was any ambition in being an English major, it was to become, perhaps, a professor of English literature or something like that. But I always loved to write. It was an influence in ways that I discover as I write. It's not as though I set out to write and say, "What did that teacher say about simile or metaphor or symbols?" I remember a professor who said something about imagery, or imagery having to do with what comes to your mind first. It has nothing to do, necessarily, with the importance or the order or the "theme" of the book, but what is the imagery that floats to your mind first when you have read a book? And then, listing those images, sort of an unconscious sense of the book, whether it had to do with its setting or emotions or all of that—that has surfaced as I write, and I remember what he said about that.

RCE: Were there any classic or canonical writers that you particularly admired?

AT: I remember one I *didn't* admire and I got chastised for it. It was Hemingway. But, you know, I was reading that in the same way that I think other people read my work at times, which is you read what the story is about and you criticize the social messages or whatever they are. I had written an essay about that and the professor trashed me in front of the class. He said [speaks in booming voice], "Who is this person to be able to criticize our world's greatest writer?!" He was a real fan of Hemingway [laughs]. I really like Hemingway's writing now; I don't read him in that way.

A lot of the writings, though, that I did read in those days were chosen for their social messages, like Theodore Dreiser or Upton

Sinclair. I'm trying to think if there were books, in general, that stood out for me [pauses] . . . and I guess the fact that I'm struggling [laughs] to come up with somebody means that I don't have anything that jumps out, meaning more than one book. I can't think of any particular writer except, maybe—I *loved* the Brontës, but that wasn't necessarily assigned as required reading; that was just some reading that I did on my own. Virginia Woolf was the only writer I read who was a woman during those years of being an English major.

RCE: I've noticed that in some of your interviews you refer to your love of music, and I'm just curious to know which composers or which kind of music you might especially enjoy.

AT: I've always loved, I think, the ones that most people would say: I love Mozart, Beethoven. I think now I would say Mahler and Stravinsky. Stravinsky I adore because his music tells huge stories. Tchaikovsky, Copland . . . and I do think that part of it has to do with who I am; that might [make it] different how I listen to music. I'm still somebody who goes to the symphony more often than I do to the movies (symphony, opera, whatever). I listen to music—classical music—a lot. And I like sound tracks because they're usually emotionally and thematically consistent. I can write to sound tracks, whereas I can't write to sonatas or symphonies that have different movements [laughs] that go from something very lively to something very quiet. In part, I think, early on in life, music to me told stories. I was forced to play the piano, and I would see stories, and I'm not sure whether it became a natural part of it or I forced myself to think of stories to just get through the one hour [of practice]. You know, sonatas, symphonies—they have a story form to them; it's built in and could easily be transferred to a traditional storytelling mode that's in a classic kind of novel. The kinds of movements that are there in a sonata are similar, and the kind of voice—you know, musical pieces have a particular voice, have particular rhythms, and they also have things that resonate and come back, and maybe have a different quality to them when they come back. So, I think that probably that, in a very big way, music had a lot to do with my [work].

RCE: One last question: What would you hope a person picking up The Joy Luck Club today for the first time would find in the book or appreciate about it?

AT: [Pauses to think] Oh . . . ah . . . umm. You know, I just know so much more about what readers get out of these books now than I did when I was writing it, and I've had so many readers say to me, "You know, I read this book and I finally understood myself and my mother, and we have a new relationship." I don't take credit for that; I think that that's again that over-layer of the reader and their history and then the story in front of them. And so, I think that's wonderful. I think that what I would hope for is what I had in writing it, which is the story itself, and when they read it they feel the story and they feel that it is honest, genuine emotion. And that they have a good time with it [laughs], that they see that there's a sense of humor in looking at things oftentimes that were in the past very painful. Other things? Well, you know, the things that you as a writer would want another writer to maybe appreciate. If you were to step away from the story—[although] you *want* people to actually stay in the story and not let the craft become the thing that they're focused on—but if they were then to step away from the story and just see it as craft, that they would say that I had put in there some things that were interesting.

RESOURCES

Chronology of Amy Tan's Life_____

1952	Amy Tan is born on February 19 in Oakland, California. Her father, John, is an electrical engineer and Baptist minister; her mother, Daisy, is a vocational nurse.
1967	Tan's older brother dies of a brain tumor, and her father dies of a brain tumor seven months later.
1973	Tan receives a bachelor's degree in English and linguistics from San Jose State University.
1974	Tan is awarded a master's degree in linguistics from San Jose State University. She marries Louis DeMattei, a tax attorney.
1976-1981	Tan works as a language-development specialist for children with disabilities.
1980-1981	Tan is employed as a project director and then becomes a freelance business writer.
1981-1983	Tan works as a reporter for *Emergency Room Reports* before being promoted to managing editor and then associate publisher of the periodical.
1983-1987	Tan works as a freelance technical writer for various corporations and takes up writing fiction in an effort to combat her workaholic habits. In 1987 she travels to China with her mother. After a literary agent gets her a contract to write *The Joy Luck Club*, Tan quits freelance work and rapidly writes the book.
1989	*The Joy Luck Club* is published and is a finalist for the National Book Award and the National Book Critics Circle Award.
1991	*The Kitchen God's Wife* is published.
1992	*The Moon Lady*, a children's book, is published.
1993	The film version of *The Joy Luck Club*, on which Tan serves as coscreenwriter and coproducer, is released.

1994	*The Chinese Siamese Cat*, a children's book, is published.
1995	*The Hundred Secret Senses* is published.
1999	Tan's mother dies; within weeks, Tan's editor and friend Faith Sale also dies.
2001	*The Bonesetter's Daughter* is published.
2003	*The Opposite of Fate*, a collection of essays, is published.
2005	*Saving Fish from Drowning* is published.

Works by Amy Tan

Long Fiction
The Joy Luck Club, 1989
The Kitchen God's Wife, 1991
The Hundred Secret Senses, 1995
The Bonesetter's Daughter, 2001
Saving Fish from Drowning, 2005

Screenplay
The Joy Luck Club, 1993 (with Ronald Bass)

Nonfiction
The Opposite of Fate: A Book of Musings, 2003

Children's Literature
The Moon Lady, 1992
The Chinese Siamese Cat, 1994

Bibliography

Bennani, Ben, ed. "The World of Amy Tan" [special issue]. *Paintbrush: A Journal of Poetry and Translation* 22 (Autumn 1995).

Bloom, Harold, ed. *Amy Tan*. Philadelphia: Chelsea House, 2000.

_____. *Amy Tan's "The Joy Luck Club."* Philadelphia: Chelsea House, 2002.

Bow, Leslie. "*The Joy Luck Club* by Amy Tan." *A Resource Guide to Asian American Literature*. Ed. Sau-ling Cynthia Wong and Stephen H. Sumida. New York: Modern Language Association of America, 2001. 159-71.

Braendlin, Bonnie. "Mother/Daughter Dialog(ic)s in, Around, and About Amy Tan's *The Joy Luck Club*." *Private Voices, Public Lives: Women Speak on the Literary Life*. Ed. Nancy Owen Nelson. Denton: University of North Texas Press, 1995. 111-24.

Chan, Mimi. "'Listen, Mom, I'm a Banana': Mother and Daughter in Maxine Hong Kingston's *The Woman Warrior* and Amy Tan's *The Joy Luck Club*." *Asian Voices in English*. Ed. Mimi Chan and Roy Harris. Hong Kong: Hong Kong University Press, 1991. 65-78.

Cheung, King-kok, ed. *An Interethnic Companion to Asian American Literature*. New York: Cambridge University Press, 1997.

Cooperman, Jeannette Batz. *The Broom Closet: Secret Meanings of Domesticity in Postfeminist Novels by Louise Erdrich, Mary Gordon, Toni Morrison, Marge Piercy, Jane Smiley, and Amy Tan*. New York: Peter Lang, 1999.

Dunick, Lisa M. S. "The Silencing Effect of Canonicity: Authorship and the Written Word in Amy Tan's Novels." *MELUS* 31.2 (Summer 2006): 3-20.

Ghymn, Esther Mikyung. *The Shapes and Styles of Asian American Prose Fiction*. New York: Peter Lang, 1992.

Huang, Guiyou, ed. *Asian American Literary Studies*. Edinburgh: Edinburgh University Press, 2005.

Huh, Joonok. *Interconnected Mothers and Daughters in Amy Tan's "The Joy Luck Club."* Tucson, AZ: Southwest Institute for Research on Women, 1992.

Kafka, Phillipa. *(Un)doing the Missionary Position: Gender Asymmetry in Contemporary Asian American Women's Writing*. Westport, CT: Greenwood Press, 1997.

Lee, Rachel C. *The Americas of Asian American Literature: Gendered Fictions of Nation and Transnation*. Princeton, NJ: Princeton University Press, 1999.

Lim, Elaine. *Asian American Literature: An Introduction to the Writings and Their Social Context*. Philadelphia: Temple University Press, 1982.

Lim, Shirley Geok-lin, and Amy Ling, eds. *Reading the Literatures of Asian America*. Philadelphia: Temple University Press, 1992.

Lin, Jinqi. *Narrating Nationalisms: Ideology and Form in Asian American Literature*. New York: Oxford University Press, 1998.

López Morell, Beatriz. "Chinese Women's Celebration in America in *The Joy Luck Club*." *Evolving Origins, Transplanting Cultures: Literary Legacies of the New Americans*. Ed. Laura P. Alonso Gallo and Antonia Domínguez Miguela. Huelva, Spain: Universidad de Huelva, 2002. 77-85.

Ma, Sheng-mei. *Immigrant Subjectivities in Asian American and Asian Diaspora Literatures*. Albany: State University of New York Press, 1998.

Mandal, Somdatta. "Ethnic Voices of Asian-American Women with Special Reference to Amy Tan." *Indian Views on American Literature*. Ed. A. A. Mutalik-Desai. New Delhi: Prestige, 1998. 141-52.

Mazzucco-Than, Cecile. "'Thinking Different' in Amy Tan's *The Joy Luck Club* (1989)." *Women in Literature: Reading Through the Lens of Gender*. Ed. Jerilyn Fisher and Ellen S. Silber. Westport, CT: Greenwood Press, 2003. 163-65.

Pearlman, Mickey, and Katherine Usher Henderson. "Amy Tan." *Inter/View: Talks with America's Writing Women*. Lexington: University Press of Kentucky, 1990.

Singer, Marc. "Moving Forward to Reach the Past: The Dialog of Time in Amy Tan's *The Joy Luck Club*." *Journal of Narrative Theory* 31.3 (Fall 2001): 324-52.

Snodgrass, Mary Ellen. *Amy Tan: A Literary Companion*. Jefferson, NC: McFarland, 2004.

Trudeau, Lawrence J., ed. *Asian American Literature: Reviews and Criticism of Works by American Writers of Asian Descent*. Detroit: Gale Research, 1999.

Ty, Eleanor. *The Politics of the Visible in Asian North American Narratives*. Toronto: University of Toronto Press, 2004.

Wong, Sau-ling Cynthia. *Reading Asian American Literature: From Necessity to Extravagance*. Princeton, NJ: Princeton University Press, 1993.

Wong, Sau-ling Cynthia, and Stephen H. Sumida, eds. *A Resource Guide to Asian American Literature*. New York: Modern Language Association of America, 2001.

Yin, Xiao-huang. *Chinese American Literature Since the 1850s*. Urbana: University of Illinois Press, 2000.

Zeng, Li. "Diasporic Self, Cultural Other: Negotiating Ethnicity through Transformation in the Fiction of Tan and Kingston." *Language and Literature* 28 (2003): 1-15.

CRITICAL
INSIGHTS

About the Editor

Robert C. Evans earned his Ph.D. from Princeton University in 1984. In 1982 he began teaching at Auburn University Montgomery, where he has been named Distinguished Research Professor, Distinguished Teaching Professor, and University Alumni Professor. External awards include fellowships from the American Council of Learned Societies, the American Philosophical Society, the National Endowment for the Humanities, the UCLA Center for Medieval and Renaissance Studies, and the Folger, Huntington, and Newberry libraries. In 1989 he was chosen Professor of the Year for his state by the Council for the Advancement and Support of Education, and in 1997 he was the recipient of a grant from the Andrew W. Mellon foundation to fund a summer seminar on critical pluralism. He is a contributing editor of the John Donne Variorum project, an editor of the *Ben Jonson Journal*, and an editor of *Comparative Drama*. He is the author or editor of four books on Ben Jonson and three on Martha Moulsworth (a previously unknown Renaissance poet whose work he rediscovered). He is also the author or editor of books on such other topics as Frank O'Connor, Brian Friel, Ambrose Bierce, short fiction, and critical theory and is the editor of a series of volumes on early modern English women writers.

About *The Paris Review*

The Paris Review is America's preeminent literary quarterly, dedicated to discovering and publishing the best new voices in fiction, nonfiction, and poetry. The magazine was founded in Paris in 1953 by the young American writers Peter Matthiessen and Doc Humes, and edited there and in New York for its first fifty years by George Plimpton. Over the decades, the *Review* has introduced readers to the earliest writings of Jack Kerouac, Philip Roth, T. C. Boyle, V. S. Naipaul, Ha Jin, Jay McInerney, and Mona Simpson, and published numerous now classic works, including Roth's *Goodbye, Columbus*, Donald Barthelme's *Alice*, Jim Carroll's *Basketball Diaries*, and selections from Samuel Beckett's *Molloy* (his first publication in English). The first chapter of Jeffrey Eugenides's *The Virgin Suicides* appeared in the *Review*'s pages, as well as stories by Edward P. Jones, Rick Moody, David Foster Wallace, Denis Johnson, Jim Shepard, Jim Crace, Lorrie Moore, Jeanette Winterson, and Ann Patchett.

The Paris Review's renowned Writers at Work series of interviews, whose early installments include legendary conversations with E. M. Forster, William Faulkner, and Ernest Hemingway, is one of the landmarks of world literature. The interviews received a George Polk Award and were nominated for a Pulitzer Prize. Among the more than three hundred interviewees are Robert Frost, Marianne Moore, W. H. Auden,

Elizabeth Bishop, Susan Sontag, and Toni Morrison. Recent issues feature conversations with Salman Rushdie, Joan Didion, Stephen King, Norman Mailer, Kazuo Ishiguro, and Umberto Eco. (A complete list of the interviews is available at www.theparisreview.org.) In November 2008, Picador will publish the third of a four-volume series of anthologies of *Paris Review* interviews. The first two volumes have received acclaim. *The New York Times* called the Writers at Work series "the most remarkable and extensive interviewing project we possess."

The Paris Review is edited by Philip Gourevitch, who was named to the post in 2005, following the death of George Plimpton two years earlier. Under Gourevitch's leadership, the magazine's international distribution has expanded, paid subscriptions have risen 150 percent, and newsstand distribution has doubled. A new editorial team has published fiction by Andre Aciman, Damon Galgut, Mohsin Hamid, Gish Jen, Richard Price, Said Sayrafiezadeh, and Alistair Morgan. Poetry editors Charles Simic, Meghan O'Rourke, and Dan Chiasson have selected works by Billy Collins, Jesse Ball, Mary Jo Bang, Sharon Olds, and Mary Karr. Writing published in the magazine has been anthologized in *Best American Short Stories* (2006, 2007, and 2008), *Best American Poetry*, *Best Creative Non-Fiction*, the Pushcart Prize anthology, and *O. Henry Prize Stories*.

The magazine presents two annual awards. The Hadada Award for lifelong contribution to literature has recently been given to William Styron, Joan Didion, Norman Mailer, and Peter Matthiessen in 2008. The Plimpton Prize for Fiction, given to a new voice in fiction brought to national attention in the pages of *The Paris Review*, was presented in 2007 to Benjamin Percy and to Jesse Ball in 2008.

The Paris Review won the 2007 National Magazine Award in photojournalism, and the *Los Angeles Times* recently called *The Paris Review* "an American treasure with true international reach."

Since 1999 *The Paris Review* has been published by The Paris Review Foundation, Inc., a not-for-profit 501(c)(3) organization.

The Paris Review is available in digital form to libraries worldwide in selected academic databases exclusively from EBSCO Publishing. Libraries can contact EBSCO at 1-800-653-2726 for details. For more information on *The Paris Review* or to subscribe, please visit: www.theparisreview.org.

Contributors

Robert C. Evans earned his Ph.D. from Princeton University in 1984. In 1982 he began teaching at Auburn University Montgomery, where he has been named Distinguished Research Professor, Distinguished Teaching Professor, and University Alumni Professor. External awards include fellowships from the ACLS, the APS, the NEH, and the Folger, Huntington, and Newberry libraries. He is the author or editor of more than twenty books and of numerous essays, including recent work on twentieth-century American writers.

Joanne McCarthy is faculty emerita, Tacoma Community College (Tacoma, Washington), where she taught literature, creative writing, and women's studies for many years.

Karl Taro Greenfeld is the author of *Speed Tribes*, *Standard Deviations*, and *China Syndrome*. His writing has appeared in *The Best American Travel Writing*, *The Best American Sports Writing*, and *The Best American Nonrequired Reading*, and his dispatch "Wild Flavor," from the winter 2005 issue of *The Paris Review*, was chosen for the 2007 anthology *The Best Creative Nonfiction*.

Camille-Yvette Welsch is a senior lecturer in English at the Pennsylvania State University. She is the director of Penn State's Summer Creative Writing Conference for high school students and the coordinator of the Red Weather Reading Series. Her work has appeared in *Mid-American Review*, *Barrow Street*, *The Writer's Chronicle*, *The Women's Review of Books*, and *Small Spiral Notebook*.

Doris L. Eder is the author of "Three Writers in Exile: Pound, Eliot, and Joyce" and some 250 contributions to books, articles, essays, and reviews. She regularly publishes biographies of writers in *Encyclopedia Americana*. She has a B.A. cum laude from Barnard College (Columbia University), a master's in English, and a doctorate in comparative literature from City University of New York (Hunter).

Neil Heims is a writer and teacher living in Paris. His books include *Reading the Diary of Anne Frank* (2005), *Allen Ginsberg* (2005), and *J. R. R. Tolkien* (2004). He has also contributed numerous articles for literary publications, including essays on William Blake, John Milton, William Shakespeare, and Arthur Miller.

Barbara Somogyi has been an editor and a freelance writer.

David Stanton has written profiles for *Poets & Writers Magazine* and articles for *The Washington Post*.

Ben Xu is Professor of English at Saint Mary's College of California. He has written extensively on China and Chinese culture and politics. His essays and articles have appeared in a number of journals, including *Literature and Art Studies*, *MELUS*, *Twenty-First Century*, *Foreign Literature Review*, *Contemporary Chinese Literature and Culture*, *Cultural Studies*, *Open Times*, and *Modern China Studies*. His books include *Situational Tensions of Critic-Intellectuals: Thinking Through Literary Politics with Ed-*

ward W. Said and Frank Lentricchia (1992), *Journey to Postmodern and Postcolonial Critical Theories* (1996), *Whither Cultural Criticism? Chinese Cultural Discussion After 1989* (1998), *Disenchanted Democracy: Chinese Cultural Criticism After 1989* (1999), *Restitution, Apology, and State Injustice* (2003), and *Intellectuals: My Thinking and Our Action* (2005).

Stephen Souris is Associate Professor at Texas Women's University. He has contributed articles to journals such as *MELUS, Thomas Wolfe Review, Southern Studies*, and *English in Texas*. He also published the book *Great American One-Act Plays* (1999).

Esther Mikyung Ghymn has taught at the University of Nevada, Reno. She is the author of *The Shapes and Styles of Asian American Prose Fiction* (1992) and editor of the volumes *Images of Asian American Women by Asian American Women Writers* (1996) and *Asian American Studies: Identity, Images, Issues Past and Present* (2000).

M. Marie Booth Foster is Assistant Professor at Florida A&M University. She has authored *Southern Black Creative Writers, 1829-1953* (1988).

Patricia L. Hamilton is Associate Professor of English at Union University. She has published essays in *MELUS* and *Eighteenth-Century Fiction*. She has also written and published poetry in journals such as *Negative Capability*, *Mobius*, *Small Brushes*, and *Pegasus*.

Patricia P. Chu is Associate Professor of English at George Washington University. She specializes in Asian American literature and cultural studies, nineteenth-century British literature, women's writing, and contemporary fiction. She has contributed chapters to several books and her book *Assimilating Asians: Gendered Strategies of Authorship in Asian America* was published in 2000.

Catherine Romagnolo is Assistant Professor of English at Lebanon Valley College. She has contributed to the volume *Narrative Beginnings: Theories and Practices* (2009) and has contributed essays to *Studies in the Novel*.

Acknowledgments_____

"Amy Tan" by Joanne McCarthy. From *Magill's Survey of American Literature*. Rev. ed. Copyright © 2007 by Salem Press, Inc. Reprinted with permission of Salem Press.

"The *Paris Review* Perspective" by Karl Taro Greenfeld. Copyright © 2010 by Karl Taro Greenfeld. Special appreciation goes to Christopher Cox and Nathaniel Rich, editors for *The Paris Review.*

"Amy Tan: An Interview" by Barbara Somogyi and David Stanton. From *Poets & Writers Magazine* 9, no. 5 (September/October 1991): 24-32. Copyright © 1991 by *Poets & Writers Magazine.* Reprinted by permission.

"Memory and the Ethnic Self: Reading Amy Tan's *The Joy Luck Club*" by Ben Xu. From *MELUS* 19, no. 1 (Spring 1994): 3-18. Copyright © 1994 by *MELUS: The Journal of the Society for the Study of the Multi-Ethnic Literature of the United States.* Reprinted here with the permission of *MELUS.*

"'Only Two Kinds of Daughters': Inter-Monologue Dialogicity in *The Joy Luck Club*" by Stephen Souris. From *MELUS* 19, no. 2 (Summer 1994): 99-123. Copyright © 1994 by *MELUS: The Journal of the Society for the Study of the Multi-Ethnic Literature of the United States.* Reprinted here with the permission of *MELUS.*

"Mothers and Daughters" by Esther Mikyung Ghymn. From *Images of Asian American Women by Asian American Women Writers*, 11-36. Copyright © 1995 by Esther Mikyung Ghymn. Reprinted by permission.

"Voice, Mind, Self: Mother-Daughter Relationships in Amy Tan's *The Joy Luck Club* and *The Kitchen God's Wife*" by M. Marie Booth Foster. From *Women of Color: Mother-Daughter Relationships in 20th-Century Literature*, edited by Elizabeth Brown-Guillory, 208-227. Copyright © 1996 by the University of Texas Press. Reprinted by permission.

"*Feng Shui*, Astrology, and the Five Elements: Traditional Chinese Belief in Amy Tan's *The Joy Luck Club*" by Patricia L. Hamilton. From *MELUS* 24, no. 2 (Summer 1999): 125-146. Copyright © 1999 by *MELUS: The Journal of the Society for the Study of the Multi-Ethnic Literature of the United States.* Reprinted here with the permission of *MELUS.*

"'That Was China, That Was Their Fate': Ethnicity and Agency in *The Joy Luck Club*" by Patricia P. Chu. From *Assimilating Asians: Gendered Strategies of Authorship in Asian America*, 141-168. Copyright © 2000 by Duke University Press. Reprinted by permission.

"Narrative Beginnings in Amy Tan's *The Joy Luck Club*: A Feminist Study" by Catherine Romagnolo. From *Studies in the Novel* 35, no. 1 (Spring 2003): 89-107. Copyright © 2003 by the University of North Texas. Reprinted by permission.

Index

Tan, Daisy, 9, 20, 52, 57, 83, 89

Tan, John, 9, 21, 52, 157

Themes, 50, 56, 65, 107, 176, 255, 282; identity, 24, 60, 69, 76, 109, 153, 170, 174, 189, 196, 200, 205, 215, 226, 273, 287; intergenerational conflict, 75, 248; miscommunication, 58, 129, 132, 142, 166, 219

Tiger imagery, 57, 61, 126, 163, 187, 189, 201-202, 215, 234, 246

Trinh T. Minh-Ha, 270

TuSmith, Bonnie, 139

"Twenty-six Malignant Gates, The" section (*The Joy Luck Club*), 129, 157, 180, 200, 276

Vacc, Nicholas, 136

Vaughan, Clarissa (*The Hours*), 67

Virtuous Woman, A (Gibbons), 113, 142

Voices, 146, 158, 166, 173, 185, 190, 240; narrative, 5, 25, 51, 65, 91, 114, 124, 131, 138, 142, 152, 162, 176, 293

Wagner, Tamara Silvia, 26

Walker, Nancy, 149

Walters, Derek, 203

Walters, Suzanna Danuta, 175

Wang, Qun, 25

Welch, Holmes, 203, 221

White, Hayden, 95

Willard, Nancy, 52, 143

Witke, Roxanne, 173

Wolf, Margery, 173, 241

Woman Warrior, The (Kingston), 19, 54, 138, 145, 149-150, 160, 170, 260

Women's Ways of Knowing (Belensky), 173

Wong, Sau-ling Cynthia, 247, 261, 287

Woo, Jing-mei (*The Joy Luck Club*), 5, 36, 70, 156, 158, 176, 180, 198, 204, 229, 256, 285; in China, 42, 56, 76, 169, 196, 220; as narrator, 49, 76, 108, 118; relationship with Suyuan, 52, 62, 73, 137, 165, 218

Woo, June. *See* Woo, Jing-mei

Woo, Suyuan (*The Joy Luck Club*), 48, 58, 65, 72, 204, 220, 239, 243; death, 5, 98, 200; Kweilin story, 97, 156, 177, 218, 273, 280, 283; relationship with Jing-mei, 53, 62, 137, 197

Woolf, Virginia, 65, 113

Wounds, 185, 274

Wu-hsing system, 57, 104, 183, 199, 203, 206, 212, 221

Wunsch, Marie, 156

Xu, Ben, 27, 204

Xu, Wenying, 24

Yalom, Marilyn, 150

Youngblood, Ruth, 201

Yuan, Yuan, 23, 287

Zeng, Li, 27

Zenobia, Mistri, 26

Zodiac, 57, 60, 146, 163, 199, 202, 211, 221